scaffolding language
scaffolding learning

PAULINE GIBBONS

∎ ∎ ∎ ∎ ∎ ∎ ∎

scaffolding language
scaffolding learning

Teaching English Language Learners
in the Mainstream Classroom

∎ ∎ ∎ ∎ ∎ ∎ ∎

SECOND EDITION

HEINEMANN
Portsmouth, NH

Heinemann
361 Hanover Street
Portsmouth, NH 03801–3912
www.heinemann.com

Offices and agents throughout the world

The author and publisher wish to thank those who have generously given permission to reprint borrowed material:

Figure 1–1: We are grateful to TESOL Italy for permission to reproduce material from Luciano Mariani's article "Teacher Support and Teacher Challenge in Promoting Learner Autonomy" that was first published in *Perspectives: A Journal of TESOL Italy*, 1997, 23 (2). http://tesolitaly.org/new/perspectives/.

Library of Congress Cataloging-in-Publication Data
Gibbons, Pauline.
   Scaffolding language, scaffolding learning : teaching English language learners in the mainstream classroom / Pauline Gibbons. — Second edition.
      pages   cm
   Includes bibliographical references and index.
   ISBN 978-0-325-05664-7
   1. English language—Study and teaching—Foreign speakers. 2. Interdisciplinary approach in education. 3. Second language acquisition. 4. Language and education.   I. Title.
PE1128.A2G48 2015
428.0071—dc23   2014018174

Editor: Holly Kim Price
Production: Vicki Kasabian
Cover design: Suzanne Heiser
Interior design: Monica Ann Crigler
Typesetter: Kim Arney
Manufacturing: Steve Bernier

Printed in the United States of America on acid-free paper
7 8 9 10 11 PAH 24 23 22 21 20
March 2020 Printing

■ ■ ■ ■ ■ ■ ■ ■

This book is dedicated to the loved ones who enrich my life:
Mark, Ben, Nadia, Safiya, and Laurie,
and in memory of my dear friend and colleague Glynis Jones

■ ■ ■ ■ ■ ■ ■ ■

■ CONTENTS ■

Acknowledgments

My thanks to the hundreds of teachers and students with whom I have worked over many years, in Australia and across the world. Thank you for sharing your classrooms with me. I have learned much from your practices and been challenged by your questions.

Thank you to the many colleagues I have worked with, for the research we have shared, and for your ongoing and loyal friendship.

My special thanks to my wonderful and ever-patient editor, Holly Kim Price, and to Vicki Kasabian and the production team at Heinemann. I have, as always, appreciated your collaborative approach in the production of this new edition.

One

Scaffolding Language and Learning

▪ ▪

I can say what I want, but not for school work and strangers.

—English language learner quoted in
The Bilingual Interface Project Report (McKay et al. 1997)

AN INTRODUCTORY STORY—AND SOME IMPLICATIONS FOR TEACHERS

In the United States, Canada, United Kingdom, and Australia there are increasing numbers of English language (EL) learners in all schools. Usually children who are at the beginning stages of learning English are supported in their learning by specialist English language or bilingual teachers. But generally this support decreases after the learner is past the initial stages of language learning, and so EL learners spend most of their school lives in regular classrooms where the classroom teacher carries the dual responsibility for the students' subject learning and for their ongoing language development. It is to these teachers, as well as to specialist English language teachers, that this book is addressed. The book is about the many ways in which teachers can provide support for EL learners through the learning contexts they provide in

1

the day-to-day life of the classroom—contexts where students are engaged in challenging tasks and have multiple opportunities for developing English-for-learning across the curriculum.

However, this chapter begins with a story that is not directly connected to the classroom. But it is a success story that educators can learn from, because it is an example of a learning context where great things were expected, great support was offered, and great outcomes achieved.

It is the story of a choir (Hawkins 2007). It was formed in 2006 in Melbourne, Australia, by Jonathon Welch, a singer with Opera Australia. It was no ordinary choir, since most of its members had no previous experience in public singing or formal music training. But more unusual was the fact that its members were a diverse group of people on the margins of society. They were there for many reasons: homelessness, drug or alcohol addiction, mental health issues, abuse, or physical disabilities such as blindness or brain injury. Not surprisingly, some people were initially skeptical about whether such a project could be achieved, expressing fears that the choir members could not be depended on to attend rehearsals regularly, or that they would simply lose interest. They were proved wrong! Less than a year after the choir was formed, they sang to more than 6,000 people at the iconic Sydney Opera House and received a standing ovation at the end of their performance. They have since recorded a platinum-selling album and have been featured on nearly every major television and radio program in the country, including a television series about the choir.

> *It is a success story that educators can learn from.*

The choir has been a life-changing experience for its members and for all those connected with its development. Some choir members have talked about how much they learned about singing. But even more spoke about their experience of being part of the choir community and how it had impacted the way they now saw themselves. Here are a few of their comments (Hawkins 2007).

> No-one has ever thought I'd achieve something, or inspire anyone, and I'm able to through the choir. (116)

> Jonathon unconditionally accepts each and every one of us. His belief in us means that each of us can sing. (47)

The choir changed my life. I haven't missed one show. And singing to the audience, it makes me proud when they are happy. (107)

The choir gives everyone the chance to show something of himself. (125)

As I watched the series over six weeks on television, it seemed to me that in working with the choir there was one principle that Jonathon Welch followed, unfailingly. He saw and treated the choir members as the people they *could become*, not as homeless people or as people with problems. From their first meeting they were treated, talked to, and trained as members of a choir. That night at the Opera House showed how they had grown into that expectation and into that new identity.

The analogies with classrooms are clear. Treating EL learners as the people they can become means that we see students not in terms of what they lack—in their case, full control of academic English—but as capable and intelligent learners who, with the right kind of support, are as able to participate in learning and achieve academically as their English-speaking peers. Today we know far more than we have ever known about the nature of language and second language development, how language can be integrated with subject learning, and what works for EL learners. There is no longer an excuse for low expectations! One of the choir members described Jonathon as a "good director who drives us to the sky and gives us courage." Another, reflecting on his life outside the choir, commented that every time he had fallen, it had reinforced what he felt about himself. Good teachers also drive their students to the sky and help them gain confidence, but through the scaffolding they provide, set them up for success rather than allowing them to fall. And as the comments from the choir members illustrate, an important part of that process lies in the relationship between teachers and students. Part of this relationship rests on how teachers talk to, and about, their students, and how students interact with each other. As the next chapter shows, every time we speak or respond to a student, we are not just talking about the particular "content" of the lesson; we are also, perhaps without being aware of it, constructing the student as a competent learner who is worth listening to, or the reverse.

EL LEARNERS IN THE MAINSTREAM CLASSROOM: SOME KEY ISSUES

The comment in the epigraph that begins this chapter was made by an eleven-year-old girl, an EL learner who was asked, "How good do you think your English is?" Her response suggests that while she feels able to communicate in general terms, she is less confident when it comes to using English at school, or with people with whom she is not on familiar terms. This may not seem surprising—it requires more linguistic skills to use language for academic purposes than it does to use it in everyday conversation. Similarly, if we are trying to use a language that we don't know very well, it is usually easier to talk to people we know well and with whom we are at ease than to converse more formally with a stranger. What some might find surprising about this comment is that this student—let's call her Julianna—was born in Australia and had been exposed to English throughout her primary education. She began school at age five, as fluent as any other five-year-old in her mother tongue but speaking little English. Yet, six years later, she felt that her English was still inadequate for certain purposes.

Why should this be? Surely, many might argue, six years is sufficient time to learn a new language given that Julianna had been living in an English-speaking country and attending an English-medium school in that time. And like many EL learners, she spoke English fluently when she played and talked informally with friends, yet had academic or literacy-related difficulties in class. To understand why this might be, we need to understand the nature of language, and in particular how it varies according to the context in which it is used.

Language and context

The theory of language on which this book draws is based on the work of Michael Halliday and other linguists working within systemic functional linguistics. These linguists argue that language is involved in almost everything we do, and whenever we use language there is a context, or, to be more precise, two kinds of context. There is, first, a *context of culture*: speakers within a culture share particular assumptions and expectations so that they are able to take for granted the ways in which things are done. Knowing how to greet someone, how to order a meal in a restaurant, how to participate in a class, or how to write a business letter are examples of this kind of cultural knowledge. While cultures may share many common purposes for using language, how these things actually get done varies from culture to culture.

A second kind of context is the *context of situation*, the particular occasion on which the language is being used. One of the most fundamental features of language is that *it varies according to the context of situation*. This context is characterized by three features: (1) what is being talked (or written) about, (2) the relationship between the speakers (or writer and reader), and (3) whether the language is spoken or written. How we use language is determined largely by these contextual features. Here are some examples of each of these three features.

- *What is being talked or written about.* Think of the differences between a conversation about teaching and another about gardening, or between a social studies text and a biology text.
- *The relationship between the speakers.* Imagine yourself chatting to a friend at a party and compare that with how you might respond to questions at a job interview.
- *Whether the language is spoken or written.* Imagine yourself watching a cooking demonstration where the cook is describing what he or she is doing. Then think about how the language would change if it were written in a cookbook.

Language varies according to the context of situation.

Halliday and Hasan (1985) refer to these contextual features as *field, tenor,* and *mode*.

- *Field* refers to the topic of the text—what it is that is being talked or written about.
- *Tenor* refers to the relationship between speaker and listener (or writer and reader), such as the level of formality required.
- *Mode* refers to the channel of communication, for example, whether it is spoken or written.

Together these three variables constitute what is referred to as the *register* of a text. As children learn their first language, they gradually learn not only the syntax or grammar of the language, but also how to vary the language they use according to the context they are in. In other words, they learn to vary the register of the language so that it is appropriate for the context. While Juliana, and many EL learners like her, learned quickly how to talk informally with her peers, she had yet to learn to use the more formal registers required in school learning, that is, the more academic subject-related language associated with school learning and literacy across the curriculum, what Julianna called "school work."

Learning to make language explicit

The ability to handle register is a both a developmental and a social process for children learning their mother tongue. One of the first things a young child learns to do is to talk about the "here and now"—to refer to the objects and goings-on in their immediate environment. Here-and-now language occurs in contexts where both speakers can see each other, and where there are visual clues, gestures, and facial expressions to help communication. What is being talked about is embedded in the visual context, such as "Put it there." The words *it* and *there* would be perfectly understandable to speakers who could see what was being referred to. But if we were speaking on the phone, we would have to express this differently. It would need to be more explicit, with more details provided: "Put the television in the corner."

If you talk with very young children you'll be aware that they do not always provide enough information for you to understand them, especially if you did not share the experience they are referring to. Last year while talking by phone to my then eighteen-month-old granddaughter, I asked her what she was doing. She replied, "I'm playing with this." Of course I had no idea what "this" was, until her father intervened and told me what it was (a toy train). What at this stage she was not able to do is what Halliday (1993) refers to as the ability to "impart meanings which are not already known" (102). He writes:

> When children are first using language . . . the particular experience that is being construed in any utterance is one that the

addressee is known to have shared. When the child says green
bus, the context is "that's a green bus; you saw it too." . . . What
the child cannot do at this stage is to impart the experience to
someone who has not shared it. [At a later stage] children learn
to tell people things they do not already know.

As children get older, they gradually become able to use language in a
more explicit or abstract way to refer to things that aren't in their immediate
surroundings, such as to tell someone about what happened at school that
day, to explain what they learned in science, or write a factual information
text. As we will see below, the ability to use language in these more explicit
ways is one of the major differences between informal face-to-face conversation and written language. Both mother tongue speakers of English and EL
learners face these increasingly complex language demands in school, but EL
learners are learning to do this in a language that is not their mother tongue.

Moving toward academic language

Martin (1984) suggests that "the more speakers are doing things together and
engaging in dialogue, the more they can take for granted. As language moves
away from the events it describes, and the possibility of feedback is removed,
more and more of the meanings must be made explicit in the text" (27). In
other words, the language itself must contain more information because it
cannot depend on the addressee knowing exactly what occurred. Consider
the differences between these four texts, which were each produced in a different context. (Note that the term *text* refers to a piece of complete meaningful language, both spoken and written.)

Text 1. Look, it's making them move. Those didn't stick.

Text 2. We found out the pins stuck on the magnet.

Text 3. Our experiment showed that magnets attract some metals.

Text 4. Magnetic attraction occurs only between ferrous metals.

Here we can see how the register of each text changes because the context
in which it was produced is different: Each text is more explicit than the one that

precedes it. Text 1 was spoken by a child talking in a small group as they were experimenting with a magnet to find out which objects it attracted. Without knowing this, it's hard to work out what's being talked about—we don't know what *them* and *those* are referring to, and the words *move* and *stick* could occur in a number of different contexts. Text 1 demonstrates how dependent "here-and-now" language is on the immediate situational context. Text 2 is the same child telling the teacher what she had learned, and is in the form of a recount in which *the pins* and *the magnet* refer to specific objects. These words make the text more explicit and therefore easier to understand. Text 3 is from her written report and contains a generalization: *magnets attract some metals.* The text is starting to sound more scientific. For example, *stick* is replaced by *attract.* Text 4, by way of comparison, is from a child's encyclopedia. The language is much denser, and the process to which the child was referring in Texts 1, 2, and 3 is now summarized in the abstract notion of *magnetic attraction.*

While the *field* of all four texts is the same (i.e., they are on the same topic), there are considerable differences in the way in which the language is used. The vocabulary becomes more technical as well as subject or *field* specific, the *tenor* of the texts becomes more impersonal (notice how the personal reference to *we* and *our* disappear), and the *mode* varies (they become increasingly more explicit and more like written language). Of course, we could continue this continuum; a tertiary text may say something like "Some well-known ferromagnetic materials that exhibit easily detectable magnetic properties are nickel, iron, cobalt gadolinium, and their alloys."

In many ways, this set of texts reflects the process of formal education: As children move through school, they are expected to progress from talking only about their here-and-now personal experiences toward using the particular registers of different curriculum areas, and be able to express increasingly more abstract ideas.

Language learning is not a simple linear process.

The four texts demonstrate that it is problematic to talk about overall "proficiency" in a language without taking into account the context in which the language will be used. As Baynham (1993) suggests, language learning is not a simple linear process but a "functional diversification, an extension of a learner's communicative range" (5). Even a fluent mother tongue speaker of English will not be proficient in every possible context: there will always be some subjects that they know very little about, so they can't talk about them. Or, perhaps there is a particular form of writing, such as a PhD proposal, that even highly educated people might not be familiar with and would need guidance in producing. So it is not simply a matter of getting the basic "grammar" correct, but of knowing the most *appropriate* language to use in a particular context, or, in other words, to know how to use the appropriate register. In the context of school the need to develop academic registers is a strong argument for *all* learners to learn through programs that integrate subject teaching with its associated language. This has implications for both program planning and for assessment.

EL learners and language learning in school

In line with this view of language, the book is based upon the assumption that language development involves a continuing process of meaning making. While the more formal and traditional aspects of language learning, such as grammar and vocabulary, cannot—and should not—be ignored, the assumption in the book is that these aspects of language are best focused on in the context of authentic meaning making, and that learning *about* language is most meaningful when it occurs in the context of actual language use.

Let's return now to Julianna, the student quoted at the beginning of the chapter. It is obvious that a second language learner is likely to have far fewer difficulties in producing something like Text 1, where the visual context provides a support for meaning making, and where fewer linguistic resources are required, than with subsequent texts that require increasingly more control over grammar and vocabulary. Cummins (2000) uses the terms *context-embedded* and *context-reduced* to refer to the distinction between the registers of everyday language and the more academic registers of school, and has suggested that whereas a second language learner is likely to develop conversational language quite rapidly—usually taking between one and two years—the registers associated with academic learning may take up to seven years for the learner to develop at a level equivalent to a competent native speaker of the same age. (A caveat to this is that students who have literacy and academic development in their first language often progress much faster.) These school-related registers, as the text examples illustrate, are more explicit, more abstract, and less personal, and they contain more subject-specific language. Julianna's comment implies she still has difficulties with this more academic language, even though she has no difficulty expressing herself in more everyday contexts.

This model of language and language development should not suggest a negative or deficit view of learners like Julianna, or of their English skills. Nor should it suggest that the development of academic language is simply a matter of time and that it will be "picked up" eventually. On the contrary, viewing language development as a process of learning to control an increasing range of registers suggests that while all children are predisposed in a biological sense to learn language, whether they actually do, how well they learn to control it, and the range of registers and purposes for which they are able to use it are a matter of the social contexts in which they find themselves.

Second language learners will have experienced a wide range of contexts in which they have learned to use their mother tongue, but probably a much more restricted range of contexts *in English*. If these children's previous language experience is not taken into account when they start school, and if they are expected not only to learn a second language but to learn *in it* as well, it is hardly surprising that without focused English language support in all subjects they may start to fall behind their peers who are operating in a language they have been familiar with since birth.

It is clear that English speakers have a head start in learning to use the academic registers of school. While the language and literacy-related demands of the curriculum—the registers of school—are unfamiliar to a greater or lesser extent to all children when they start school, and English-speaking children are also learning new concepts and new registers, they are doing so through the medium of their mother tongue. EL learners are not. In an English-medium school, English speakers have largely already acquired the core grammar of the language they are learning in and the ability to use it in a range of familiar social situations. EL learners have not. But as Cummins (2000) points out, we cannot put EL students' academic development on hold while they are learning the language of instruction. Ultimately, if second language learners are not to be disadvantaged in their long-term learning, and are to have the time and opportunity to learn the subject-specific registers of school, they need ongoing language development across the whole curriculum and the recognition by all teachers that they are teachers of English, not simply of subject "content." Only in this way will EL students have access to, models of, and practice in using the range of academic language they need for learning.

Merely exposing EL learners to content classrooms, however, is not an adequate response: Simply placing them in an English-medium classroom in itself "cannot be assumed to provide optimal language learning opportunities as a matter of course" (Mohan 2001, 108). But the integration of language, subject content, and thinking skills suggested in this chapter is not a straightforward task. It requires systematic planning and monitoring. The following chapters suggest some of the ways that teachers can respond to the language-learning needs of EL students within the context of the regular school curriculum.

VIEWS OF TEACHING AND LEARNING

The "lone" learner

Since public education began, there have been two major and competing ideologies about the goals of education and the means by which it is to be accomplished (Wells 2000). The first of these can be described as the "empty vessel" model of teaching and learning, whereby teachers "transmit" skills or knowledge into the "empty" minds of their students. The teaching–learning relationship is one of transmission and reception. Language, if it is thought about at all, is seen simply as a conduit or carrier of knowledge. The second ideology, sometimes referred to as "progressive," appears at one level to be very different. The learner is placed at the center of the educational process and education is seen not as a matter of receiving information but of intelligent inquiry and thought. In the way that this has been interpreted in some classrooms, the major organizing principle is seen to be the individual child's active construction of knowledge, with the teacher's role being to stage-manage appropriate learning experiences. In this model of learning, a child's language abilities are seen as largely the result of more general and cognitive abilities.

Both orientations have been critiqued from the standpoint of minority students and second language learners (Cummins 2000). Transmission models tend to work against what is now accepted as one of the central principles of language learning—namely, that using the new language in interaction with others is an essential process by which it is learned (Swain 2000). Transmission pedagogies are also criticized as presenting a curriculum sited solely within the dominant culture, providing little or no opportunity for minority students to express their particular experiences and nonmainstream view of the world. Unfortunately, transmission-based approaches have tended to dominate the education of so-called disadvantaged students. Many compensatory programs have focused on drilling students in low-level language and reading skills that are excised from any meaningful context, at the expense of any authentic intellectual challenge involving higher-level thinking and literacy development. The ongoing effect of such programs is that further disadvantage may become structured into the curriculum of the school. As Carrasquillo and colleagues suggest: "ELLs' lack of oral [English] language proficiency has often hindered their opportunity to receive cognitively stimulating and content-level appropriate instruction in school" (Carrasquillo, Kucer, and Adams 2004, 30).

Progressive pedagogy has also been criticized, in particular for its lack of explicit language teaching, which, it has been argued, places a disadvantage on those who are least familiar with the language and assumptions of a middle-class, English-medium school curriculum. In relation to the teaching of writing, such approaches have been criticized in particular for their focus on the *processes* of language learning, at the expense of focusing sufficiently on the actual production of written texts, especially nonnarrative texts that will allow learners to participate in the dominant society. This is a powerful argument and is taken up again in Chapter 5.

Though very different in the way that they view learning and the role of the teacher, both ideologies have an individualistic notion of learning: the child as a lone learner. Whether you view the learner as an empty vessel waiting to be filled with appropriate knowledge, or as an unfolding intellect that will eventually reach its potential given the right environment, both views see the learner as "self-contained" and learning as occurring *within* an individual.

There is an alternative model, however, one that is increasingly influential in classroom practice and with which most teachers are now familiar. Based on the work of Lev Vygotsky (1978, 1986), this pedagogical approach emphasizes the social and collaborative nature of learning and language development. It sees learning as occurring *between* individuals. The roles of teacher and learner are interrelated, with both taking active roles in the learning process. The next section discusses this approach.

A social view of learning

The Russian psychologist Lev Vygotsky lived at the beginning of the twentieth century but his work was not widely translated until the 1960s. Since the 1980s, his work has exerted a major influence on Western education in Europe, North America, and Australia, and it is increasingly influential in today's classrooms. Together with the work of other Soviet cognitive researchers—including Luria, Leont'ev, and the literary theorist Bakhtin—and interpretations of this work by scholars and educationists such as Wertsch, Mercer, and Wells, Vygotsky's perspective on human development and learning, broadly termed *sociocultural*, offers a very different perspective from that offered by earlier Western psychological theories. Sociocultural theory sees human development as social rather than individualistic. An individual's development is thus to a significant extent a product, not a prerequisite, of education—the result of his or her social, historical, and cultural experiences. Thus, as suggested earlier in this chapter, while we are all biologically able to acquire language, what language we learn, how adept we are at using it, and the purposes for which we are able to use it are a matter of the social contexts and situations we have experienced. In a very real sense, what and how we learn depends very much on the company we keep!

The zone of proximal development

The educational basis for a child's development is encapsulated in what Vygotsky terms the *zone of proximal development*, by which he refers to the distance or the cognitive gap between what a child can do unaided and what the child can do jointly and in coordination with a more skilled expert. Anyone who has been involved with young children is familiar with what this looks like in practice. When children are learning to feed or dress themselves, the adult at first has to perform the whole activity. Then the child gradually performs parts of the activity, with the parent still assisting with the more difficult parts. Finally, the child is able to do the whole thing unaided. In other words, successful coordination with a partner—or assisted performance—leads learners to reach beyond what they are able to achieve alone, to participate in new situations and to tackle new tasks, or, in the case of second language learners, to learn new ways of using language.

Vygotsky sees the development of cognition itself also as the result of participation with others in goal-directed activity. A child initially engages in joint thinking with others through the talk that accompanies problem solving and social participation in everyday activity. Imagine, for example, a child doing a jigsaw puzzle with a parent or caregiver. They will probably talk about the shapes of the pieces, what piece might go where, how to match up colors and images, and so on. Vygotsky would argue that this external, social dialogue is gradually internalized to become a resource for individual thinking, or what he refers to as "inner speech." The child's external dialogues with others later become an inner personal resource for the development of thinking and problem solving; eventually the child will do jigsaw puzzles without the need for external dialogue. The child doing the puzzle with the adult is, of course, not only learning how to do that particular puzzle but is also becoming familiar with the kind of processes to go through for completing subsequent puzzles. The goal of this kind of learning is to go beyond simply learning items of knowledge to being able to use that knowledge in other contexts—in other words, to learn *how* to think, not simply *what* to think.

As pointed out earlier, second language learners are both learning a new language and learning other things through the medium of the language. If we accept the premise that external dialogue is a major resource for the development of thinking, and that interaction is also integral to language learning, then it follows that we must consider very seriously the nature of the talk in which learners are engaged in the classroom. (This topic is the focus of Chapters 2, 3, and 4 but is a continuing theme throughout the book.)

This social view of teaching and learning moves us away from the often polarized (and not very helpful) debate about teacher-centered versus student-centered learning. It suggests a more unified theory of "teaching-and-learning," in which both teachers and students are seen as active participants, and learning is seen as a collaborative endeavor. In line with these collaborative principles, the achievements of second language learners cannot be seen as simply the result of aptitude, background, or individual motivation. They are also dependent on the social and linguistic frameworks within which their learning takes place: language learning is a socially embedded, not simply a psychologically driven, process. Thus what teachers choose to do in classrooms, and in particular the kinds of support they provide, is of crucial importance in the educational success of their students. It is to the nature of this support, or *scaffolding*, that we now turn.

What is scaffolding?

Here is an example of scaffolding in action: The father and mother are talking with their son Nigel, who at the time was around fourteen months (taken from Halliday 1975, 112). Earlier Nigel had been to the zoo, and while he was looking at a goat it had attempted to eat a plastic lid that Nigel was holding. The keeper had explained that he shouldn't let the goat eat the lid because it wasn't good for it. As you read this dialogue, look particularly at what the parents are doing and the effect this has on Nigel's language.

Nigel	try eat lid
Father	what tried to eat the lid?
Nigel	try eat lid
Father	what tried to eat the lid?
Nigel	goat, man said no, goat try eat lid, man said no
	Later
Nigel	goat try eat lid, man said no
Mother	why did the man say no?
Nigel	goat shouldn't eat lid, (*Shaking head*) good for it
Mother	the goat shouldn't eat the lid, it's not good for it
Nigel	goat try eat lid, man said no, goat shouldn't eat lid, (*Shaking head*) good for it.

Notice the kind of scaffolding that the parents provide. Nigel's initial utterance is far from explicit—no one who had not shared the experience with him would be able to understand the significance of what he is saying. At first it is not clear what or who Nigel is referring to, and the father's question *what* shows Nigel what information he needs to provide. Having extended the initial three-word utterance to something significantly more complete, Nigel relates this more extended version to his mother, who pushes the dialogue forward with the question *why*. While Nigel does not take up his mother's use of *it's not* (using instead the strategy of indicating a negative by shaking his head), he does provide the reason his mother is seeking (*it's not good for it*), and by the end of these two small conversations he has elaborated on and made more explicit his original short utterance. Most important, what Nigel achieves—the final story he tells—has not simply come from him and his own linguistic resources, nor has it been "provided" by the parents. Rather, this story is a collaborative endeavor, and it has been *jointly* constructed.

The term *scaffolding* was first used by Wood, Bruner, and Ross (1976) in their examination of parent–child talk in the early years. It is a useful metaphor that we will employ throughout the book. Scaffolding—in its more usual sense—is a temporary structure that is put up in the process of constructing or repairing a building. As each bit of the new building is finished, the scaffolding is taken down. The scaffolding is temporary, but essential for the successful construction of the building. Bruner (1978) describes scaffolding in the metaphorical sense in which we are using it here, as "the steps taken to reduce the degrees of freedom in carrying out some tasks so that the child can concentrate on the difficult skill she is in the process of acquiring" (19). In the classroom it portrays the "temporary, but essential, nature of the mentor's assistance" in supporting learners to carry out tasks successfully (Maybin, Mercer, and Stierer 1992, 186). *Scaffolding*, however, is not simply another word for *help*. It is a special kind of help that assists learners in moving toward new skills, concepts, or levels of understanding. Scaffolding is thus the temporary assistance by which a teacher helps a learner know how to do something so that the learner will later be able to complete a similar task alone. It is future-oriented and aimed at increasing a learner's autonomy. As Vygotsky has said, what a child can do with support today, she or he can do alone tomorrow.

It can be argued that it is only *when* teacher support—or scaffolding—is needed that learning will take place, since the learner is then likely to be working within his or her zone of proximal development; Vygotsky's work

(1978) suggests that learning leads development. While this idea does not ignore the notion that teaching experiences should not be completely beyond the capacity of the learner, it does challenge the notion of learner "readiness" by suggesting that it is the teacher who is largely responsible for initiating each new step of learning, building on what a learner is currently able to do alone. It challenges teachers to maintain high expectations of all students as well as provide adequate scaffolding for tasks to be completed successfully.

A high-challenge, high-support classroom

Mariani (1997) has provided a useful diagram (Figure 1–1) to illustrate these ideas. It is particularly useful because it relates scaffolding to the degree of intellectual challenge of the task that the student is carrying out. In the diagram the vertical "challenge" axis refers to what the students are doing. They may be engaged in a high-challenge classroom, where they regularly participate in intellectually challenging tasks and higher-order thinking, or in a low-challenge classroom, where the tasks involve simple, low-level tasks and drills, or the tasks may lie somewhere along this continuum. The horizontal

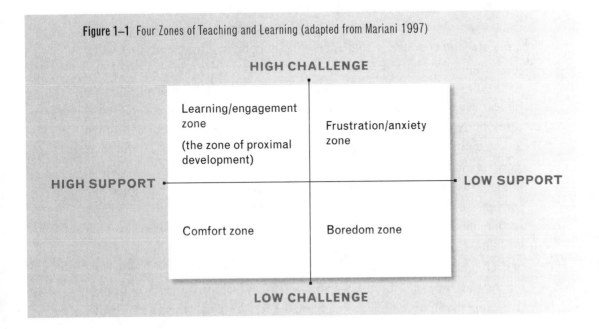

Figure 1–1 Four Zones of Teaching and Learning (adapted from Mariani 1997)

"support" axis refers to what the teacher is doing. He or she may be providing high or low levels of scaffolding. The four quadrants illustrate four kinds of classroom environments: (1) high challenge, low support; (2) low challenge, low support; (3) low challenge, high support; and (4) high challenge, high support. Pause in your reading at this point to consider how you might feel in each of these four zones as a learner. Which one is most likely to engage you and provide you with the most productive learning environment?

Considerable research over a number of years suggests that a high-challenge, high-support classroom benefits all children. Thomas and Collier's research (1999) has shown that where the teachers' expectations of their students were high, EL learners' achievement was also high. Other studies have also found that in a high-challenge/high-support curriculum equity gaps diminish and all learners, regardless of background, achieve at higher levels (Newmann and Associates 1996; Gibbons 2008; Hammond 2008; Walqui 2007). And as Chapter 2 points out, research on second language development would suggest that the inquiry-based and dialogic orientation that such a curriculum provides also provides a context that fosters the language development of EL learners.

For EL students, a high-challenge, high-support classroom suggests a very different orientation to learning tasks than has often been the case in the past. As far as possible, all learners, including EL learners, need to be engaged with authentic and cognitively challenging learning tasks. This means that rather than simplifying the *task* (and ultimately risking a reductionist curriculum), we should instead reflect on the nature of the *scaffolding* that is being provided for learners to carry out that task. It is the nature of the support—support that is responsive to the particular demands made on children learning through the medium of a new language—that is critical for success. For example, all learners might be expected at some point to write a persuasive text. Some, though, may write part or all of this in their mother tongue. For others the teacher may provide a scaffold that provides the connectives that start each section: *first, my second point, on the other hand*. For a student who as yet has very little English, the teacher might also provide the first sentence (or more) of each part of the text. Or they may provide, in addition to all these, and by talking with the student, a list of words or phrases that the student will need to use. Or perhaps some students might do the task in pairs, others individually.

In this way, the outcomes (here, the type of text) are similar for all students; what differs is the nature and amount of scaffolding provided, and the route by which the outcomes are achieved.

> *All learners need to be engaged with cognitively challenging tasks*

This book offers many suggestions for scaffolding learning for EL learners in the regular classroom. However, it is worth remembering that the presence of EL children in a school, while posing a challenge for many mainstream teachers, can be at the same time a catalyst for the kind of language-focused curriculum that will benefit all children. As a result of poverty or social background or nonstandard dialect, native speakers of English may also have difficulty with the specialized registers of curriculum subjects. Recognizing that the language of these subjects cannot be taken for granted but has to be taught, finding stimulating and effective ways to do so, and critically examining how language is currently being used in one's own classroom will assist not only EL learners but also many of their monolingual-English peers.

AN OUTLINE OF THE BOOK

In the past fifty years there has been much research in what is most often referred to as "second language *acquisition*," or SLA. In this book, along with others who view the development of language and learning as social in origin, I have used the term "second language *development*" to better suggest that, for the learner, learning a language is an active and collaborative process. I have also retained, for ease of reference, the use of the traditional term "second language," but I acknowledge that in reality English may be a third or subsequent language for some students. "Mother tongue" is also a problematic term for those children who regularly operate in several languages. I have retained the use of this, however, to refer to the learner's most dominant or strongest home language. I have also used the term *EL* (English language) *learner*, since at the time of writing it is a commonly used term for those students who are learning *through* a language of instruction (English) in which they are not yet fully familiar, or that is new to them. *EAL* (English as an additional language) is another term used when referring to the multilingual skills that some children possess. While I acknowledge, and agree with, those researchers who are wary of the use of such "labels," arguing that we should not think of learners in terms of deficit, I have retained them for ease of reference to talk about the heterogeneous group of learners that are the subject of this book.

Many of the teaching activities discussed in the book involve the integration of all four areas of speaking, listening, reading, and writing. However, they have been separated in the chapters so that the implications for EL learners can be more fully discussed. The layout of the chapters is not intended to suggest that the four skills should be regularly taught discretely or in isolation!

- ◆ **Chapter 2** begins with a brief summary of some of the central ideas from research about second language learning that are most relevant for classroom talk, and it introduces the idea of "dialogic talk." The chapter goes on to give examples of teacher-talk that is supportive of EL students' language development.
- ◆ **Chapter 3** also draws on the research discussed in Chapter 2, this time with a focus on student-centered pair and group work, and it includes a number of strategies and activities that can be used across the curriculum.
- ◆ **Chapter 4** discusses in more detail the spoken-written continuum introduced briefly in this chapter, and it shows how talk can be a "bridge" into literacy.
- ◆ **Chapter 5** discusses the teaching of writing. It describes the major linguistic features of a range of writing forms common in primary schools, and it suggests a teaching model by which specific forms of writing—text types or genres—can be developed across the curriculum.
- ◆ **Chapter 6** focuses on the teaching of reading, and it includes examples of a range of activities that help students access the meaning of texts and model what effective teachers do.
- ◆ **Chapter 7** focuses on listening and discusses what kind of listening demands are made on listeners in different contexts, and it offers a range of activities aimed to improve effective listening.
- ◆ **Chapter 8** draws together the theories and practical activities of the previous chapters to focus on language learning across the curriculum. It provides a rationale for integration and guidance about how to

plan and implement an integrated program. Assessment is presented as "assessment-for-learning," which can be used to inform future program planning and feedback to students, parents, and other teachers.

- **The Glossary of Teaching Activities** is included at the end of the book. Activities that are included in the glossary are designated in bold type in the text.

In Summary

This chapter has foreshadowed the major themes of the book.

- Language varies according to the context in which it occurs.
- Second language learning in the school context requires learners to develop more "academic" language in an increasing range of subject contexts.
- This academic language development requires planned English language support across the whole curriculum and throughout the school.
- Learning is essentially collaborative and social, and it is a partnership between teacher and students.
- EL learners need the same access to intellectually challenging work as all other students.
- A high-challenge classroom requires high levels of language support (scaffolding).

To Think About

1. In your own school context, are there students like Julianna? How are they viewed by their teachers? What kind of support do you think is most important for learners like her?
2. The chapter suggests that simply exposing EL learners to English is insufficient by itself to lead to effective language learning. Do you agree? What happens to some EL learners when they are immersed in content classrooms and taught as if they are fluent in English?

3. Do you agree that it is problematic to talk about overall "proficiency" in a language without taking into account the context in which the language will be used?
4. Look at the four quadrants in Figure 1–1. Where do you think *most* of your own teaching is concentrated?
5. What points in the chapter affirm or challenge your current practice? What represents the most important learning in the chapter for you?
6. Tell a success story! In your own classroom, think about when you could have said, "Great things were expected, great support was offered, and great outcomes were achieved."

Suggestions for Further Reading

Cummins, J. 2000. Chapter 3, "Language Proficiency in Academic Contexts." In *Language, Power and Pedagogy: Bilingual Children in the Crossfire*, ed. J. Cummins. Clevedon, UK: Multilingual Matters.

Genesee, F., K. Lindholm-Leary, B. Saunders, and D. Christian. 2006. *Educating English Language Learners: A Synthesis of Research Evidence*. New York: Cambridge University Press.

Gibbons, P. 2009. Chapter 1, "English Learners, Academic Literacy, and Thinking." In *English Learners, Academic Language, and Thinking*. Portsmouth NH: Heinemann.

Gibbons, P. 2013. "Scaffolding." In *The Routledge Encyclopedia of Second Language Acquisition*, ed. P. Robinson, 563–64. London: Routledge.

Mohan, B. 2001. Chapter 6, "The Second Language as a Medium of Learning." In *English as a Second Language in the Mainstream: Teaching, Learning and Identity*, ed. B. Mohan, C. Leung, and C. Davison. London: Longman.

Walqui, A. 2007. "Scaffolding Instruction for English Language Learners: A Conceptual Framework." In *Bilingual Education: An Introductory Reader*, ed. O. Garcia and C. Baker, 202–18. Clevedon, UK: Multilingual Matters.

TWO

Classroom Talk

- -

Creating Contexts for Language Learning

*Language is our cultural tool—we use it to share experience and so to
collectively, jointly, make sense of it . . . Language is therefore not just
a means by which individuals can formulate ideas and communicate
them, it is also a means for people to think and learn together.*

—Neil Mercer, *The Guided Construction of Knowledge*

This chapter and the following chapter focus on one of the most fundamental
things that goes on in all classrooms—talk. This chapter focuses on teacher
talk and how teacher–learner interactions can facilitate language development. Chapter 3 focuses on talk between students in small-group and pair
work. As both chapters illustrate, a classroom without a well-planned spoken
language program denies all students a major resource for learning and denies EL learners the kinds of contexts that foster language development. Yet,
compared to the time that has been put into literacy programs, curriculum
development, and syllabus design, it is probably still the case that in some
classrooms spoken language is the "poor relation" to the teaching of the written mode. And, according to some researchers, in some classrooms students

may still spend over 90 percent of their time listening to teachers or doing individual seatwork (Pianta et al. 2007).

For EL children, classroom tasks and conversations must provide the same rich opportunities for learning as for all other children, but they must in addition create the conditions that will foster second language development. This chapter begins with a summary of the most important of these conditions and includes some practical ideas that illustrate how they can be built into a subject-based program. The remainder of the chapter looks at teacher talk from the perspective of these principles, focusing on how a teacher working with a whole class can provide opportunities for language development through the ways in which they make what they say comprehensible to learners, and the ways in which they respond to what children say.

> *Classroom conversations must create the conditions that will foster language development.*

WHAT HELPS LEARNERS TO LEARN A NEW LANGUAGE?

What follows is a brief summary of some of the central research-based principles about what supports second language development, together with some classroom ideas about how each of these principles can be put into practice. Note that all the named activities (identified in bold text) are explained more fully in later chapters, and they are also listed in the glossary with the chapter reference in which they first appear.

Learners need to understand what is said to them and what they read

Krashen (1982) refers to this need for learners' to understand as *comprehensible input* and suggests that it is fundamental to successful language learning. Comprehensible input is not the same as "simplified" input, however. As the notion of the zone of proximal development (ZPD) suggests, learners need access to language that is ahead of what they are yet able to produce themselves. But there are many ways to make subject-based language comprehensible to EL learners without resorting to ongoing simplification. For example:

- Use practical demonstrations (such as a science experiment) and familiar language to talk about the new ideas *before* talking about related abstractions in complex language.
- If possible, use the mother tongue to introduce a topic or key concept, before using English.
- Build talk on something children have experienced, such as a school excursion, or on previous learning.
- Use pictures, diagrams, or graphic outlines to illustrate complex ideas.
- Draw on the resources of technology, including interactive texts.
- Link what you are talking about to what children already know.
- Express the same idea in more than one way (see the section about "message abundancy" later in this chapter).
- When helping children comprehend written texts, build up relevant background knowledge *before* they are expected read. As they are reading, draw attention to pictures, diagrams, or subheadings that will help them comprehend the text (see Chapter 6).

Learners need to use the new language themselves

While comprehensible input is a necessary condition for second language learning, it is not sufficient by itself for language development. Merrill Swain (2000, 2005) has written extensively on the need for learners to participate in contexts where they also use the language themselves. She refers to the learner's use of language as *comprehensible output*. Children need to have opportunities to talk in more extended ways, so that, for the benefit of their listeners, they begin to focus not only on what they are saying but how they are saying it. Swain argues that, unlike what happens when we listen or read, a focus on making language comprehensible to others encourages learners to process their own language more deeply. She suggests that this is likely to lead to more comprehensible, coherent, and grammatically improved discourse. Swain also points to the value for language development of problem-solving dialogue where small groups or pairs of learners solve a problem collaboratively. The pair and group activities below all create contexts for learners to use extended language in interaction with others:

+ **Barrier games,** such as the **Find the Difference** game (Chapter 3)
+ **Paired problem solving** (Chapter 3)
+ Solving subject-based problems, for example, developing recommendations for improving the school environment
+ **Dictogloss** or **Picture Prompt** activities that are related to the topic under study (Chapter 7)
+ Reporting back in small groups to the rest of the class about something their group has done or learned (Chapter 4)
+ Jigsaw reading (Chapter 6).

Learners need opportunities to use "stretched" language

In the course of producing comprehensible output, students will at times be pushed to go beyond their current English language abilities, and to move out of their comfort zone. If you have traveled overseas and have been in situations where you have struggled to make yourself understood in a foreign language, you will have experienced what Merrill Swain (2000) refers to as "stretched" language. This is when the situation you face requires you to use language that is beyond what you know how to do. You are pushed to go beyond the language you can control well and to try out ways of saying something that requires you to use language you are still unsure of, probably using faulty grammar or inaccurate vocabulary. Yet these moments of struggle are often significant moments in language learning, especially if you are speaking with a helpful interactant. Often at these times you become aware of what you are not yet able to do. Or you may notice what the interactant says to you in reply, since it is immediately relevant to what you want to say. Or you are pushed to rethink how to express something and then have another go at saying it. And if you are in the same situation again, you are likely to do better!

So some struggle with the language—stretched language—is necessary for ongoing language development.

The classroom implication for comprehensible output and stretched language is not that language "form" per se should become the only teaching focus, but that it is important, at times, for learners to have opportunities to use stretches of discourse in contexts where there is a press on their linguistic resources, and where, for the benefit of their listeners, they must focus on how they are saying it. All the activities mentioned in relation to comprehensible output will for some students be beyond what they can do easily. What is important is that this challenge occurs in a context where students feel their efforts are acknowledged and supported. The ideas below will help to provide a supportive context in which students feel able to take risks with language:

> *Moments of struggle can be significant moments in language learning.*

- ◆ In activities, such as barrier games that involve a single pair of students (i.e., student A and student B), try using two pairs of students (i.e., two As and two Bs) so that students have a buddy to help them participate in the activity.
- ◆ Build up students' confidence when they are talking by affirming that you can understand what they are trying to say (even if it is inaccurately worded): *Yes, I see what you mean.*
- ◆ In interactions with students, allow time for them to attempt to self-correct what they say, or to reword an idea, before you provide the wording they are seeking. Processing what is said and how you will reply requires much more time when you are using a new language, so allow students time to think before you are tempted to tell them the answer or reword what they have said!
- ◆ Encourage students to go beyond what is easy and familiar, and take risks with their language use.
- ✳ BUT, don't allow a student to struggle to the point of giving up, becoming embarrassed, or losing confidence; and do ensure that the student is in a supportive environment, as in, for example, working with a friendship group.

Learners need models of new language, especially the academic registers of school

In a classroom where there are large numbers of EL learners, group work cannot by itself provide models of the academic language that students are not yet familiar with. If students are to move forward in their development of the academic registers of school, the teacher's role in modeling this language is essential (Schleppegrell 2012). It is likely therefore that the modeling of academic language will need to be in whole-class formats with the teacher explicitly leading the learning, or in contexts where the teacher is interacting with individual learners.

- Teach subject-based language explicitly; academic language is not simply "picked up."
- Plan the specific language (spoken and written) that will be integrated with a particular unit of work (Chapter 8).
- As you talk with students, model academic language by building on, extending, and rewording what students say. For example,

    Student   it all got dried up
    Teacher   yes the water dried up, it evaporated.

- Talk about the way that language varies according to the context in which it is used (see the discussion on field, tenor, and mode in Chapter 1).
- As far as possible, talk *about* language in the context of using it, rather than in isolation (see, for example, Joint Constructions below). Introduce key grammatical terms (often referred to as *meta-language*) in context.
- In your writing program, include **Joint Constructions**, where teacher and students write a text together; these allow you to model the process of writing and to talk about language (such as overall structure, connectives, sentence grammar and vocabulary) in the context of actually using it (Chapter 5).
- Display **Writing Frameworks** for particular genres in the classroom so that students can refer to them as they write Chapter 5).

◆ Together with students, develop criteria for effective writing, in
each genre.

◆ Draw attention to the way that many nonfiction texts are structured,
for example, through the conjunctions and connectives that begin
paragraphs (Chapters 5 and 6).

Learners need opportunities to build on the resources of their mother tongue

It is beyond the scope of this book to discuss bilingual approaches in detail,
since its primary concern is with the development of English, but this should
not suggest that the first language be neglected. There is a very large body of
research carried out over many years and in a wide range of countries and contexts that illustrates the relationship between first and subsequent languages.
Recent research has suggested that bilingual learners use all of their linguistic
resources when reading or producing texts (Hornberger and Link 2012; Garcia
2009). Much research also shows that for EL learners the stronger
their first language is, the more likely it is that they will be successful learners of English and/or subsequent languages (Cummins 2000). In the process of learning English, children's primary
cultural and linguistic identities should not be submerged, nor
should the process of learning a new language and culture be
a one-way journey away from family and community. Here are
some ways that the mother tongue can be incorporated into an
English-medium classroom and used as a *resource* for learning.

> *Bilingual learners use all of their linguistic resources when reading or producing text.*

◆ Allow students, at times, to work with others who speak the same
language—for example, in some problem-solving situations, in some
prereading activities, when being introduced to complex concepts,
when listening to instructions about what to do, or for some barrier
activities. Ideally, use of the mother tongue in these contexts will
precede related work in English.

◆ Encourage students who are already literate in another language
to read and write in it, especially (though not exclusively) in the
early stages of their English learning. Literacy in their first language

is a significant part of their identity as learners, which is all too often ignored.

- Invite students to develop bilingual books for younger learners.
- Encourage students to build up their own subject-based bilingual dictionaries.
- If you have bilingual teachers in your school, have them discuss new concepts in the children's mother tongue *before* they are introduced to them in English; learners are then able to make use of their total language resources.
- Talk about other languages, for example, by comparing them with English. Your learners make good informants and, given the opportunity to do so, they can often talk in very sophisticated ways about how language works and how they use their other languages in learning English. Such conversations will also give you valuable insights into what students are able to do in their mother tongue, and are, in addition, important learning for monolingual English speakers.

Second language learning is facilitated when students are using the new language to learn other things, such as subject content

Many researchers have suggested that subject-based learning can be a highly effective context for language development as long as a language focus is carefully planned, integrated, and scaffolded into the teaching program (Gibbons 2009, 2012; Walqui and van Lier 2010; Mohan, Leung, and Davison 2001; Cloud, Genesee, and Hamayan 2000). Since subject-based language learning is at the heart of this book, specific strategies are not listed here.

There is a clear teaching implication from all these studies for second language learning: that how successful school-age EL learners are in developing English depends largely on how classroom discourse is constructed and how well it fulfills the principles and conditions discussed in this section. It is important to remain mindful of these conditions and principles when you are planning any teaching program designed to be inclusive of EL learners, whether your focus is speaking, reading, or writing, or you are deciding on specific classroom activities. Given the emphasis on spoken language in learning, we look now at one of the most common patterns of interactions associated with learning in school.

CLASSROOM TALK AND EL LEARNERS

The IRE pattern

Think for a moment about the patterns of interaction that typify many classrooms. There is a particular kind of three-part exchange between teacher and student that is very familiar to all teachers (and to their students), and it has been identified over a long period by many researchers of classroom discourse (Mercer 1995; Mehan 1979; Sinclair and Coulthard 1975). In this pattern of interaction, the teacher first asks a question (almost certainly one to which she or he knows the answer); the student responds, often with a single word or short answer; and then the teacher responds by evaluating the answer. Such interactions are often referred to as IRE (Initiation, Response, Evaluation). Here is an example:

Initiation	**Teacher**	What season comes after fall?
Response	**Student**	Winter.
Evaluation	**Teacher**	Right, good. Winter.

The IRE pattern is based on a teacher-generated "display" question, a question that is primarily designed for students to display their learning. It remains a common pattern in traditional classrooms, especially where the teacher sees his or her role primarily as transmitting a body of information. Of course, such interaction patterns are sometimes very useful: for example, when the teacher's questions serve to provide a framework for a logical thought process, such as talking students through the steps of a math problem. It also enables teachers to quickly check students' understanding of particular subject content and, used well, can also be used to probe thinking. So it would be foolish to suggest that teachers should avoid all such interactions altogether.

However, if we look at the IRE pattern above, it's easy to see that what it doesn't fulfill is the need for students to produce comprehensible output or stretched language. When teacher initiations lead only to single-word or single-clause responses, there is little opportunity for the learner's language to be stretched, for students to focus on how they are saying something, or for giving them practice in using the language for themselves. And what they do say only makes sense when heard in conjunction with the question: there is no opportunity for the student to express a complete thought or idea. In a traditional IRE pattern, the teacher in fact says far more than the students! Teacher–student talk of this kind therefore actually deprives learners of just those interactional features and conditions that the research cited earlier suggests are enabling factors in second language learning. A classroom program that is supportive of second language learning must therefore create opportunities for the more varied and dialogic interactional patterns described in the previous section to occur.

A dialogic approach

The importance of talk in learning has long been understood (see, for example, Bruner 1978; Barnes 1976). More recently, largely influenced by the work of Vygotsky, the social and cultural basis for learning has been increasingly recognized (Gibbons 2013; Walqui and van Lier 2010; Mercer 2000; Wells 2000). As we saw in Chapter 1, this perspective puts interaction and dialogue at the heart of the learning process because they construct the resources for thinking. We also saw how the development of the spoken forms of language is essential for all learners because they can serve as a bridge to the more academic language associated with learning in school, and with the development of literacy. Recent research points, too, to the important role talk plays in the development of reading comprehension (Harvey, Goudvis, and Wallis 2010). For all these reasons, then, it follows that the *quality* of the dialogues that children are engaged in—not simply the quantity—must be viewed critically. Increasingly, researchers in recent years have focused on the quality of talk between teachers and students, and talk between children. Although these researchers have "named" this talk in different ways, there are striking resemblances in the way they describe it.

Wegerif and Mercer (1996) refer to *exploratory talk*, which they see as stimulating "thinking aloud." Exploratory talk allows learners to explore and clarify concepts or to try out a line of thought, through questioning, hypothesizing, making logical deductions, or responding to others' ideas. In the *Productive Pedagogies* framework, developed by the Teaching and Learning Branch, Education Queensland, talk like this is referred to as "substantive conversation." *Substantive conversation* is described as extended talk around "big ideas" and leads to increased understanding of subject content and to a more nuanced understanding of key issues. Like exploratory talk, it creates shared understanding and space for children to explore new ideas, clarify understandings and perceptions, and make their reasoning visible to others. It is reciprocal conversation, not dominated or controlled by a single person (as in teacher-led recitation), so that participants address their comments, questions, and statements directly to each other. Where the talk is teacher-led, exchanges are extended beyond students offering only one-word or short answers, and there is a sustained and topic-related series of exchanges.

> *The quality of the dialogues that children are engaged in, not simply the quantity, must be viewed critically.*

Some researchers refer to talk like this as *dialogic* teaching (Mercer, Dawes, and Kleine Staarman 2009; Alexander 2008; Haneda and Wells 2008; Lyle 2008). Ball and Wells argue that "students' understanding of new material is most effectively achieved when curriculum is co-constructed through dialogue, in which students are able to make connections to previous learning both in and out of school and are encouraged to voice their ideas and opinions in the knowledge that they will be taken seriously by the teachers as well as their peers" (Ball and Wells 2009, 371).

Whatever we call this kind of talk, it is clear that it is very different from the IRE pattern described earlier, and that it is most likely to occur in an intellectually challenging curriculum that is inquiry oriented and cognitively engaging. For EL learners in particular, dialogic talk needs also to be associated with high levels of teacher support (look again at Figure 1–1 in Chapter 1). Compared to the traditional tightly controlled IRE exchange, a dialogic approach offers EL students an increase in comprehensible input, since there will be far more opportunities to have ideas clarified and revisited, and more opportunities to make sense of and engage in the academic language related to subject learning. In addition, there will be many opportunities for students to engage in using the language themselves, to produce

this is what I want

more extended, reasoned, and complex contributions, and to learn how to interact and collaborate with peers.

Chapter 3 focuses on group and pair work where there are many opportunities for substantive conversations and the kind of dialogic interactions and substantive conversations that this section has described. However, with some modification to the IRE pattern, more traditional teacher-to-student talk can also encourage this kind of talk and be very effective in supporting language development. This is the focus of the following section.

Teachers talking with children

There will be many times when the whole class works together with the teacher in traditional position at the front of the class. Often, as we have suggested, the kind of interaction in which teacher and students commonly engage in such situations is not supportive of EL development. Yet even in teacher-centered situations, traditional interactions can still allow for a more equal distribution of speaking rights. Two examples of this are given below.

In Chapter 1 we saw how the notion of a zone of proximal development presents learning as something accomplished through collaboration, where a more-experienced participant supports the less-experienced participant with those aspects of the task that the learner is not yet able to do alone. In the examples shown in Figures 2–1 and 2–2, children are taking part in what I refer to as *teacher-guided reporting*. This refers to those times when a student is asked to report to the whole class about what he or she has done or learned. It's probably an activity that you use yourself; you may refer to it as "reporting back" or "reporting to the class" or "reviewing." I have adopted the term *teacher-guided reporting* to make more explicit the role of the teacher in providing scaffolding for the learner. Children may not always find it easy to explain clearly to others what they have done or learned, and for EL learners in particular this may be a daunting task that pushes them beyond what they would be able to do *alone* in English. But in teacher-guided reporting, the teacher provides scaffolding by clarifying, questioning, and providing models for the speaker so that the learner and teacher together collaboratively build up what the learner wants to say. In addition, through their responses, teachers can model the kind of thinking aloud that characterizes substantive conversations and dialogic talk. Just as the father and mother provided interactional scaffolding to Nigel in the "goat text," whereby he was able to reach further in his language than he could have done alone, so too can a teacher provide scaffolding for learners so that the interaction becomes a supportive context for second language development. In this process students can also learn how to make their thinking explicit.

The examples of classroom talk in this book are authentic. Traditional punctuation is therefore not used, since the excerpts are transcriptions of spoken language. A single dot represents approximately a one-second pause, two dots a two-second pause, and so on. A *turn* refers to what a single speaker says.

Example 1: "Miss C., I can't say it."

	Student	Teacher	Commentary
1		what did you find out?	*T begins the conversation with an open question.*
2	if you put a nail . onto the piece of foil . . and then pick it . pick it up . . the magnet will . . . . that if you put a . nail . under a piece of foil . and then pick . pick the foil up with the magnet . . still . still with the nail . . under it . . . it won't		
3		it what?	*It what?* = it does what? T is looking for a verb.
4	it won't / it won't come out		
5		what won't come out?	*What* = what does *it* refer to?
6	it'll go up		
7		wait just a minute . . can you explain that a bit more, Loretta?	*T asks L to clarify.*
8	like if you put a nail and then foil over it and then put the nail on top . of the foil . . the nail underneath the foil . Miss C., I can't say it		

Figure 2–1 Teacher-Guided Reporting   *(continues)*

	Student	Teacher	Commentary
9		no, you're doing fine I . I can see	*T encourages L. Affirms she understands what L is trying to say.*
10	Miss forget about the magnet/em the magnet holds it with the foil up the top and the nail's underneath and the foil's on top and put the magnet in it and you lift it up . . . and the nail will em . . . hold it/stick with the magnet and the foil's in between		
11		oh . so even with the foil in between . the . magnet will still pick up the nail . alright does the magnet pick up the foil?	*T "recasts" what L has said.*
12	no		

Figure 2–1 *Continued*

Loretta, the student, had been separating a number of objects into two groups, magnetic and nonmagnetic. She had discovered first that a nail was magnetic and that aluminum foil was not. She had then placed a piece of aluminum foil between a magnet and a nail, discovering that the magnet still attracted the nail.

Explaining this makes considerable linguistic demands on Loretta, and she clearly finds it very difficult to verbalize what she wants to say. Her comment in turn 8, "Miss C., I can't say it," gives some indication of just how difficult the task is for her. Also note how much she pauses and how hesitant she appears at the beginning. As you read, consider how the teacher provides scaffolding for the learner, so that with this guidance Loretta is able to complete the task successfully. Notice too the overall pattern. Although this is a teacher-controlled interaction, the teacher doesn't dominate; as you can see from the transcript, the learner, in fact, says far more than the teacher.

In terms of language learning, this exchange with the teacher is very supportive for Loretta. Notice that each of her three attempts to report what she has done (turns 2, 8, 10) becomes progressively less hesitant and more understandable for those listening, with the last attempt being a greatly improved version on her initial attempt (2). How has the teacher modified the IRE pattern to make this happen?

First, the teacher begins with an open question to which there is no prescripted reply, rather than a "display" question to which she already has a "correct" answer in her own mind. Having observed Loretta in the group, she had some idea of what Loretta had done, but it is left to Loretta herself to initiate what she wants to talk about. In other words, she enters the conversation on her own terms. In general, it is a much easier task for EL learners to initiate what they want to talk about than to respond to what someone else wants them to talk about.

Second, the teacher provides very specific scaffolding for precisely those language items that need to be clarified for the listeners: the action being referred to (3) and the thing being referred to (5). She gives a word of encouragement, but she resists rewording or evaluating what Loretta says until turn 11. This added time allows Loretta two more attempts to explain what she is trying to say and more opportunity to focus on *how* she is expressing it. In fact, what students say in these kinds of conversations with the teacher is often not the outcome of previous learning, but the process of language learning itself.

Example 2: "What do you think he was thinking?"

In the text that follows, the action of one of the students in previous small-group work, Mahmoud, led to the teacher drawing the class' attention to what he might have been thinking, thus making explicit his reasoning. He had been testing a range of objects to decide what was magnetic and what was nonmagnetic. A gold-colored nail was eventually shown to be nonmagnetic, but not before—without any prompting from the teacher—Mahmoud had ruled out the possibility that its nonattraction was simply the result of the nail's weight. To test this he had used two, then three magnets to find out whether their combined strength would be enough to attract the nail. During the following teacher-guided reporting, the teacher is discussing the reason why he might have done this with Mahmoud and five other students from his group (Gina, Colin, Fabiola, Rana, and Amanda). The remainder of the class is seated on the floor in front of the teacher.

	Student	Teacher	Commentary
1	Mahmoud: we put three magnets together / it still wouldn't hold the gold nail . . . even though we had three magnets it still wouldn't stick		
2		so he put three magnets together . . . because he was concerned about that gold nail . . . and he said / he thought well . . . maybe one magnet wasn't strong enough / is that what he was thinking Gina?	*T repeats what Mahmoud has said more explicitly for the benefit of other listeners.*
3	Gina: he was thinking to try each end [pole] like if one end isn't good then something like that?		
4		is that what you were thinking Mahmoud?	*T defers to Mahmoud to respond to Gina.*
	Mahmoud shakes his head.		
5		Colin what do you think he was thinking?	
6	Colin: he was thinking the gold nail was stronger . . . . couldn't make the magnet go on . . . it was too heavy		
7		he was thinking that the nail was a bit heavy so he thought maybe one magnet wasn't strong enough but then with three magnets it still wouldn't attract	*T rewords and extends on what Colin has said, so that all the students can understand what he was thinking.*
8	Mahmoud: ten magnets wouldn't still		
9	Colin: if you did twenty it wouldn't still		
10	Fabiola: yeah hundred!		*It is clear that the students understand that the weight of the nail is not relevant here.*
11	Rana: and we thought how about if the gold screw is . . gold and the thumbtack color gold as well . . how come the thumbtack stick and the gold screw didn't? and we thought that they might be different metals		*Rana's contribution is not the result of the teacher's nomination, but suggests her engagement in the conversation.*

Figure 2–2 Teacher-Guided Reporting *(continues)*

	Student	Teacher	Commentary
		aah! that was good that was very good the way they were talking about that . . . see here's Rana's argument look (*demonstrating*) same colour but the magnet didn't attract this (*gold screw*) but it did attract this (*thumbtack*)	*T gives positive feedback about "the way they were talking about that."* *She defers to the Rana by referring to the hypothesis as "Rana's argument."* *Then, through demonstration, she gives a concrete example of what Rana has said.*
12	Amanda: magnets only stick to some kinds of metal		*Amanda makes a significant contribution to the conversation.*
13		so Amanda say that again . . it's different kinds of metal *therefore*	*T repeats what Amanda has said. Note the emphasis on* therefore, *signaling that what follows is significant.*
14	Amanda: magnets only stick to some kinds of metal		*Amanda repeats what she said in turn 12.*
15		only *some* metals	*T again repeats the key words in what Amanda said, emphasizing "some."*
16	Amanda: yes		
17		only *some*	*The third repetition of "only some" underlines for the children the significance of this piece of information.*

Figure 2–2 *Continued*

Most teachers would agree that part of what they aim to do in the classroom is to teach children to think! In Example 2 we see how the teacher focuses on helping the children make their thinking and reasoning explicit; this is in fact a major part of the conversation. The main piece of scientific information—that magnets only attract certain metals (no matter how many magnets you use you still can't pick up something that is nonmagnetic)—is co-constructed between students and teacher, and highlighted in the teacher's talk through repetition and emphasis. The students' thinking is valued—note the way in which the teacher defers to individual students: *was that what you were thinking Mahmoud?*; *that was good the way they were talking about that*; *here's Rana's argument.* The teacher also makes the students' thinking explicit in her own talk: *he thought maybe one magnet wasn't strong enough.* This conversation is a model for the kind of dialogic talk described earlier, where students are free to contribute to the conversation without teacher-nomination (see turns 8, 9, 10, 11) and where there is an expectation that ideas and opinions should be justified and supported.

There is much we can learn by listening to how teachers talk with and respond to students. Examples 1 and 2 indicate the potential that thoughtful teacher talk can have for supporting language development. Here are some ideas to consider in your own interactions with EL learners.

Find a balance between straight "display" questions and those that allow learners to decide what they want to talk about

When you are questioning children about what they have learned, possible openers could include: *Tell us what you learned. Tell us about what you did. What did you find out? What would you like to tell us about? What did you find most interesting?*

Try monitoring your own talk to see what openers you use most often.

Respond to meaning

This involves really listening to what the students say rather than listening for the answer you expect! While in Example 1 the teacher's scaffolding could be seen as a focus on form—that is, on the grammar and structure of the language—everything she says is ultimately in the service of meaning making, not for the sake of practicing grammar. As Lily Wong Fillmore (1985) says in her seminal study of effective teachers of very young EL learners, the teachers "were effective communicators . . . because all of them were concerned with communication" (40).

Slow down the dialogue

This doesn't mean that you should speak excessively slowly, but that the overall pace of the conversation should allow sufficient time for learners to think about what they are saying, and thus how they are saying it. This can be achieved in two ways:

- ◆ By increasing "wait time"—that is, the time you wait for the learner to respond. Increasing this by just a few seconds makes a big difference to how much students say, how clearly they say it, and how far they are able to demonstrate what they understand.
- ◆ By allowing a student more turns before you evaluate or recast (reword) what the student has said. The teacher in the transcript shown in Figure 2–1 made a significant choice: she could have reworded what Loretta was attempting to say at turn 3 but she chose not to, instead waiting until turn 11. In this way Loretta was given the opportunity to have several attempts to explain what she had done, offering much more opportunity for student output. This extends the conversation and leads to a much longer exchange between a teacher and a student than is often the case in whole-class work. The teacher uses a simple strategy, which is to ask Loretta herself to clarify meaning, rather than take responsibility for doing this herself. The teacher's responses to her do not simply evaluate what Loretta has said; instead, they prompt her to have another go: *Can you explain that a bit more?* Other ways of extending a conversation in similar situations include: *I don't quite understand, can you tell me that again? Tell me a little more. Can you just expand on that a little more? That was a really good comment, explain it to us again.*

> *The pace of the conversation allows sufficient time for learners to think about what they are going to say.*

Whenever you say something like this, you are slowing down the often-fast pace of the discourse, and giving learners time to formulate, as far as they are able, a more explicit way of saying what they want to say. And there is considerable evidence that learners who have more opportunities to reflect on and improve their own communication receive more long-term benefits for language learning than those who constantly have communication problems solved *for* them by the teacher. Of course, you need to use your own judgment in relation to individual learners, and decide how much responsibility for clarification you put onto them, but almost certainly most EL students will be able to say more if they are given more time during the process of an interaction.

just for ELs →

Allow thinking time before students are expected to answer

For example, tell students they have thirty seconds (or more) to think of an answer before you nominate someone to answer. Or give students time to talk with a partner and share their answers before you ask someone to share their ideas with the whole class. All children are likely to benefit from this extra processing time, but it is a particular advantage for EL learners to be able to "rehearse" what they want to say before they are asked to respond. And, in addition, the whole class is engaged in thinking about and formulating a possible answer.

Help students to explain their reasoning, not just give information

Making thinking explicit and explaining reasoning is a central part of dialogic talk and substantive conversation. When teachers encourage this through their own conversations with children, it helps not only the speaker but also those listening to better understand key concepts and "big ideas," and in turn it provides them with the skills to share their thinking with others in small-group work.

Treat students as worthy conversational partners

Build on and extend their ideas. Ask for clarification. Defer to specific students when referring to their ideas. In modeling this behavior you are affirming and constructing children as capable learners, and you are also modeling two of the attributes of effective dialogic talk: (1) to show respect and interest toward the contributions of others, and (2) to explain the basis for an opinion.

Using "message abundancy"

In this section we focus on how teacher talk can be made comprehensible to learners. Before considering this, however, it is important to keep two things in mind. First, not all learning happens as a result of teacher-led talk. Second, how comprehensible teacher talk is to EL learners is largely to do with what they already know about the topic, including what they know in their mother-tongue/other languages. As Chapter 4 will illustrate, learners' prior learning and concrete experiences provide significant scaffolding for comprehension. But there will still be times where more extended teacher talk will occur and where students need further support to fully comprehend what is said, especially as new subject language is introduced.

When I have talked with EL learners about the difficulties they have in learning in school, there is one problem that they often identify: they complain that the teacher talks too quickly. When we talk further, it often becomes clear that they are talking not about the speed at which their teachers speak, but rather the speed at which new ideas and concepts are being presented. When we are listening to someone talking in a language that is new to us, we need a lot more time to process what is being said in order to make sense of it. In a fast-paced classroom, where a teacher moves quickly from one new idea to the next, EL learners may be unable to keep up. By the time they have processed the first piece of information the teacher has already moved on to the next, so as the talk continues EL learners may fall further and further behind, resulting in a kind of information backlog. To support students' understanding of new or more complex ideas, we need to consider how this information backlog for students can be avoided. In Figure 2–1 where the teacher was talking with a student, we saw the importance of the teacher slowing the interaction so that the student had more time to express herself. In a longer stretch of teacher talk, a sequence of new ideas or information may also need to be slowed, and carefully spaced. One way to do this is through "message abundancy." As an illustration of message abundancy, here is an example from outside the classroom.

My work in schools has often required me to do a considerable amount of driving. This has not always been problem free, since I admit to having a very poor sense of direction. Unlike many I know, I find it difficult to memorize a map route ahead of time, so I often need to stop to check where I should be going (or where I am). Listening to a complicated set of directions rarely helps either, as often they are given quite quickly (perhaps because it is a familiar route for the person explaining it!). Driving somewhere new was always a challenge that often involved taking wrong turns and getting lost. So now I use a GPS system. It gives me the same information as a map or a set of spoken instructions, but with one important difference: it presents this information in more than one way, using a range of spoken and visual modes.

Here is an illustration of how my particular system works:

- The spoken instructions are given in small bites of information and are repeated several times: *left hand turn coming up; turn left in 600 metres/turn left in 500 metres/turn left in 400 metres,* and so on, until the turn is reached and the voice then says something like *turn left, Epping Road; turn left now.*
- Accompanying the spoken language, and representing the same information, is a map on screen that moves in synchrony with the progress of the car. The visual representation closely matches the oral instructions. To make the route clearer, it is indicated in color, with the left-hand turn indicated by an arrow.
- At the bottom of the screen is another representation of the spoken instructions using symbols and numbers: there is an arrow (in this case, pointing left) along with numbers that match the countdown of the spoken instructions (600 metres, 500 metres, and so on).
- Significant landmarks are indicated on the map as they are reached so that the driver knows exactly where he or she is: traffic lights, gas stations, bridges, parks, rivers, and so on.

What the GPS system does, therefore, is to present the same information in different ways: through spoken language with key information repeated several times; through visual symbolic representations such as maps, arrows, and numbers; and through highlighting techniques such as the use of color. These things are happening *alongside* the spoken language: they are integrated with what is being said. This is what I am referring to as *message abundancy*. It gives a listener more than one chance to access information: if any part of the spoken language is missed, then there are other systems of meaning occurring simultaneously by which the same information can be accessed. To put it another way, message abundancy gives a listener more than one bite of the apple!

Message abundancy is a significant aspect of comprehensible teacher talk and is central to effective learning. When teacher talk is integrated with other systems of meaning, it is much more likely to be understood. In one Year 4 classroom the children were learning about the rotation of the earth. In a previous lesson they had been introduced to the concept of the earth turning. As a reminder to the children of what they had talked about, the teacher is now holding a globe. She turns it, asking the children, *what does the earth do?* Several children respond with, *it turns.* The teacher affirms the answer and writes what the children said, using a blue marker, on the whiteboard. Then she tells the class that they are going to learn a new word and reminds them that scientists often use "special words" when they talk about science. Here is what she says. The dots denote pauses and the bold type denotes a strong emphasis on the word.

Message abundancy gives a listener more than one bite of the apple!

> it's quite right what you all said . . the earth **turns** . . . (*Writes "the earth turns" on the whiteboard in blue*) but there is another word that we can use . . a special word that scientists use, a **scientific** word . . . so we can say the earth . . **rotates** . . it **turns** . . . it **rotates**, look (*Demonstrating with the globe, as several children repeat the word* rotates) . . . . so what's it doing? . . it's rotating, it's turning . . . so the earth **rotates** . let's write that up, too, beside what you told me before . the earth **rotates** (*Writes "the earth rotates" in red marker on the whiteboard, beside "the earth turns"*).

good example of message abundance

If you had been an EL learner in that classroom, you would have had several opportunities to understand the concept and the new word.

- ◆ The teacher drew on prior knowledge.
- ◆ She demonstrated the meaning of *rotate* using a concrete demonstration.
- ◆ The children heard both the everyday and more academic terms used *together*.
- ◆ They could see the everyday and more academic terms written on the board.
- ◆ The two sentences were side by side on the board, and were color-coded, indicating that while the meaning is equivalent, the register is different.

- The teacher paused between each key point, and immediately before introducing the new word, and used emphasis for key words.
- She talked about how language is used, referring to "special"/"scientific words."

Here are other ideas for providing message abundancy. As you are talking:

- Refer to visuals, such as diagrams, mind maps, or graphic outlines.
- Intersperse what you say with other sources of input, such as a video or a diagram.
- Give students an outline of key points and a highlighter for them to indicate key words as you introduce them, or a diagram, flow chart, or sequence of pictures that represent the most important information.
- If relevant, draw attention to other written texts where the same information is presented.

What the teacher did in the small fragment of talk above is not unusual, of course, and many teachers would be able to see their own practices mirrored there. However, while there are EL learners who struggle to follow the meaning of what goes on in the classroom, the use of message abundancy, where information is amplified rather than simplified, is a significant aspect of scaffolding for EL learners. This is a message that needs to go beyond those who are EL specialist teachers!

In Summary

This chapter has discussed the nature of classroom talk, focusing on teacher talk and teachers' interactions with students.

- An effective spoken language program needs to be underpinned by an understanding of the key principles of second language development.
- Learners need access to comprehensible input and models of new language across the curriculum, as well as opportunities for comprehensible output, stretched language, and using the resources of their other languages.

◆ A classroom where there is an overuse of the IRE pattern cannot provide for these conditions.

◆ Using a dialogic approach, including making some adaptations to teacher-led talk, gives EL learners increased opportunities for understanding subject content in tandem with the development of English.

◆ Message abundancy, where the same information is given in a variety of ways, increases comprehensibility of input for EL learners.

To Think About

1. How important is it for all teachers of EL learners, not only specialist language teachers, to be familiar with second language development principles?
2. If appropriate, audio-record yourself in class talking with a group of EL learners. Listen to your responses and consider how well you provided opportunities for students to talk. Who spoke most? Why?
3. What do you see as the key features of "dialogic talk" or "substantive conversation"?
4. What points in the chapter affirm your current practice? What is the most important learning for you?
5. Tell a success story that is based on a spoken language activity you designed for your class or talk about an individual student's growth in oral language development.

Suggestions for Further Reading

Alexander, R. 2008. *Towards Dialogic Thinking: Rethinking Classroom Talk*, 4th ed. North Yorkshire, UK: Dialogos.

Carrasquillo A., S. Kucer, and R. Abrams. 2004. Chapter 2, "English Literacy Development and English Language Learners: A Theoretical Overview." In *Beyond the Beginnings, Literacy Interventions for Upper Elementary English Language Learners*. Clevedon, UK: Multilingual Matters.

Gibbons, P. 2009. Chapter 7, "Planning Talk for Learning and Literacy." In *English Learners Academic Literacy, and Thinking*. Portsmouth, NH: Heinemann.

Haneda, M., and G. Wells. 2008. "Learning an Additional Language Through Dialogic Inquiry." *Language and Education* 22 (2): 114–36.

Mercer, N., L. Dawes, and J. Kleine Staarman. 2009. "Dialogic Teaching in the Primary Classroom." *Language and Education* 23 (4): 353–69.

Wallace, C. 2013. Chapter 3, "Bilingual Learners in a Multilingual Primary School." In *Literacy and the Bilingual Learner*. London: Palgrave Macmillan.

Walqui, A., and L. van Lier. 2010. *Scaffolding the Academic Success of Adolescent English Language Learners*, 25–41. San Francisco: WestEd.

Three

Collaborative Group Work and Second Language Learning

··

Language is our cultural tool—we use it to share experience, and so to collectively, jointly, make sense of it . . . Language is therefore not just a means by which individuals can formulate ideas and communicate them, it is also a means for people to think and learn together.

—Neil Mercer, *The Guided Construction of Knowledge*

As we saw in the previous chapter, where language development is a major objective of a teaching program, alternatives to IRE patterns need to be consciously planned and set up. The previous chapter discussed teacher talk. This chapter focuses on the use of group work, again drawing on the research of second language development discussed in Chapter 2. It begins with an illustration of how a group of children, working together, were able to achieve more than they each could have done individually. It continues with a discussion of criteria for making group work effective, then suggests some group and pair work activities that are easily integrated with subject-based work across the curriculum. The chapter concludes with suggestions for the development of the interpersonal language that is necessary for effective collaborative work.

Well-designed and well-run group work offers many affordances for language learning and has important advantages for second language development. Learners have more chances to interact with other speakers, and therefore the amount of language they use is also increased. They tend to take more turns, and in the absence of the teacher have more responsibility for clarifying their own meanings: it is the learners themselves who are doing the language-learning work. What learners hear and what they learn is *contextualized*: language is heard and used in an appropriate context and used meaningfully for a particular purpose. For EL learners, comprehension is also increased, because asking questions, exchanging information, and solving problems all provide a context where words are repeated, ideas are rephrased, problems are restated, and meanings are refined. The need to get information or clarify meaning also increases the opportunities for learners to ask questions that genuinely seek new information, and thus there is further input and practice in authentic communication. Well-designed group work therefore offers a particular kind of language-rich context that cannot be duplicated in whole-class work. In addition, group work may have positive affective consequences: learners who are not confident in English often feel more comfortable working with peers than performing in a whole-class situation.

Here is a classroom example that illustrates how children working together can do more collaboratively than they can individually, and it demonstrates the collaborative nature of learning discussed in Chapters 1 and 2. It is taken from the science classroom mentioned in the previous chapter, where different groups of children had each done a different experiment designed to show the effects of magnetic repulsion. Prior to the reporting-back session described earlier, the teacher had told the children they would report to the rest of the class about what happened in their own group, and what they had learned from doing their particular experiment. Time was given for the children to rehearse what they might say later to the whole class. The teacher explained to the students that they needed to make what they said clear and comprehensible to their listeners, and they needed to remember that the rest of the class did not know what each group had done. She explained that their language needed to be very clear and precise so that everyone could understand what happened, and suggested to the reporters that they should help their listeners to "try to get a picture in their mind of what you did." This time for rehearsal was also a time when children could clarify common understandings and new learning. This rehearsal for reporting is transcribed and begins on the next page.

In the group were four children. All of the children except Emily, who was a fluent bilingual in Chinese and English, were identified as having EL needs. Milad and Maroun were in the early stages of learning English. For their experiment, the group followed instructions to construct a small polystyrene block into which a number of popsicle sticks (referred to by the children as paddle pop sticks) were inserted to form a fence-like framework that would hold a bar magnet in place. The group was asked to test the effect of a second bar magnet when it was placed above the first, and then to reverse the position of the second magnet. They recorded their results. (Depending on the relative position of the poles, the magnets either attract or repel. When repulsion occurs, the top magnet is suspended in mid-air and appears to be floating above the bottom magnet.) In the dialogue that follows, the children are planning how they will report back to the class about this science experiment.

Emily	we have to talk about what we did last time and what were the results . . .
Milad	we got em . . . we got a . . . thing like . . . this . . . pu- we got paddle pop sticks and we got
Maroun	we put them in a pot
Milad	and have to try and put
Gina	wasn't in a pot . . . it's like a foam . . .
Milad	a foam
Emily	a block of foam
Gina	and we put it
Emily	we put paddle pops around it . the foam and then we put the magnet in it
Gina	and then we got
Emily	and then we got another magnet and put it on top and it wasn't touching the other magnet . .
Maroun	when we . . . when we turned it the other way . . . it didn't stick on because . . . because
Gina	because?

Maroun   because em . . . it was on a different . . . side

Milad   Emily your go

Emily   OK. last week we . . . we . . . did an experiment . . . we had a em a block of foam and we um . . . stuck paddle pop sticks in it and we put . . . a magnet a bar of magnet . . . into the em cradle that we made with the paddle pop sticks . then we put another magnet on top and the result of this was . . . the magnet that we put on top of the cradled magnet did not stick to the other magnet

Gina   then when we turned it around . when we turned the other magnet around it . . .

Maroun   stuck

Milad   it stuck together because

Maroun   and it stuck together because it was

Emily   it was on a different side

Gina   it was on a different side and the other one's and

Emily   and the poles are different

Gina   and the poles are different

Milad   and em when . . . we put on the first side it stuck together . . .

Gina   because em it was on different sides, because we put it on the on the thin side and it didn't and we didn't . . . it didn't stick . .

Maroun   because the flat side is stronger than the thin side?

Emily   no because the poles are different

Milad   because the poles are different . alright?

What can we learn from this example? It is clear that a lot is being learned in this group talk, both about science and about how to talk about it. The conversation also serves the purpose of clarifying what happened in the group. All the children participate in *jointly* constructing this discourse. For example, the term *block of foam* is finally reached through a progressive clarification of an appropriate way to name it, and this is built up by three speakers: *a pot, not a pot, a foam* (repeated), *a block of foam.* Students complete one another's remarks and prompt one another to continue. The main scientific understanding of the experiment is built up across seven turns that together construct the statement: *when we turned the other magnet around it stuck together because it was on a different side and the poles are different.* Through the process of joint construction, the wording is gradually refined toward more explicit and written-like language, and scientific understandings are reworked and modified (note that *different sides* becomes *different poles*). Individual students are therefore scaffolded by the contributions of the group as a whole.

This talk is not a functionally empty language exercise, but the result of a real and shared purpose.

This kind of collective peer scaffolding is at times as useful as that provided by the teacher. No student, except perhaps Emily, possessed the ability to construct this oral report alone, but *collectively* the students are able to reach an appropriate wording. Note, however, that this talk is not a functionally "empty" language exercise, but the result of a real and shared purpose for the students, who knew that one of them would be expected to share his or her learning with the class. Gina, who was chosen by the teacher for this task, explained her group's experiment like this:

> We put paddle pop sticks around the block of foam . . . and then . . . we got a magnet and put it in . . . and we got another magnet and put it on top but it wasn't touching the other magnet and then . when we turned it around it attach together . the two magnets . . when we put it on the side they attach . because . . because the poles are different.

It is unlikely that Gina would have been able to speak as fluently as this without the initial group talk that helped her to clarify the information. Notice that what she says here is beginning to sound more like "written" language. Oral reporting to others, where what is being talked about is not supported by the visual context and where the listeners did not participate in the original task, is an example of "literate talk." Literate talk like this serves as a bridge to reading and writing, and it is discussed further in Chapter 4.

Peer scaffolding is at times as useful as that provided by the teacher.

MAKING GROUP WORK EFFECTIVE

How then should group work be organized if it is to be effective for EL learners? Here are some suggestions.

Clear and explicit instructions are provided

This may seem very obvious, yet it is often at the setting-up stage that even a well-designed task can go wrong. As you have probably observed in your own teaching, one of the hardest listening tasks for EL learners is to understand and remember a string of instructions. While a single instruction may cause no problems, instructions that involve a number of sequenced steps are often far more difficult. Try giving the same instructions in several ways: use message abundancy! For example, after you have explained to children what they are to do, ask someone to retell what you said to the rest of the class, or ask individual children to tell you each step in turn. Write it on the board as they say it. Written instructions on cards are also useful and will help keep children on task. And remember that it is often better to demonstrate a game or activity with a student as your partner than to give an explanation in words. In some tasks, and particularly with beginners, the language of the explanation can be more complex than the language involved in the task itself!

Here is an example of a teacher giving instructions to a group of EL children who are about to carry out the science experiment described earlier; it is a good example of message abundancy. First, she read from written instructions:

> Place a bar magnet into the cradle made by the paddle pop sticks. Place a second bar magnet on top. Observe and record what happens. Repeat, alternating the poles. Observe and record what happens.

Figure 3–1 is a transcript of what the teacher then says. The right-hand column explains what the teacher was doing physically and comments on the language she used. You will see that as she worked through each step of the instructions, she provided scaffolding for the children to ensure that the

Teacher's words	Commentary
You have to place a magnet, put a magnet, into the cradle, and place another magnet on top of the cradled magnet	*Teacher refers to the written instructions, introduces less-well-known word* place *alongside more familiar word* put.
So you've got one magnet in here	*Pointing*
then you have to put another magnet on top, right?	*Holding the second magnet, indicating where it must be placed but not actually placing it*
. then you have to alt-ern-ate the magnets.	*The word* alternate *is said slowly and with emphasis.*
It says "alternating the poles" . . . changing the poles.	*Models the more formal word* (alternate) *but uses this along with a familiar "everyday" word* (change); *also holds the second magnet and indicates how the magnet should be turned.*
So if you put it facing like this . . . you've got it one way like this,	*Demonstrating*
then you change the poles around	*Indicating the movement by turning the second magnet in the air but not placing it*
change it to the other side, alternate the poles.	*Switches between more and less formal terms.*
So you're trying it each way	*Summarizing what the children should do.*

Figure 3–1 Scaffolding Instructions

written instructions were comprehensible. After this careful scaffolding, each group was given a copy of the instructions.

Notice how the teacher introduced the use of more formal terms (such as *place* and *alternate*) alongside more usual and familiar terms (*put* and *change*) so that through this parallelism children could see the equivalencies in meaning. At the same time, she demonstrated the meaning of what she was saying by physically handling the materials with which the children would be working. Finally, the children had a set of written instructions to which they could later refer (which also modeled a more formal example of language use). Note that the teacher was not simply giving the children a set of *simplified* instructions. On the contrary, the written instructions were fairly typical of more formal written language and were appropriate for the age level of the children. What the teacher did was to build "bridges" into this written text so that the learners were given access to new and more formal language. She *amplified*, rather than *simplified*, the language.

Talk is necessary for the task

A group task should *require*, not simply *encourage*, talk. Let's imagine that you are working with the topic of insects. If you ask groups of children simply to "talk about" a picture of insects, there is no real reason or need for the picture to be discussed, and probably not all children will join in. In this case talk is invited, even encouraged, but it is not *required*, since there is no authentic purpose for using it.

> *The teacher amplified rather than simplified the language.*

However, if a pair of children is given two similar pictures of insects that differ in some details (see Figure 3–2) and they are asked to find the differences between them without showing each other their pictures, then talk is *required*: without interaction, the task cannot be carried out. This kind of activity is a **Find the Difference** game. Each student needs to describe his or her picture in order to determine in what ways it differs from his or her partner's picture. Encourage children to ask questions of their partner if they need clarification and to provide as much detail as they can about their own picture for the benefit of their partner.

Tasks that require talk often involve some kind of *information gap*—that is, a situation whereby different members within a group, or individuals in a pair, hold different or incomplete information, so that the only way that the task can be completed is for this information to be shared. Pair activities like this are sometimes called "barrier games," referring to the fact that partners do not show each other their information, so they have to complete the task through language alone. Many of the activities described later in this chapter also have an information gap of some kind.

It is possible to use the information gap principle with a whole class. In the science classroom discussed in Chapter 2, the teacher had set up five different

Figure 3–2 Find the Difference

experiments, all designed to develop students' understanding of the concepts of magnetic attraction and repulsion. The teacher's original plan was for all groups of students to do each of these experiments over the course of a couple of weeks, and then to report to the whole class about what they had learned. On reflection, the teacher decided against this, since this would have resulted in students talking about what was already familiar to the rest of the class (given that they would all have done the same things). Instead, the teacher revised her plan and decided that each group would do a different experiment so that when the time came for reporting what they had learned, each group would be talking about something unknown to their audience—they would be the "experts" in what they had done, and there would be an authentic context for information sharing. Talking about something that the rest of the class hasn't experienced themselves also requires students to be very explicit about what they have learned, and to focus on making what they say comprehensible to the rest of the class.

Organizing the class into **Jigsaw Groups** is another way to fulfill the principle of creating an information gap with a whole class. Jigsaw groups operate on the principle that different groups of learners become "experts" in a particular aspect of a topic and then share this with other learners who are experts in a different aspect. For example, in a topic about insects, each group may choose to research a particular insect under certain agreed headings, such as *description*, *habitat*, *food*, *life cycle*, and *interesting facts*. After each group has become an expert in one particular insect, the students go into new groups so that one person from each expert group is in each new group. Then each person shares his or her "expert" knowledge with the other group members.

In this way, each individual becomes an expert in the new group and now has the responsibility of sharing what he or she knows, while the nonexperts make notes. Through this process all information is shared, and the resulting notes may become the basis for a piece of writing.

There is a clear outcome for the group work

In well-designed activities, something *happens* as a result of the language being used. There will be an outcome, a result, such as the solving of a problem or the sharing of information. Learners should be clear about what this outcome should be. For example, in the Find the Difference game, they should know the number of differences they are looking for, and know that they must name them. In the jigsaw activity described above, the outcome will be that all children will have a set of written notes based on what others have said and on their own research. It's important to make the outcome of the task explicit to students when you are setting it up so that they understand the purpose of what they are doing.

The task is cognitively appropriate to the learners

As far as possible, the task should be at an appropriate level of cognitive challenge for the age of the learners. The high-challenge, high-support quadrant illustrated in Figure 1–1 in Chapter 1 is where students will have the most opportunity to engage in the kinds of conversations and contexts that best support language development.

For learners who are at the very early initial stages of learning English, tasks need to be cognitively challenging while at the same time providing high levels of language scaffolding so that the task is not simply beyond what the student can achieve at that time. This is not always an easy task. But it is often the nature of the *scaffolding* that makes the difference between a student's success or failure, rather than the cognitive challenge of the task. Older learners are also likely to have some literacy skills, and it may be that part of the task can draw on first language resources. For example, students may initially discuss, read, or write in their first language (see also Chapter 1). Beginners in English will also be able to participate in tasks that are less dependent on language, such as science experiments or mathematics activities. And remember that such tasks provide an essential respite from the intense demands of continuously operating in an unfamiliar language.

The task is integrated with a broader curriculum topic

We have seen in Chapter 1 how a functional view of language relates language to the context in which it is used. We do not first "learn" language and then later "use" it. EL learners do not in any case have the time to study English as a "subject" before they use it to learn other things: they must begin to use it as a medium for learning as soon as they enter school, simultaneously developing academic English hand in hand with curriculum knowledge. As Mohan (2001) points out, we cannot place EL students' academic development on hold while they are learning English. And so, as far as possible, language-learning tasks should be integrated with learning across the curriculum. Language tasks and exercises that are simply an add-on to the curriculum not only work against this, but are a frustrating experience for the teacher who then has to find time for such extra work. In Chapter 8 we will look in more detail at how program planning can incorporate both language and content objectives. Here I will note only that one of the advantages of situating language teaching within a curriculum area is that language development and subject development

We cannot place EL students' academic development on hold while they are learning English.

support each other: through the focus on language, the concepts and content associated with particular curriculum knowledge are recycled, while familiar content provides a meaningful context for language development. Most of the activities and tasks listed in the Glossary can be situated within a range of subject areas and integrated with the particular topic being studied.

All children in the group are involved

As a teacher, you will no doubt have had students who don't participate in group work, perhaps because of different cultural norms, or because they feel insecure about their contribution, are dominated by others in the group, or simply prefer not to work in this way. There are two ways in which you can help ensure that all children are involved.

First, the overall organizational structure should be such that it requires the participation of all group members. Jigsaw groupings, for example, require that all members carry out their particular responsibilities, otherwise the group will not have all the information it needs. And the peer group is very good at making sure this work gets done! As I overheard one learner insist to another when a group was sharing information on insects, "Go on, you tell us, *you're* the butterfly!" Students are urged to take responsibility because the group wants them to, not just because the teacher expects them to. In this way, group work serves as an effective prompt for learning and helps students develop a sense of personal worth and responsibility.

Second, until children are used to working in groups, members of the group should each have a role to play. These can include a timekeeper, a recorder, a reporter, someone who keeps the group on task, someone who ensures everyone has an opportunity to contribute, and so on. Not only does this give a special responsibility to all the members of the group, but it also helps ensure that the group work runs effectively and makes more explicit what makes a group function well.

Students have enough time to complete tasks

The question of time is a very important one: too much, and children may waste it; not enough, and they are unlikely to learn effectively or be able to engage in the activity as fully as they could. EL students are likely to take longer to complete language-based tasks, since they need longer to process what they hear and to respond to language that is directed to them. Less-experienced teachers may sometimes design a wonderful set of tasks but aim to do too much in one lesson, so that children are no sooner into one task than another one is begun. Well-designed tasks are worth exploiting! Don't underestimate the time it takes to give clear instructions, for the task to be completed and for summing up what students have done or learned. Each of these processes also involve language and are an opportunity to model, recycle, and revise what students have done and learned. They can be as important a part of the learning as the end product.

Students know how to work in groups

Working in groups is a learned skill—even some adults are not good at it! If learners are unable to work collaboratively, even the best-designed teaching activities are unlikely to be successful. Effective participation implies the taking of initiative, and this is only possible when students understand and subscribe to the "rules" of classroom behavior. While most classrooms have some agreed-upon rules for behavior, group work is often based on "unwritten" and assumed knowledge about how to work together. Making such knowledge explicit is helpful for all children, but especially for those less familiar with the learning culture and norms of the school.

Here is an example of one teacher talking with her students about working collaboratively in a group. As a conclusion to work on magnets, the children are about to design a game based on the properties of magnets. The teacher is talking with the children about what makes group work a success.

> **Teacher** you're going to come up with *one* game . . OK . . . so you have to do a lot of negotiating because you're all going to have lots of good ideas . . but is . . . is it going to be like this . . . get into the group . . and say, "I know what we're doing, me me me . I've decided?" is that how we work in groups?
>
> **Students** no.
>
> **Teacher** what sorts of things can we remember? Simon?
>
> **Simon** em . . . share your ideas?

Teacher	good take turns share your ideas because four people's ideas or three people's ideas have to be better than one person's ideas, don't they? we'll get a lot more . . Fabiola?
Fabiola	communicate with your group.
Teacher	how do you *communicate* with your group . . . that's very true, but how do you do it?
Fabiola	like instead of . . em when you start with your group you don't em shout, and don't . . . "I know what we should do and this is what we can do" . . and if someone want to talk it over say "no, *this* is what we're going to do."
Teacher	OK . . so it's a lot of . . . first of all, turn taking, and quiet group-work voices, and maybe sharing your ideas . . certainly . "oh, an idea I have" or "one idea I have" or "a suggestion that I have" . . put it forward as a suggestion or an idea . . people will be much more willing to listen to it than if you say . . "this is what we're going to do" . . so be careful with the sort of group-work language that you use
Gina	Miss how about if like . . . you have four people in your group and one want [sic] to do something and another one want to do something else and they all want to do different things?
Teacher	they've all got different ideas? good . good question . . does anyone have any suggestions for Gina? if you get into your group and everyone says "well this is my idea," "this is my idea," "this is my idea," "this is my idea" . . and no one wants to . . . move from their idea?
	Lots of students indicate they have ideas.
Teacher	what could be some strategies? Duncan.
Ducan	em, you could put them all together . . . like . . . like make them one.
Fabiola	make up into one game
Teacher	OK so maybe try to combine the ideas to make up one game, that could be one thing . . what if they don't go together, though? what if the ideas are very very different? how could you work with it then Anna?

Anna   em you could em find a piece of paper and write it and scrunch up and put it into a hat

Teacher   OK choose it . . . maybe say "Alright, we can't decide . . . so that's the most fair way to do it" . . that could be one way . . that's another suggestion . yes Charbel?

Charbel   do an arm wrestle? (*Laughing*)

Teacher   oh probably not the most appropriate way . certainly an idea. (*Laughing*) yes . we might get ourselves into real trouble though . . . thank you, I don't think Mr. W. [the principal] would be too impressed if he walked in and saw us arm wrestling over what we decide to do . he probably wouldn't think that was appropriate group-work behavior . (*Laughing*) Robert?

"Do an arm wrestle?"

Robert   miss if you can't think of one you can em . . . you can you can . . . play it? and see which one's a good one.

Teacher   OK good suggestion . . yes, Andre?

Andre   Oh Miss like . . . you're going to vote for which one is the most fun

Teacher   that's a good idea. maybe you could say you can't vote for your own but you can vote for one of the others . sometimes though it's just . . . not being stubborn . . . you know . thinking . really trying to step back and think "well, it doesn't matter whose idea it is, but what would be the best idea for the task that we're trying to complete?"

This kind of talk makes explicit to children some of the ways they will be expected to work. But perhaps even more important is the fact that the "rules" are collaboratively built up, with the children's contributions being valued by the teacher and expanded on. In this process, the teacher also provides models of what (and what not!) to say in the context of group work. This introduces us to an area of language that is often not explicitly taught: the interpersonal function of language. The interpersonal dimension of language describes how language is used to develop and maintain relationships, so it is an important part of successful group work where the aim is to work collaboratively. It is discussed in more detail at the end of the chapter.

Finally, remember to talk with the children about what the teacher shown here referred to as "quiet group-work voices"! Encourage children to speak as quietly as possible to avoid the situation all too familiar to teachers—when noise levels steadily increase as everyone seeks to make themselves heard above the others. Remember that for EL learners, a noisy environment makes comprehension that much harder.

SOME SUGGESTIONS FOR GROUP AND PAIR ACTIVITIES ACROSS THE CURRICULUM

All the activities described here require authentic spoken communication among learners. Most are intended for small-group or pair work. All can be adapted for a range of age levels and subject areas. They are not, however, intended to be used in isolation, but should be integrated into a broader subject-based topic.

Paired Problem Solving

This activity is useful in those situations where something is to be made, such as in art, in design and technology, or in science. In the following example, which is taken from the work of Jenny Des-Fountain and Alan Howe (1992), pairs of students are engaged in two different problem-solving activities, based on a book they have read. One group of pairs have the task of designing a mobile, and the other of designing a boat made out of newspaper that will keep afloat twenty marbles. When the groups have finished, different pairs come together to cross-question each other about what they did, how they did it, and what problems they faced. One of the boat-builders is Manzeer, an early EL learner. The pair had a problem! In the children's words:

> **Sylvia**   It kept on sinking, and the newspaper, it kept on . . .
>
> **Manzeer**   Leaking.
>
> **Sylvia**   Breaking.

Sylvia and Manzeer continue by describing what they did and what happened. Their first attempt at making the boat had fallen apart. As Manzeer said, "It looked like a bit of food; all cut up." The other pair then questioned them about the shape, and one student made the suggestion that perhaps it should have been flat bottomed. There is a real point to this discussion, since the next part of the activity is for each pair to complete the other activity.

This kind of hands-on, problem-solving activity is an excellent one to use with EL learners. First, at the stage when the boat was being constructed, those with little English (like Manzeer) can participate on a more equal footing, since this stage of the activity will be less language dependent. As we suggested in Chapter 1, language that is "situation embedded" is easier both to produce and to understand. Second, new language will be heard in context, and it is more likely to be noticed and taken up since the need to use it will be immediate. Third, the activity as a whole can be pitched at an appropriate cognitive level—it is a challenging task that demands critical-thinking and problem-solving skills, not simply language "rehearsal."

During the discussion that follows the hands-on activity, three particular aspects of language are likely to be modeled and reinforced by more competent English speakers. The activity provides an authentic context for EL learners to hear this language:

> ➤ *Reporting.* The two pairs must first report what they did to each other. This requires them to give information to others who did not share in the experience, and thus to use the kind of explicit language discussed earlier. (If the teacher wishes to focus on this, it would also provide an authentic context for using the past tense.)
> ➤ *Questioning.* The children must ask questions of each other. Here the two children questioning the boat-builders asked, "What happened to yours? What happened in the end? Did you make a newspaper boat first? Did you do a flat bottom?" As we noted earlier, children often have few opportunities to ask these kinds of questions, and this is a very good opportunity to practice question forms in an authentic context.

➤ *Making Suggestions.* The discussion requires the listeners to make constructive suggestions. In this case, one of the speakers in the group provided a good model of how to offer a suggestion when she suggested how to improve the design of the boat: "Do you think you should have done a flat bottom?" As discussed earlier, this kind of language is not necessarily just "picked up" by EL students, and the context of this activity would be an excellent one for the teacher to focus on some specific ways of making suggestions: "Do you think you should . . . Maybe you could . . . How about if you had . . . Perhaps it would be better if. . . ." This could be a focus in the initial setting up of the activity as a whole.

Note that this activity exemplifies a number of principles for well-designed group work in an EL classroom: (1) there is a real need to talk because there is an authentic purpose for it, (2) it has a built-in information gap, since pairs hold different information, (3) all children are involved, (4) it is cognitively demanding, and (5) it can be embedded in a curriculum topic that the children have been studying.

Donut Circles

This is a well-known activity that is can be useful for students with low levels of English. Children are in two concentric circles with equal numbers of students in each circle. The outer circle (circle A) faces inward, and the inner circle (circle B) faces outward so that each student is facing someone from the other circle. The pairs talk in turns to each other for a minute or two (or less for beginners) about a teacher-nominated topic. After both students have had a turn, one of the circles moves clockwise to face a new person, while the other circle stands still, so that everyone is now opposite a new partner. The process of exchanging information is then repeated, and the same circle then moves once more. This process continues as many times as the teacher feels is useful. Simple topics for young learners could include what they did the previous weekend, what work they would like to do when they leave school, what they like doing in their spare time, or who they would most like to meet. Donut activities can also be used for responding to more complex subject-based questions or for sharing opinions about an issue.

There are two advantages for EL learners in an activity like this. First, similar to a jigsaw activity, it allows for practice and rehearsal of an idea or a sentence structure, since the student can repeat the same thing to each new partner as the circle moves on. Second, it allows for peer scaffolding. One group of very young learners, all beginners in English, were asked to tell their partners one thing they had done the previous weekend as a preparation for later writing one or two sentences. One student began the activity by consistently beginning with "I goed. . . ." About halfway round the circle, after hearing most of the class say, "I went . . . ," he began to self-correct, and by the time he came back to his original position in the circle he was using "I went . . . " quite spontaneously, and subsequently used the correct form in his later writing.

Hot Seat

Seat children in a circle, with one chair being designated the "hot seat." The student in the hot seat portrays a character from a book that has been shared by the class or a historical character. Other students ask him or her questions to find out more about the character's life. You can change the time frames, too, moving back into the past or forward into the future, so that the person in the hot seat imagines the character older or younger. Of course, if the character is historical, details must be correct.

Talking Points

This activity has been developed by Dawes (2008) and described by Mercer, Dawes, and Kleine Staarman (2009). It is a simple activity for stimulating speaking, listening, thinking, and learning. It consists of a list of statements that may be factually accurate, wrong, or contentious, all related to a particular topic. In the process of assessing the validity or otherwise of the statements, children's understanding and thinking about the topic is stimulated. Through making their opinions explicit, and justifying them, they are helped to come to a better understanding of the issue. This small-group discussion is followed by a whole-class feedback session.

Progressive Brainstorm

This is an interactive activity where children share what they know about a topic. It can occur at the beginning or end of a unit of work (or both, as an evaluation for children of what has been learned).

> ➤ Divide students into small groups. Each group has a large sheet of paper with the topic or a question written in the center (what we know about earthquakes, insects, spiders, healthy eating, etc.). Each group must have a different colored pen.
> ➤ Children spend 5–10 minutes brainstorming what they know in the small group and write down words or concepts associated with the topic, as in a mind map or semantic web.
> ➤ After 5–10 minutes, each group moves to the next group's table, leaving their paper behind but keeping their own color pen.
> ➤ On the next group's paper they add ideas, using the ideas there as a springboard for things they hadn't thought of earlier, adding things that are missing, or adding to the ideas already there with further examples or details.
> ➤ The groups continue moving every 5–10 minutes until they are all back in their original places.
> ➤ Each group then discusses what is now on their original sheet, noting additions or critiquing anything they disagree with. Allow time for some whole-class discussion or a "show and tell" for each group.

This activity generates a lot of talk, especially as children come to read what has been written on other papers and on their own.

Opinion Clines

The aim here is for students to arrange themselves in a line representing a continuum from strongly agreeing to strongly disagreeing with a controversial statement. They will need enough knowledge to be able to make a decision that they can support. Those who strongly agree with the statement stand on the left, and those who strongly disagree stand on the right. Other students (with views in between) range themselves as a cline between the two extremes. To do this there needs to be considerable discussion among individual students about how their views fit in with those standing on each side of them. This activity requires students not only to give their opinions, but also to make explicit the reasons they have for holding these opinions.

Opinion clines may be a precursor or a follow-up to a small group or whole-class discussion, and they are also useful scaffolding for a written Argument or Discussion (see Chapter 5).

Problem Solving

Contexts for group problem solving occur in all curriculum areas, often followed by students reporting back to the class about their solutions. As we saw in Chapter 2, problem-solving dialogue is a good context for second language learning.

Questions or problems whereby students are encouraged to think laterally, in unusual and creative ways that are less bound by the constraints of formal logical thinking, can also provide fun contexts for spoken language and can serve as useful warm-up activities. Many of them allow for EL beginners to participate easily, especially if they are presented visually (as in the first two examples below), or they use simple grammatical structures. Here are some examples:

How can you combine two of the following to make something new: a paintbrush, a wheelbarrow, a garbage bin, four wheels, a spade, a tent?

Sample answer: *Put the tent on the wheels to make a mobile home.*

How many uses can you think of for an old car tire?

Sample answers: *grow flowers in it; use it as a swing*

Think of five things that you can't photograph.

Sample answers: *the camera while you are using it to take the photo; the back of the moon*

The answer is "midnight." What is the question?

Sample answer: *What time is it when the clock strikes 12 and it's dark outside?*

Picture Sequencing

For this activity, you will need a set of picture cards that tell a simple and predictable story or illustrate a predictable sequence or set of instructions (see Figure 3–3). Give each student in the group one card (there should be the same number of students as there are picture cards). Tell the students not to show their card to others in their group. Each student describes their card (it doesn't matter who starts), and when they have all finished describing the cards, the group decides on the basis of the descriptions which card should come first, which second, and so on. On the basis of the order decided, the students put down their cards in sequence. For younger students and those very new to English, make sure that cards are placed from left to right. This activity can provide scaffolding for several forms of writing, such as a narrative based on the pictures, or a description of a sequence of events, or a set of instructions.

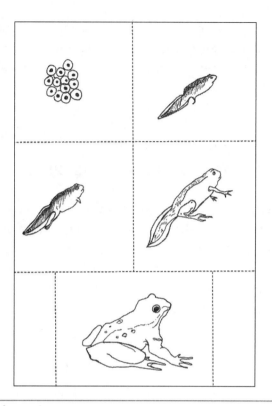

Figure 3–3 Picture Sequencing

ACTIVITIES ESPECIALLY FOR BEGINNERS

All of these activities can be integrated with particular subject topics.

Inquiry and Elimination: Practices question forms and helps develop logical thinking.

Choose a large picture showing a range of objects within a set, such as a picture showing a number of different animals. One member of the group chooses an animal and the others must guess which one it is by asking *yes/no* questions only. It's important to restrict the number of questions that can be asked so that guesses are not just random. Instead, encourage children to ask those questions that elicit the maximum amount of information. For example, the answer *yes* to the question *Does it fly?* immediately eliminates all of those animals that don't fly.

I'm Thinking of . . . : Practices describing things and their functions, and sentence structure.

Use a set of pictures of objects related to a particular topic being studied, such as sets of dinosaur pictures, animals, tools, food, and forms of transport. Each student in the group says "I'm thinking of something that is . . . " and then proceeds to describe the object. Whoever guesses the object then takes the next turn, or the group members may each take a turn.

Describe and Draw: Practices giving instructions; describing objects; describing position—under, near, next to, to the left of, and so on.

Children work in pairs, and each has a blank sheet of paper and drawing materials. Child A describes to Child B what she or he is drawing, and Child B reproduces the drawing according to A's description. This is a barrier game—they should not be able to see each other's work.

Find My Partner: Practices question forms and describing.

Deal four to six pictures to the group, two of which are identical, with the others having minor differences. Pictures can be related to a curriculum topic. One of the two identical pictures should be marked with an X, and whoever is dealt that card has to find the other picture by questioning other members of the group. (See Figure 3–4.)

What Did You See? Practices vocabulary.

On a table, place a selection of objects, or pictures of objects, that are related to a topic being studied. After children have looked at them for a few moments, cover the objects with a cloth and see how many objects children can remember.

There are many other activities that require students to use language with each other and many ways of grouping students (for more examples see, for example, Brady 2006). But as a general

Figure 3–4 Find My Partner

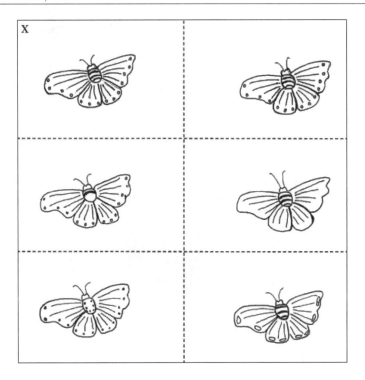

checklist for effective, collaborative pair and group activities with EL learners, here are some questions to think about:

> ➤ Is talking really necessary for the task or activity to be completed?
> ➤ Is thinking involved?
> ➤ Are content areas of the curriculum being reinforced?
> ➤ Does the structure of the activity provide sufficient scaffolding for all students, including beginners (e.g., repetition of ideas or language structures, time for rehearsal of language)?
> ➤ Are children using stretches of language?
> ➤ Are all children participating in some way?

DEVELOPING AND MAINTAINING RELATIONSHIPS

Earlier in this chapter an example was given of a teacher modeling examples of how students might come to a consensus, in ways that encourage supportive and productive relationships between group members. Being able to use this interpersonal function of language appropriately in collaborative work is an important dimension to knowing how to work in a group. The interpersonal function of language concerns itself with *how* a message or idea is given to others rather than on the content of the message itself. For example, a teacher reminding her class that an assignment is due could present this "message" in a number of ways. She could say any of the following:

- ◆ OK guys, hand your assignments in by the end of the day, please.
- ◆ Please everyone, I would like you to hand in your assignments by the end of the day.
- ◆ Could everyone please hand in their work by the end of the day?
- ◆ Everyone must hand in their work by the end of the day.
- ◆ All assignments are to be handed in by the end of today!

Although the overall message is the same—every example contains the words *assignments* and *hand in by the end of the day*—the way it is delivered creates a different relationship with the listeners. Similarly in the examples of teacher–student talk in Chapter 2, we saw how when we are teaching subject content, we are also showing—through the way we question and respond to what they say—how we see our students. We use language in subtly different ways depending on whether we see them as worthy conversational partners with interesting things to say, or the reverse.

In Chapter 1 we referred to this variation in how things are said as *tenor*. The tenor, or tone, that we use when we speak to someone varies for many reasons, and it reflects what we are feeling or how we perceive our relationship with the listener. For example, we are likely to vary how we say something depending upon whether we feel angry or irritated or happy, how fond we are of someone, whether we see someone as our boss or as our equal, whether someone is a stranger or a close friend, or whether we feel confident about what we saying or feel tentative. When people talk together there is always an interpersonal dimension embedded in everything they say! So it is important to remember that the language of the classroom is never simply the language of the subject being studied. It includes these interpersonal aspects, too, and is reflected in how teachers talk with students and how students interact with each other.

The interpersonal aspect of language is reflected in how teachers talk with students and how students interact with one another.

A successful discussion in most Western and many other cultures is marked by speakers' willingness to listen to others, acknowledge contributions, build on others' ideas, offer their own opinion and, when they disagree, to challenge others' thinking respectfully. If at times EL learners seem impolite or abrupt, they are probably not being discourteous. Rather, it may simply be that they have not had access to the appropriate models in English, and such language has never been made salient or explicit to them, or perhaps because their own language marks respect in different ways. So being aware of the interpersonal function of language in your teaching and talking about it explicitly at those times when it is most relevant—such as prior to group work—is as an important part of language teaching as teaching subject-related language.

There are many examples of useful "group-work language" that can be modeled explicitly and built over time with learners. A few examples are shown in Figure 3–5 together with the purpose or specific function they serve.

Purpose	Example
Agreeing	Yes, I think that's right.
Disagreeing	I don't think that's quite right because . . . I understand you, but . . .
Acknowledging a contribution	That's a really interesting idea.
Asking for clarification	I don't really understand. Can you explain that a bit more?
Making reasoning explicit	I think . . . because. . . .
Including others in the discussion	Maroun, what do you think?
Posing a question	What do you/we think . . . ? What about . . . ?
Summing up/clarifying the group's idea	So what we are saying is. . . .
Giving advice, making a suggestion	Maybe we could . . . ? It might be a good idea if . . . .

Figure 3–5 Examples of the Interpersonal Function of Language

In Summary

This chapter has focused on the opportunities for language learning offered by small-group work and the principles of effective group work. It has provided a number of examples of pair and small-group activities.

- ◆ When children work collaboratively on a group task they often work at higher cognitive and language levels that they would working individually.
- ◆ Well-designed and well-run group work offers EL learners many opportunities for language development. It increases comprehension, provides opportunities for student output and peer scaffolding, and increases students' confidence.
- ◆ There are number of principles for effective group work. These include providing clear and explicit instructions, ensuring that talk is

required for the task, making expected outcomes clear, ensuring the task is cognitively appropriate, integrating the task with a curriculum topic, ensuring all group members are involved, allowing appropriate time, and helping students understand how to work in groups.

♦ Developing students' ability to use the interpersonal function of language appropriately is important for successful collaborative work and should be included as part of any language teaching program.

To Think About

1. Choose three activities described in this chapter, and discuss how you could use them in any curriculum area or topic.
2. When your students are engaged in group tasks, what difficulties have you or they encountered? Discuss with a partner how you might respond to these difficulties.
3. The chapter makes the point that an interpersonal dimension is embedded into everything we or our students say. How important do you think it is to focus on the interpersonal dimensions of language discussed in this chapter? In relation to your own students, what other examples would you add to Figure 3–5?
4. What points in this chapter affirm your own practice? What is the most important learning for you?
5. Tell a success story. Describe a small-group activity you have used in any curriculum area successfully, and suggest why it was successful. Refer to the principles for effective group work in the chapter summary above. Are there additional principles that you think should be added?

Suggestions for Further Reading

Alexander, R. 2008. *Towards Dialogic Teaching: Rethinking Classroom Talk*, 4th ed., with revisions up to 2011. North Yorkshire, UK: Dialogos.

Brady, L. 2006. *Collaborative Learning in Action*. Frenchs Forest, NSW, AU: Pearson.

Haneda, M., and G. Wells. 2008. "Learning an Additional Language Through Dialogic Inquiry." *Language and Education* 22 (2): 114–36.

Mercer, N., L. Dawes, and J. Kleine Staarman. 2009. "Dialogic Teaching in the Primary Science Classroom." *Language and Education* 23 (4): 353–69.

Four

From Speaking to Writing in the Content Classroom

▪ ▪

*Prior experience becomes a context for interpreting the
new experience . . . prior experiences serve as the contexts
within which the language being used is to be understood.*

— Lily Wong Fillmore, "When Does Teacher Talk Work as Input?"

In this chapter we look more closely at the relationship between talking and writing. Chapter 1 briefly discussed the concept of register and introduced the terms *field*, *tenor*, and *mode* as the variables that impact on the way that language is used in any particular context. In Chapter 3 we looked at the notion of tenor, the way that language varies according to the relationship between speaker and listener. This chapter explores the notion of *mode*, that is, the channel of communication; broadly, this refers to whether the language is spoken or written. The chapter illustrates how spoken language and written language are better understood as a continuum rather than as two discrete forms of language. It illustrates how a classroom program can be planned to move along this spoken–written continuum, so that the teaching and learning sequence moves from the kind of language that occurs in a face-to-face context toward the more academic written language of schooling.

USING THE MODE CONTINUUM: FROM SPEAKING TO WRITING

In Chapter 1 we compared four short science texts. Here are four similar texts, this time as more extended pieces of language. They illustrate how certain language features change as the language becomes increasingly closer to written forms, and how they represent a continuum from spoken to written language. We will refer to this sequence as a *mode continuum*.

Text 1: Spoken by three ten-year-old students, with accompanying action

this . . . no, it doesn't go . . . it doesn't move . . . try that . . . yes, it does . . . a bit . . . that won't . . . won't work, it's not metal . . . these are the best . . . going really fast.

Text 2: Spoken by one student about the action, after the event

we tried a pin . . . a pencil sharpener . . . some iron filings and a piece of plastic . . . the magnet didn't attract the pin.

Text 3: Written by the same student

Our experiment was to find out what a magnet attracted. We discovered that a magnet attracts some kinds of metal. It attracted the iron filings but not the pin.

Text 4: Taken from a child's encyclopedia

A magnet . . . is able to pick up, or attract, a piece of steel or iron because its magnetic field flows into the magnet, turning it into a temporary magnet. Magnetic attraction occurs only between ferrous materials.

Text 1 is typical of the kind of situation-embedded language produced in face-to-face contexts. Because everyone can see what is being talked about, objects need not be named; instead, a speaker can use reference words (such as *this, these, that*), to verbally "point" to things in the immediate environment and know that the other participants in the conversation will understand what is being referred to.

In Text 2 the context changes because the student is telling others what she learned and no longer has the science equipment in front of her. She must now reconstruct the experience through language alone, so she has to make explicit the things or people she is referring to (*we, pin, pencil sharpener, iron filings, piece of plastic*) and name what is happening (*attract*). That is, for the benefit of her audience, she needs to use what we described in Chapter 2 as "literate talk."

Text 3 is a written text and, since the audience is now unseen, the writer can't rely on shared assumptions: she can't assume that readers of the text will know anything at all about the particular events she is describing. So, once again, the writer must re-create the experience through language alone, but this time she also needs to provide an orientation for the readers in order to provide a context for what follows: *Our experiment was to. . . .*

In Text 4 there is no reference to a specific experiment. The magnet referred to here as *a magnet* is generic: its properties are those of all magnets. There is an increase in technical terms and in the density of the text; a lot of information is being packed in. One way of packing information into a written text is to use a *nominalization*, meaning that a process or verb (*attract*) is turned into a noun (*attraction*). Nominalizations are typical of much written language because it is very often a general concept or phenomenon we want to talk about, rather than the people and processes around a specific event. For example, in Text 4, what is significant is not the idea that a particular magnet attracts a pin, but rather the process itself, which is now encoded as the noun *attraction*. Academic abstract language is therefore not simply about vocabulary, but is also reflected in the grammar.

While spoken and written language obviously have distinctive characteristics, this continuum of texts illustrates that there is no absolute boundary between them. Technology increases this blurring. Leaving a detailed message on an answering machine, for example, may be quite linguistically demanding since, in the absence of two-way contact, and without (initially at least) the shared understandings and expectations that are implicit in two-way, face-to-face communication, we are required to "speak aloud" the kind of language that would more usually be written. An email is written language, yet an email to a close friend sounds a lot like spoken language. And texting, too, has further blurred the distinction between spoken and written language, for example, by introducing visual emoticons and other ideographs that "fill in" the writer's emotions that would normally be part of the context of face-to-face spoken language. So, in terms of the mode continuum, it is perhaps more appropriate to describe texts as "more spoken-*like*" or "more written-*like*."

As these four texts illustrate, texts that are most spoken-like (Text 1) are often dependent for their interpretation on the situation in which they occur: they are situation embedded. More written-like texts are not embedded in the situation itself; rather, they must be complete enough in themselves to create their own context for the listener or reader. Thus as we move along the mode continuum, texts are no longer dependent on the situation in which they occur: if we read a book while at the beach, for example, our understanding of what we read and how we interpret the language usually has nothing to do with the fact that we are sitting on a beach.

As Chapter 1 pointed out, an EL learner is likely to have fewer difficulties with producing something like Text 1, where the situational context itself provides a support for meaning. Thus there are fewer linguistic demands than with more written-like texts, where a greater control of the lexico-grammar (grammar and vocabulary) is required. It is worth noting, too, that when children are expected to write simply on the basis of personal experiences, they are being asked to take a very large linguistic step (as can be seen by comparing Texts 1 and 3), one that is beyond the current English language resources of some EL learners.

If you reflect back on the spoken language activities described in the previous chapter, you'll see that most of them require learners to use more explicit spoken language (i.e., like Text 2). This is the reason why barrier games such as Find the Difference are designed the way they are. If students were to show each other their pictures, they would be using language as in Text 1. By not showing each other the pictures, they are using language more like Text 2, and thus are practicing more written-like talk. Chang and Wells (1988) refer to this more written-like spoken language as "literate talk." This is a useful term because it draws an important distinction between different *kinds* of spoken language, so this is the term that will be used throughout this book.

We turn now to how one teacher used the notion of the mode continuum as a major organizing principle in the planning of her classroom program. (For a fuller description of this program, see Gibbons 2001.) For all but two of her students, English was a second or subsequent language, and therefore her whole curriculum needed to be supportive of language development as well as to focus on appropriate content. Using the mode continuum as a language framework, she designed teaching activities that were sequenced from most situation-embedded, or most spoken-like (and thus for ESL learners the most easily understood), to least situation-dependent, or most written-like (in this instance, a learning journal).

A major focus for the teacher was to help students use literate talk in the way that Text 2 illustrates. Remember, this is spoken language that is not dependent on the immediate situational context in which it occurs. This literate talk serves as a language "bridge" between the talk associated with experiential activities and the more formal—and often written—registers of subject learning.

Based on the science topic of magnetism, the teacher planned teaching and learning activities to reflect points along the mode continuum so as to offer a logical development in terms of language learning. Here are the stages that the children moved through:

1. *Doing an experiment* (small groups). Learners initially participated in small-group learning experiences based on a number of science experiments in which the language used was tied in with the situation the children were in. What they talked about referred directly to the actions in which they were taking part and to what was happening in front of them.

2. *Introducing key vocabulary* (whole class). At this point the teacher briefly introduced the words *attract* and *repel* to the children.

3. *Teacher-guided reporting* (whole class). Groups of students, with the help of the teacher, shared their learning with the whole class. Since this did not involve the use

> *Literate talk serves as a bridge between activity-related talk and more formal written registers of subject learning.*

of the concrete materials, students had to use language more explicitly, which provided a linguistic bridge into journal writing. (You will remember from Chapter 2 that the children were given a time to rehearse what they would say.) During this part of the cycle, the teacher also helped the children build up generalizations by directing their attention to the commonalties in each group's findings.

4. *Journal writing* (individual). This was the final activity of the cycle and linguistically the most demanding.

This cycle was repeated several times during the unit on magnets, based on different initial activities.

The stages are described below, together with examples of the language the children used. You will see that the children gradually learn to use language in ways that are more appropriate to the context they are in (learning and talking about science). Note the significant role that the teacher–student talk in Stage 3 plays in this development.

Stage 1: Doing an experiment

In many elementary schools, it is usual for students to rotate through a number of activities over the course of one or two lessons. However, as suggested in Chapter 2, this kind of organizational structure negates any authentic purpose for reporting back to others, since children are likely to have shared very similar experiences. Here, the teacher made an attempt to set up a genuine communicative situation by having each group of children work at different (though related) science experiments. And so, by the time they had completed their experiments, each group of children held different information from other class members. In its communicative structure, the classroom organization was based on what we referred to in the previous chapter as an information "gap," so there was an authentic exchange of information at the reporting stage.

In Text 1 (which follows) children were carrying out the experiment described in Chapter 2. Prior to beginning the activity, they were told that they would later describe to the rest of the class what happened, and attempt to explain why. The texts that follow occurred as students were engaged in this activity.

Text 1

Hannah	try . . . the other way
Marco	like that
Hannah	north pole facing down
Joanna	we tried that
Daniella	oh!
Hannah	it stays up!
Marco	magic!
Daniella	let's show the others
Joanna	mad!
Daniella	I'll put north pole facing north pole . . . see what happen
Marco	that's what we just did
Daniella	yeah . . . like this . . . look

The dialogue continues for several minutes longer as the students try different positions for the magnet, and then they begin to formulate an explanation.

Hannah	can I try that? . . . I know why . . . I know why . . . that's like . . because the north pole is on this side and that north pole's there . . . so they don't stick together
Daniella	what . . like this? Yeah
Hannah	yeah . . . see because the north pole on this side . but turn it on the other . . this side like that . . . turn it that way . . yeah
Daniella	it will stick
Hannah	and it will stick because . look . . the north pole's on that side because . .
Daniella	the north pole's on that side yeah

At this stage, the children do not know the terms *attract* and *repel*. Instead, they use familiar words like *stick* or *push away*. (Sometimes this led to very interesting comments—one child was overheard to say, as he was holding two magnets that were repelling each other, "It feels like a strong wind!")

What can we learn from this example? First, we can see again how small-group work supports learning. Together children explored and developed certain scientific understandings, namely that the position of the poles is significant in how the magnets behave. They also attempted to hypothesize about the causal relations involved (note the use of the connectives *so, because*). So, even though they were not using what we might think of as science language, they were learning a lot about science. As the discourse progresses, individual utterances became longer and more explicit, and this occurred as the students began to formulate explanations for what they saw. The teacher's instruction to "try to explain what you see" was significant here, since it extended the task from simply "doing" to "doing and thinking." Wegerif and Mercer (1996) suggest that it is through this kind of exploratory talk "that knowledge begins to be built up and reasoning is made more visible" (51). This piece of learning later became shared knowledge when the children reported to the rest of the class, and it was the basis upon which the teacher next introduced subject-specific vocabulary such as *attract* and *repel*.

Stage 2: Introducing key vocabulary

Before the children reported to the rest of the class, the teacher introduced a new vocabulary item, drawing on the experiences the children had just had and at the same time demonstrating the meaning physically:

> now I'm going to give you another word for what Joseph was trying to say one more scientific word . some of you were saying it pushes away . . . or slips off . . . so instead of saying the magnet pushes away I'm going to give you a new word . . . *repel* [said with emphasis] . it actually means to push away from you [demonstrating with her arm] . *repel*

From the point of view of second language development, it is important to note that in this classroom the children were given an opportunity to develop some understandings about magnets *before* they were expected to understand and use more scientific discourse and vocabulary. It is not until after the group work that the teacher introduced the scientific terms *attract* and *repel*—that is, at a time when students had already expressed these meanings in familiar everyday language. There is some parallel here to the principle within bilingual programs suggesting that learning should occur first in the mother tongue as a basis to learning in the second language, but here the issue is one of register (learning and explaining phenomena through more everyday language before being introduced to new academic language).

Stage 3: Teacher-guided reporting

Science educator Rosalind Driver made the important point that "activity by itself is not enough. It is the sense that is made of it that matters" (1983, 49). In teacher-guided reporting, the role of the teacher is to help children make sense of learning activities through talking with them, and in this process, introduce new language. As children are supported to clearly describe events and consolidate what they have learned in words, they are helped to understand and gain access to academic language (Haneda and Wells 2008; Wegerif and Mercer 1996).

In the classroom example shown here, the overall aim of the teacher-guided reporting was to extend children's linguistic resources and focus on aspects of the specific discourse of science. As the teacher expressed it to the children, "Now we're trying to talk like scientists." She also anticipated that the reporting stage would create a context for students to rehearse the language and vocabulary that were closer to written discourse—what we referred to earlier as "literate talk." This shift toward more literate talk involves the juxtaposition of everyday and scientific ideas, a shift that Mercer, Dawes, and Kleine Staarman (2009) suggest is essential for the meaningful learning of science.

"Now we're trying to talk like scientists."

In the text shown in Figure 4–1, Hannah is explaining what she learned. The teacher's role in guided reporting is crucial, especially for EL learners; the text provides an example of how her interactions with individual students provided scaffolding for their attempts, allowing for communication to proceed while giving the learners access to new ways of expressing the meanings they wanted to make.

	Student	Teacher
1		try to tell them what you learned . . . OK . . . (*To Hannah*) yes?
2	when I put/when you put . . . when you put a magnet . . . on top of a magnet and the north pole poles are . . . . (*Seven-second pause, Hannah is clearly having difficulty expressing what she wants to say.*)	
3		Yes, yes you're doing fine . . you put one magnet on top of another . . .
4	and and the north poles are together er em the magnet . . . repels the magnet er . . . the magnet and the other magnet . . . sort of floats in the air?	
5		I think that was very well told . . . very well told . . do you have anything to add to that Charlene? (*The teacher invites other contributions, and then asks Hannah to explain it again.*)
6		now listen . . now Hannah explain once more . . . alright Hannah . . . excuse me everybody (*Regaining class' attention*) . . listen again to her explanation
7	the two north poles are leaning together and the magnet on the bottom is repelling the magnet on top so that the magnet on the top is sort of . . . floating in the air	
8		so that these two magnets are repelling (*Said with emphasis*) each other and . . . (*Demonstrating*) look at the force of it.

Figure 4–1 Teacher-Guided Reporting

This interaction between teacher and student is different in several small but important respects from the traditional IRE pattern. As we saw in Chapter 2, the IRE pattern occurs in fairly predictable ways, usually involving a question to which the teacher already knows the answer, followed by a student answer (often brief), and finally a teacher evaluation relating to the correctness (or otherwise) of the answer. These kinds of questions are often framed in ways that do not allow for students to make extended responses. In contrast, in the text shown in Figure 4–1, the interactions approximate more closely what occurs in mother tongue, adult–child interactions outside of the formal teaching context (see, for example, the seminal work of Halliday 1975 and also Painter 2000).

During teacher-guided reporting, the teacher begins the exchange by inviting students to relate what they have learned, rather than with a known answer or display question. In this way the teacher sets up a context that allows students to initiate the specific topic of the exchange. When learners initiate what they wish to talk about, language learning is facilitated because they enter the discourse on their own terms, rather than responding to a specific request for information from the teacher. In the text shown in Figure 4–1, the student takes on the role of "expert." Although the teacher is in control of the knowledge associated with the overall thematic development of the topic, the individual exchanges locate that control in the student.

This increase in the equality of teacher and student roles leads Hannah to produce longer stretches of discourse than often occurs in classroom interaction. The teacher can be described as "leading from behind." At the same time, while the teacher follows Hannah's lead and accepts as a valid contribution the information the child gives, she also recasts or reformulates what Hannah says, modeling alternative forms of language that are more appropriate in the context of talking about science.

Chapter 2 introduced the notion of "stretched" language and comprehensible output. From the perspective of second language learning, it is clear that teacher-guided reporting encourages learner language to be stretched. Hannah is going beyond what is unproblematic for her, but, because she is allowed a second attempt, she has an additional opportunity for comprehensible output. Hannah's second attempt at her explanation is considerably less hesitant and syntactically more complete than her first, and it is produced this time without the help of the teacher. As I discussed in Chapter 1, Vygotsky (1978) suggests that learning occurs, with support from those more expert, at the learner's zone of proximal development—that is, at the "outer edges" of a learner's current abilities. In turn 2, Hannah appears to have reached her own zone of proximal development for this task, since she hesitates for a considerable time and can presumably go no further alone. The recasting and support she receives from the teacher (turn 3) is precisely timed for learning to occur and helps Hannah continue with what she wants to say.

As this text illustrates, the reporting context also gives students opportunities to produce longer stretches of discourse that are more written-like than those that occurred in the small-group work. Often this required the teacher to increase wait time, on occasions for as long as eight seconds. Much research has suggested that when teachers ask questions of students, they typically wait one or two seconds for the students to begin a reply, but that when teachers wait for three or more seconds, there are significant changes in student use of language and in the attitudes and expectations of both students and teacher (see, for example, Stahl 1994; Rowe 1986). It would seem likely that increased wait time—perhaps *thinking time* is a better term—is even more important for students who are formulating responses in a language they do not fully control. Equally important, we can see from the example in Figure 4–1 that scaffolded interactions like this support learners in completing what they want to say successfully, so they are positioned as successful interactants and learners. In addition, since it is the immediate need of the learner that is influencing to a large extent the teacher's choice of actual wording, it seems likely that this wording will be more salient to the learner—more likely to be taken note of—than if it had occurred in a context that was less immediate.

> *Increased wait time—perhaps thinking time is a better term—is even more important for students who are formulating responses in a language they do not fully control.*

Another significant mode shift occurred toward the end of most reporting sessions, where the teacher used children's personal knowledge to show how generalizations might be generated. For example, her questions at this point included:

Can you see something in common with all these experiences?

What's the same about all these experiments?

Such questions require the students to do more than simply produce a personal recount of what they did; they must now express their learning in terms of generalizations. Note how in the next examples, taken from the following lesson, the children no longer mention themselves in the discourse:

> the north pole of the magnet sticks . . attracts . the second magnet . the south pole of the second magnet . if you put the south and north together then they will . . attract but if you put north and north or south and south . together . . they won't stick . attract

The teacher-guided reporting stage, then, both in the way language is used and in the ways that children are encouraged to generalize from their learning, serves to create a bridge for learners between personal ways of understanding a phenomenon through everyday language, and the broader concepts and language associated with the science curriculum.

Stage 4: Journal writing

After the students had taken part in the reporting session, they wrote a response in their journals to the question "What have you learned?" These were intended as informal responses that would later serve as a source of information in the writing of more formal reports about magnets. What is particularly significant is that these journals indicated that the teacher-guided reporting sessions influenced the way the students *wrote*: their writing reflected wordings that they had used in interaction with the teacher or that had been part of the teacher's recasting. This was particularly evident when the students themselves had had opportunity to reformulate their *own* talk. Here, for example, is what Hannah eventually wrote:

Students' writing reflected the wordings that they had used in interaction with the teacher or that had been part of the teacher's recasting.

> I found it very interesting that when you stuck at least 8 paddle pop sticks in a piece of polystyrene, and then put a magnet with the North and South pole in the oval and put another magnet with the north and south pole on top, the magnet on the bottom will repel the magnet on the top and the magnet on the top would look like it is floating in the air.

And here is an excerpt from the journal writing of a student who had *listened* to the talk between Hannah and the teacher but who was not part of the group that had carried out the experiment. The conversation influenced her writing, too.

> The thing made out of polystyrene with paddle pop sticks, one group put one magnet facing north and another magnet on top facing north as well and they repelled each other. It looked like the top magnet was floating up in the air.

SOME IMPLICATIONS FOR THE CLASSROOM

While this teacher's program illustrates the value of learning by doing (especially for EL learners where concrete experiences help make language comprehensible), it also illustrates the critical role of teacher–student talk in children's learning and language development. Regular teacher-guided reporting, with its focus on literate talk, is one way of providing an authentic and meaningful context for students to develop the more academic registers of school.

We can also see that it is not simply the linguistic features of language itself that affect students' comprehension (for example, the simplicity or otherwise of the grammatical structures), but also the previous knowledge they bring to the new language they are hearing. Note that in this classroom the new language introduced by the teacher occurred *after* students had already developed some understanding of key concepts through the small-group work, so new language was more readily interpretable by the students. What preceded this new language—in this case the learning that the students had gained through their participation in the small-group work—was therefore an important factor in students' understanding of it and their ultimate ability to use it. Prior knowledge provided a cognitive "hook" on which to "hang" new language.

One implication of this for teaching is that language that would normally be beyond EL students' comprehension is much more likely to be understood when students can bring their experiences and understandings as a basis for interpretation. This broad principle is illustrated at other points in this book, in particular in the chapters on reading and listening. In the words of Wong Fillmore (1985) at the beginning of this chapter, written in relation to her study of kindergarten EL learners, "prior experiences serve as the contexts within which the language being used is to be understood" (31).

This overall sequence of activities also presents a challenge to more traditional ways of sequencing teaching and learning activities in the second language classroom, where a new topic very often *begins* with the preteaching of vocabulary or a grammatical structure. While this approach may be appropriate at times, it is worth remembering that it is underpinned by the notion that learners must first "learn" language before they can "use" it. As we have seen, however, EL learners must from the outset use their new language for curriculum learning, and they need many contexts in which they can do this. In this class, students used their current language resources at the beginning of the unit while the focus on new language occurred at later stages, a sequence that allowed for students to build on their existing understandings and language, and to link old learning with new. In effect, they moved successfully *toward* the language of the curriculum throughout the unit of work, rather than being expected to master it prior to their learning of science.

> *The learning that the students had gained through their participation in the small-group work provided a cognitive "hook" on which to hang new language.*

The work described in this chapter also challenges the notion that EL learners need to first "learn English" before they can learn subject content. As we have seen, in a well-planned integrated curriculum where there is a dual focus on both content and language, students have many opportunities to develop subject knowledge and relevant academic language simultaneously.

In Chapters 2, 3, and 4, we have seen that allowing talk to occur is not enough. Productive talk does not just happen—it needs to be deliberately and systematically planned, just as we plan for literacy events. Julianna's comment in Chapter 1—"I can say what I want, but not for school work and strangers"—reminds us that developing a language for learning is not a matter of chance. How tasks are designed, how group work is set up, and how teachers respond to students all impact on how effective classroom talk is in supporting language development. And sometimes, as we have seen, even quite small changes in how opportunities for talk are set up can have significant effects on how the discourse is played out. It is not an exaggeration to suggest that classroom talk determines whether or not children learn, and their ultimate feelings of self-worth as learners. Talk is how education happens.

In Summary

This chapter has discussed the "mode continuum" and illustrated how it can provide an important organizing principle for planning a unit of work.

- The differences between spoken and written language can be understood as a continuum that moves from the most contextually embedded language (e.g., in interactions that take place in face-face contexts) to denser, abstract written language.
- *Literate talk* refers to spoken language that makes explicit the ideas of the speaker in ways that take account of the needs of listeners, who may not have shared the experiences of the speaker.
- Literate talk can serve as a bridge to literacy.
- Academic language is more easily understood when it builds on the foundation of relevant prior learning and experience, such as hands-on concrete activities.
- Teacher-guided reporting provides a context for explicit scaffolding of academic language.

To Think About

1. In this chapter the use of the mode continuum was illustrated through a science unit around magnets, but this approach could be used in any curriculum area and with many topics. In what other topics or subject could a similar approach be taken? (Begin by thinking of units of work that could begin with a concrete experience.)
2. Apart from teacher-guided reporting, in what other classroom contexts will children use literate talk?

3. What do you think Driver means when she suggests that "sense must be made" of activity? Do you agree? Why, or why not?
4. In what ways did this chapter affirm your own practice?
5. What is the most important learning for you in this chapter? What implications, if any, are there for your own teaching practice?

Suggestions for Further Reading

Ball, T., and G. Wells. 2009. "Running Cars Down Ramps: Learning About Learning Over Time." *Language and Education* 23 (4): 371–90.

Gibbons, P. 2003. "Mediating Language Learning: Teacher Interactions with ESL Students in a Content-Based Classroom." *TESOL Quarterly* 32 (2): 247–73.

Halliday, M. 1993. "Towards a Language-Based Theory of Learning." *Linguistics and Education* 5: 93–116.

Mercer, N., L. Dawes, and J. Kleine Staarman. 2009. "Dialogic Teaching in the Primary Classroom." *Language and Education* 23 (4): 353–69.

Five

Learning to Write in a Second Language and Culture

▪ ▪

*In the absence of an explicit focus on language, students from
certain social class backgrounds continue to be privileged and
others to be disadvantaged in learning, assessment, and promotion,
perpetuating the obvious inequalities that exist today.*

—Mary Schleppegrell, *The Language of Schooling*

Literacy in today's world is very different from literacy as it was understood in the nineteenth century and in the early part of the twentieth century. Many children at the beginning of the nineteenth century were required to do little more than write their name. As late as the 1930s, the level of literacy required in many contexts was still quite minimal, and it was represented by the capacity to read and copy simple passages and to write an occasional short text, such as a letter or a passage on a given topic (Christie 1990).

By contrast, the contemporary world in the first quarter of the twenty-first century demands a level of sophistication in literacy skills greater than ever before, including the many forms of digital literacy, in order to access information and ideas and participate meaningfully in society and the global community. As sociologists have pointed out for many years, the relationship between illiteracy, social alienation, and poverty is also too acute to be ignored. Today's children are entering a world in which they will need to be able to read and think critically, embrace new technologies, live and work in intercultural contexts, solve new kinds of problems, and be flexible in ever-changing work contexts—in short, to make informed decisions about their own lives and their role in a multicultural and multilingual society.

This chapter discusses some of the challenges that EL students may have in learning to write in English, including issues of language and culture, challenges that are likely to be greater for those not already literate in another language. It discusses in detail the language demands of some of the types of writing that children are asked to do in school, and it describes a teaching cycle that models and makes explicit these forms of writing, or genres.

SOME CHALLENGES FOR EL LEARNERS

First, drawing on your knowledge of your own students, consider some of the characteristics of good writers and less effective writers.

Effective writers are likely to think about and plan their writing, at least in a general way, before they begin. They understand that writing is a recursive process—that writers continually revise and edit at all stages of their writing, from first draft to final product. They are also able to anticipate the needs of the reader; they do this by including enough information about the topic so that the reader can make sense of what she or he is reading and by using clear signaling devices such as connectives and conjunctions to indicate how ideas are linked. Effective writers are aware of the linguistic differences between writing and speaking (Chapter 4), and they know that written language is not just speech written down. They understand the cultural purpose of the text and how to organize the major ideas coherently.

By contrast, poor writers are much less likely to take account of these things. They may focus primarily on the mechanics of writing, such as the spelling, and are often overly concerned with "correctness." As a result, they may lack confidence to write at length or in new ways. They tend not to plan at a whole-text level, and they are less able to anticipate the language and content information that a reader will require to fully understand their writing. Their writing tends to sound like "speech written down," and they probably have difficulty revising and editing their own work.

Young EL learners learning to write in English who are not already literate in another language have even more to learn about writing. Trying to grasp concepts of print—such as sound–symbol relationships, directionality, and the notion that written symbols are not arbitrary but fixed—is much more difficult if you are learning to do it in a language in which you are not strong. EL students are also less likely to be familiar with the particular organizational structure of different kinds of writing and the cultural norms and grammatical structures of English. Some may also be faced with learning a new script.

Many literacy practices may also be built on the (often incorrect) presumption that EL learners have already developed strong spoken-language skills in English, and that these learners have internalized the same kinds of understandings about how to use it as fluent English speakers of the same age. Thus learners' apparent lack of progress may be viewed as lack of ability or effort. There is also a strong tendency in the national curriculum and assessment documents of several English-speaking countries to assess EL learners as though they have identical language resources to English mother tongue speakers. Consequently they may fail to recognize what EL learners actually do achieve in their learning of English. In addition, assessment systems designed for English speakers rarely acknowledge that many EL students are literate in another language, so the full extent of the learners' language resources is not acknowledged and their progress and achievements as *biliterate* learners not considered (Olivos and Sarmiento 2006; Hornberger and Link 2012). It is therefore increasingly important that classroom teachers are aware of what language knowledge their students bring to the classroom and to build on this as a significant resource for the development of literacy.

WHAT IS A GENRE?

In this section we look at some of the types of writing that are common in school, and we consider some of the cultural and linguistic knowledge needed to produce these forms successfully.

Different forms of literary writing, such as poems, plays, or novels, are often referred to as *genres*. These general distinctions are often further categorized: adventure novels, detective novels, romance novels, and so on. However, the word is now used with a much broader meaning, to refer to the range of ways in which things get done through language in a particular society or culture (Schleppegrell 2012; Martin and Rose 2008; Christie 1990).

Under this broader definition, the notion of genre in English-speaking cultures would encompass things as diverse as the TV news, a marriage service, a game show, a lesson, a joke, a telephone conversation with a friend, a newspaper report, a set of written instructions, or a written persuasive text. Of course these are very different kinds of genres, but we can say of each of them that it:

The full extent of EL learners' language resources is often not acknowledged.

+ occurs within a culture
+ has a specific social purpose
+ has a particular overall organizational structure
+ is characterized by specific linguistic features.

Discussion of each of these characteristics follows.

Occurs within a particular culture

Genres are *cultural* and shared by members of that culture. The previously mentioned genres would be familiar to most people reading this book. You would be able to recognize each of them, and the social context in which it would occur, often from just hearing or reading a few words. Other cultures, of course, also have particular ways of doing similar things, but they may do so very differently—think of the many different cultural ceremonies for weddings or funerals. So although similar social purposes are common to many cultures, the genres of a particular culture may look very different from culture to culture. Even within English-speaking cultures there are differences in cultural knowledge, often depending on where one spends most of one's life. Most North Americans are not familiar with cricket, whereas I have little understanding or experience of the traditions, activities, and language of baseball.

As Chapter 1 pointed out, knowing the cultural context is a part of being able to understand and use language appropriately. Some years ago I received a letter from overseas that began:

> I am immensely delighted and profoundly honored to send you this letter. Please accept my deepest esteem, my warmest, kindest regards, and sincerest wishes of constant happiness, good health, and ever-increasing prosperity and success in all your endeavours. . . .

Four paragraphs later it concluded:

> Deeply grateful to you for each second you have so graciously spent reading my letter. Please do accept once more my profoundest esteem, deepest thanks for your gracious attention and consideration, and my most genuinely sincere wishes of constant happiness, success, peace, and prosperity, now and in the future.

The writer was requesting a copy of a book. The letter was completely accurate in terms of the grammar, but to a writer from an English-speaking country the language sounds excessively "flowery," ornate, and even servile. In the writer's culture, however, such language is entirely appropriate, whereas an equivalent letter from someone who has grown up in an Anglo-Saxon culture would be seen as deeply impolite and abrupt. So, more than just correct grammar is involved here. What learners must also know is the most *appropriate* language to use and the most *appropriate* ways to get things done. For language teaching purposes, "a useful way of viewing a culture is in terms . . . of its purposeful activities" (Painter 1988). Learning a second language thus means learning the different kinds of spoken and written genres needed to participate in the second language culture.

The notion of culture can also be applied to the contexts of school learning. Historians, scientists, mathematicians, social scientists, environmentalists, economists, artists, and all other subject disciplines each have their own "culture," their own valued ways of thinking, talking, and writing. So, within a school there are also learning communities, each with their own culture. As students study each subject, they need to learn the language of that subject, and how to think and reason in the subject. This includes learning to read and write the key written genres used in the subject. In this way students are gradually apprenticed into being members of that culture.

A specific purpose

Each of the examples listed above has a specific social purpose or goal: to give information about the current news, for people to be married, to provide amusement, to teach students, to persuade someone to think a certain way, and so on. This social purpose is reflected in the way that the genre is structured. A set of instructions, such as a recipe, intended to tell someone how to do something, will be organized in sequence, so that each step follows from the one before. Genres, then, are goal oriented and have a specific purpose.

A particular overall structure

Every genre has a particular structure. For example, in Australia a news program will begin with the most important and recent news, which may often include reports on international events; it goes on to less important, domestic, or local news; it gives a summary of the economic forecast and concludes with a sport's review and the weather forecast. If a news program started with a minor piece of news, or with the weather forecast, it would be unexpected. Similarly, a written narrative is structured differently from a report or a discussion.

Specific language features

Each genre also has a number of likely language features that make it distinctive from other types of genres. It will also have particular features in common with, or very similar to, other genres of the same type. For example, most newspaper reports are likely to make use of the past tense, to name particular people and events, and to say when the particular event took place. They are also likely to include a quotation or two from key participants in the event. Sets of instructions will contain action verbs and often make use of the imperative. Narratives frequently use the past tense, contain dialogue, and make use of adjectives and adverbs to describe characters, things, and actions.

More than just correct grammar is involved when writing in a new language.

Different genres also have different ways of linking the key ideas. A persuasive, or opinion, text is likely to contain conjunctions and connectives that organize and introduce the writer's arguments: *first, second, in addition, however, therefore*, whereas a narrative, such as a folktale, is likely to be organized along a timeline and so use time connectives to structure the story: *once upon a time, one day, and then, finally*.

THE GENRES OF SCHOOL

A number of written genres associated with learning in school have been identified by a group of linguists working in Sydney, Australia, including, among many others, Jim Martin, Joan Rothery, Frances Christie, Beverley Derewianka, David Rose, and Jenny Hammond. These genres include Recounts, Narratives, Information Reports, Procedures, Arguments, Discussions, and Explanations. (Note that in this book the names of the genres are capitalized to avoid confusion between the genre and more generalized meanings.) For a linguistic description of each of these genres see Figure 5–2.

Two of these genres—Narrative and Argument—are described in detail below. The Narrative is one of the most common genres (and ironically, probably one of the most complex to write successfully) that children are expected to use early on in their school life. But in recent years, national curriculum documents in the United States (Common Core State Standards), Australia (Australian National Curriculum), and the United Kingdom (National Curriculum) have increasingly recognized the importance of students writing nonfiction texts, and in particular being able to present well-reasoned personal opinions or a persuasive text in writing, which in this book are referred to as Arguments and Discussions. The distinction between these two is discussed later.

Narrative

Narratives, like all text types, have a *purpose*, which may be to entertain or perhaps to teach (as fables do). They also have a *particular organizational structure*, which is typically displayed in traditional stories. First, there is an *orientation*, the purpose of which is to set the scene, introduce the characters, and say when and where the narrative is set. Then there are a number of *events*, which lead to some kind of problem, sometimes referred to as a *complication*. Finally, the problem is resolved in the final part of the story, the *resolution*. Figure 5–1 contains a short version of the story of "Jack and Beanstalk," which illustrates how each of these stages is integral to the story.

There are also particular connectives or conjunctions that structure the text. Narratives are sequenced in time, and this is often signaled by the conjunctions or connectives that are used. In the beanstalk story, the time

Once upon a time there was a boy named Jack, who lived with his mother in a small village. They were very poor and their only possession was a cow, which gave them milk, and an old axe, which hung on the wall of their house.	Orientation: *Sets the scene; gives details of who, when, and where.*
One day his mother said to Jack, "We are so poor that we must sell the cow. You must take it to market and sell it to buy food." So Jack took the cow and set off to market. On his way there he met an old man who offered to exchange Jack's cow for some beans. Jack said, "My mother will be very angry with me if I don't take back money. We need to buy food." "Don't worry," replied the old man. "These are no ordinary beans. They are magic beans, and they will bring you good luck!" Jack felt sorry for the old man, for he looked even poorer than Jack, and so he agreed to exchange the cow for the magic beans. You are a kind boy," said the old man, "and you will be well rewarded." When he got home and told his mother what he had done, she was very angry. "You stupid boy," she shouted. "You have sold our most valuable possession for a handful of beans." And she threw the beans out of the window. The next day, when Jack woke up, there, in the garden, where his mother had thrown the beans, was a huge beanstalk. It was as thick as a tree and so tall it seemed to go right up into the sky. Jack stared and stared at the beanstalk, and remembered the old man's words. Taking his axe, he began to climb up the beanstalk. Up and up he climbed. For many hours he kept climbing until, at last, he could see the top of the beanstalk. Right at the top of the beanstalk, asleep on the ground, was a huge, ugly giant. And in front of him lay a heap of treasure. There were gold and silver coins, and piles of precious jewels. Very quietly, so as not to wake the giant, Jack started to fill his coat pockets with the giant's treasure.	Events: *Relates a number of events in sequence.*
Just as Jack had taken all he could carry, the giant opened one eye and saw Jack. "Who are you?" he roared. He opened the other eye, and then he stood up. Jack could hardly see his head it was so far away. He turned and ran and started to climb down the beanstalk as fast as he could. The giant strode after him, and Jack felt sure he was about to die!	Complication: *States the problem.*
But as the giant was about to reach down and grab Jack, Jack remembered the axe. He swung it backward and then, as hard as he could, he chopped into the beanstalk just above his head. Again and again he chopped until, at last, the top of the beanstalk crashed down out of the sky, carrying the giant with it. With a loud roar he disappeared and fell to earth. And Jack climbed safely down the beanstalk carrying enough jewels to look after his mother and himself for the rest of his life.	Resolution: *Relates how the problem is solved.*

Figure 5–1 Organizational Structure of a Narrative

connectives that sequence events include *once upon a time, one day, when, the next day, for many hours, at last, and.*

There are typical *language features* common to narratives:

- They usually use the past tense.
- They use many action verbs that describe what people do. In the beanstalk story, the action verbs include *took, met, threw, woke, climbed, stood, turned, ran, strode, chopped, swung, crashed, disappeared.*
- They often contain dialogue, so they also contain "saying" verbs that explain how people speak; the narrative above uses *said, replied, shouted, roared.*

Argument

An Argument aims to persuade people to take a particular view about an issue. Sometimes an Argument is referred to as an opinion piece or as a persuasive text. In this book, Argument is differentiated from Discussion. Argument is used to describe a piece of writing that provides only one perspective on an issue (that taken by the writer). Discussion provides two or more opposing perspectives. Discussion discusses both sides of a case, so it includes counter-arguments. Usually the writer states some opinion based on all the arguments presented. Discussion is therefore a more mature and more complex form of writing involving critique and an understanding of others' perspectives.

Argument:
The purpose of an Argument is to take a position on an issue and justify it, in order to persuade others of your point of view.

Organizational structure:
The text broadly follows the structure below.

- A statement by the author of his or her position, sometimes accompanied by some background information about the issues in question, and a preview of arguments.
- Argument 1 supported by evidence (for example, statistics, quotes, examples).

- ◆ Argument 2 supported by evidence.
- ◆ Argument 3 supported by evidence, and so on.
- ◆ Summing up of the author's position in light of the arguments presented and reaffirming of the initial statement. Sometimes a recommendation for action is also included.

Connectives and conjunctions that structure the main ideas:
An Argument is sequenced logically, and connectives are associated with reasoning (unlike Narrative where they are associated with time). Logical connectives introduce and sequence each argument, and they often occur at the beginning of a paragraph, where they signal to the reader the overall structure of the text. For example:

First . . . (Argument 1)

Second . . . (Argument 2)

In addition . . . (Argument 3)

In conclusion . . . Finally . . . Therefore.

Language features:

- ◆ Vocabulary that relates to the issue.
- ◆ Sometimes evaluative vocabulary that indicates the writer's stance or feeling toward the issue, as in: It is *extremely* unfair that . . . I *strongly* believe that . . .

For teacher reference, the key features of some of written genres of school are summarized in Figure 5–2 and described under the headings *Purpose, Organizational Structure, Connectives (Linking Words),* and *Other Language Features.* You will see that each type of genre is distinctive: they have different purposes, a different overall structure, different ways of organizing or linking ideas, and different grammatical features. Of course, not all the possible genres are included, and two columns have been left blank so that you can add other genres you think are significant. Try to fill in the purpose, overall organization, connectives, and other language features following the models provided.

As the next part of the chapter will demonstrate, being aware of the most important linguistic features of some of the text types in school will help you

Creative and Personal Genres

Type of text	Recount	Narrative	Other?
	Our class excursion	*The elephant and the mouse*	
Purpose	To tell what happened	To entertain, teach	
Organization	• Orientation (tells who, what, where, when) • Series of events • Personal comment/conclusion	• Orientation (tells who, what, when) • Series of events • Problem • Resolution	
Examples of connectives (to structure ideas)	To do with time (*first, then, next, afterward, at the end of the day*)	To do with time (*one day, once upon a time, later, afterward, in the end*)	
Other language features	• Past tense, tells about what happened • "Action" verbs, e.g., *left, arrived, ate, went* • Words to describe people, events, and actions	• Past tense, tells about what happened • "Action" verbs, e.g., *ran, took, sold* • "Thinking" verbs, e.g., *thought, wondered, hoped* • May have dialogue and "saying" verbs, e.g., *said, replied, asked, shouted*	

Factual Genres (to reproduce knowledge)

Type of text	Information Report	Procedure	Other?
	Insects	*How to make a healthy meal*	
Purpose	To give information about something	To tell how to do something	
Organization	• General statement • Characteristics (e.g., habitat) • Characteristics (e.g., appearance) • Characteristics (e.g., food, etc.) • May have subheadings	• Goal • Steps in sequence	
Examples of connectives (to structure ideas)	• May not be used • Subheadings structure information • If report describes life cycles, time connectives such as *first, two weeks later, then, finally*	To introduce each step, e.g., *first, second, third*	

Figure 5–2 Some School Genres   *(continues)*

Factual Genres (*continued*)

Type of text	Information Report	Procedure	Other?
Other language features	• Generalizations using present tense: *it eats, it lives* • Often uses *to be* and *to have* for descriptions; e.g., *A fly is an insect. It has six legs.* • Specialized vocabulary about insects	Uses "action" verbs to give instructions, e.g., *take, mix, chop, bake*	

Analytical Genres (to reflect on and analyze knowledge)

Type of text	Argument	Discussion	Other?
	Should smoking be made illegal?	*Should smoking be made illegal?*	
Purpose	To persuade others, to take a position and justify it, showing one side of an argument	To persuade others, to take a position and justify it, showing two or more sides of an argument	
Organization	• Personal statement of position • Argument 1 and supporting points/evidence; Argument 2 and supporting points/evidence, etc. • Conclusion and possible recommendation	• Identification of the issue • Argument 1 and supporting points/evidence; Argument 2 and supporting points/evidence, etc. • Counterarguments • Conclusion and possible recommendation	
Examples of connectives (to structure ideas)	• To introduce each argument, e.g., *first, second, in addition, finally* • To introduce the conclusion, e.g., *therefore, in conclusion*	• To introduce each argument, e.g., *first, second, in addition* • To introduce each counterargument, e.g., *however, on the other hand, nevertheless* • To introduce the conclusion, e.g., *therefore, in conclusion*	
Other language features	• Subject-related vocabulary • Evaluative vocabulary that indicates writer's belief (*it is <u>extremely</u> likely that*)	• Subject-related vocabulary • Evaluative vocabulary that indicates writer's belief (*it is <u>extremely</u> likely that*)	

Figure 5–2 *Continued*

make these explicit to students, and they will help guide your assessment. Note though that the descriptions of the genres in Figure 5–2 are not intended to be passed directly onto students as they stand; a section later in this chapter describes a teaching process for supporting learners in developing a range of text types.

EXPLICIT TEACHING ABOUT WRITING

In the 1970s and 1980s there was a strong reaction against traditional teacher-controlled ways of teaching writing. This reaction was embodied in what became known as progressive approaches, with great importance placed on the processes of learning (see, for example, Graves 2003). An underlying assumption in many classrooms was that, given the right classroom environment and a climate that expects a quantity of writing across a range of purposes and forms, children would learn to write on a variety of subjects and in many forms, just as they learned to speak without formal instruction. While the move away from the traditional teacher-centered classroom was generally welcomed, there were also a number of critiques of progressive approaches in relation to EL learners and others less familiar with the language of school. Many teachers of EL learners began to argue the need for more explicit instruction in the structures of language and the conventions of writing for EL learners. A number of researchers also argued that purely process-oriented approaches tended to reinforce existing social inequities since what was expected of learners was often not made explicit, and that this lack of explicitness may actually prevent some students from achieving educational success, as Mary Schleppegrell's words that begin this chapter suggest. Educators thus have a responsibility to intervene in the learning process (Martin 1986, 1989; Martin, Christie, and Rothery 1987; Delpit 1988).

Lisa Delpit (1988) wrote in a similar vein in the context of the education of African American students in the United States, arguing that the conventions of writing need to be explicitly taught, and that they will not simply be "picked up" by students for whom the language and assumptions of the school are unfamiliar. As she argued, if you are not already a participant in the dominant culture, being told the rules of that culture explicitly makes acquiring power easier. On behalf of parents, she argued that those who may not themselves function well in powerful dominant cultures "want to ensure that the school provides their children with discourse patterns, interactional styles, and spoken and written language codes that will allow them success in the larger society" (285).

So what does it mean to teach "explicitly"? Let's begin with what it *doesn't* mean! It doesn't mean a return to the teaching of traditional grammar and to meaningless drills and exercises devoid of functional and communicative purpose. Nor does it mean that grammar is taught separately from the authentic use of language. Neither does it mean a breaking up of language into its component parts of speech; or a fragmentation of the timetable into spelling, dictation, composition, and so on; or a separation of the macro skills of reading, writing, listening, and speaking. It *does* mean that students are encouraged to reflect on how language is used for a range of purposes and with a range of audiences, and that teachers focus explicitly on those aspects of language that enable students to do this. Explicit teaching is related to real-life use, so that understanding *about* language is developed in the context of actual language use. It aims to foster active involvement in learning, independence in writing, and the ability to critique the ways that language is used in authentic contexts, such as the ways it is used to persuade and control. And, as we suggested in Chapter 1, explicit teaching reflects Vygotskian notions of learning, with its emphasis on the need for learner guidance by the teacher.

> *Explicit teaching reflects Vygotskian notions of learning, with its emphasis on the need for learner guidance by the teacher.*

THE TEACHING AND LEARNING CYCLE

Let's turn now to what this might look like in the classroom. The pedagogical approach described here began in Australia in the 1980s. It grew out of collaborative work between teachers and linguists working within the perspective of functional linguistics. They were working in schools (often in low socio-economic areas) where for many students English was a new language. The teachers and researchers at that time were concerned about the low levels of achievement in writing, especially in schools where there were high levels of students from low socioeconomic groups and also where there were large numbers of EL learners. They noted the repetition and lack of variety in what children were attempting to write (almost all the pieces of student writing they examined were personal and everyday recounts of things students had done). To address this, the teachers and researchers took an explicit approach to the modeling and development of writing, along with a deliberate strategy to introduce a wider range of genres integrated across the curriculum.

Derewianka (1990) and others involved in the "genre" movement in Australia have identified four stages (often referred to as the Teaching and Learning Cycle) through which a particular genre can be made explicit to students. At the same time, the importance of students understanding the *processes* of writing is not ignored. These four stages are generally known as *building the field*; *modeling* or *deconstructing the genre*; *joint construction*; and *independent writing*. Each of these stages has a particular teaching purpose:

- *Stage 1: Building the field.* In Chapter 1, *field* was described as the topic of the text. In this stage the aim is to make sure that learners have enough knowledge of the topic to be able to write about it. The focus here is primarily on the content, or information, of the text. At this stage, children are a long way from writing a text themselves, and activities will involve gathering relevant information through speaking, listening, reading, note-making, and other research to gain information, including the use of technology.

- *Stage 2: Modeling the genre (sometimes referred to as "Deconstructing the genre").* The focus here is on the form and the function of the particular genre that the students are going to use in their own writing. The aim is for students to become familiar with the purpose, overall structure, and linguistic features of the type of text they are going to write (see Figure 5–2).

- *Stage 3: Joint construction.* Here, the teacher and students write a text together so that students can see how the text is written. The focus is on illustrating the process of writing a text, while also discussing with students the language features associated with the genre, and the content.

- *Stage 4: Independent writing.* At this stage students write their own text, using the appropriate processes of drafting and conferencing.

It's important to recognize that, integrated with subject teaching, these four stages may take several weeks or longer to work through with students, especially if the focus genre is one that students are unfamiliar with. The Teaching and Learning Cycle itself could, if you wish, provide an organizing framework for an entire unit of work. But it is never a single lesson!

Here are some classroom activities that you might find useful for each of the stages. Not all activities will be appropriate for all ages, and they are not all appropriate for use in the teaching of every genre. In addition, from your general teaching experience you can no doubt think of other language-focused activities and ways of developing the topic. However, the activities suggested here illustrate how this approach to writing integrates speaking, listening, reading, and writing, and how it authentically integrates language with curriculum content.

As a starting point, begin with the topic itself, choosing a genre that will occur naturally in the subject content you plan to use. It's important that the Teaching and Learning Cycle is not seen as an "add-on" to what you would normally be teaching but is located within the regular curriculum. As an example to illustrate each of the four stages of the Teaching and Learning Cycle, let's imagine that you are teaching a unit of work on dinosaurs, and that within this unit you have decided to focus on an Information Report.

Stage 1: Building knowledge of the field (topic)

The focus here is *what* children will write about: the content of the writing. Knowing a lot about the subject matter is essential for all writers, and this is true for all forms of writing, fiction as well as nonfiction. Writers always need to know a lot more than their readers, even though they may in the end not use in their writing all of the information they now possess. The writer J. K. Rowling once described in an interview how she developed biographies for each of her characters even though not all of these details were directly referred to in her books. If writers are to sound convincing, they need a stock of information to select from and an understanding of their topic. So, the aim of this stage is to ensure that learners know enough about the subject to have something worth writing about. One of the advantages of integrating the writing program with subject teaching is that children will already be developing this knowledge base as they learn about the topic.

The activities described below all involve research for what children will eventually be writing about and the pooling of information and ideas. As they build up their knowledge it can be organized through, for example, data banks, matrix charts, flowcharts, mind maps, and anchor charts, including sharing information electronically. Most of the activities below can be used across the curriculum. Since the aim of this stage is to build up a knowledge base, many could be carried out by groups of students in their mother tongue, although they will also need to use English to share the information with others.

One way of building up topic knowledge is the jigsaw grouping described in Chapter 3. In the example we are using here, groups of four to six carry out research on a particular dinosaur. Once they have become "experts," the students regroup so that each new group contains one or two students from each of the "expert" groups. The job of the experts is to share what they have learned with the rest of the new group. Jigsaw activities involve note-taking, listening, speaking, and reading, and they provide an authentic context for interaction.

Here are some other ways to build up a shared knowledge of the topic.

- Find out what students already know by building up a class **Mind Map** of their current knowledge of the topic. Discussing what students know also provides a context for extending vocabulary associated with the topic.
- Use a **Wallpaper Activity** to collect ideas based on students' current knowledge.
- Gather a list of questions from the children of things they would like to find out about (for example, *Why did the dinosaurs disappear?*). For beginner EL students, encourage questions in the mother tongue and help students also word it in English.
- Read about the topic with students using shared reading or big books. These could include both nonfiction and fiction texts. If you use both kinds, there is an opportunity to discuss with students the different purposes of each. With a narrative text you could also talk about what is fact and what is fiction, and ask children what facts (if any) they have learned about dinosaurs from the story.

- Use the Internet to access additional information online. Here is a context where you could use a jigsaw grouping.
- Get students to match labels to drawings, introducing relevant vocabulary (*horns, jaws, curved teeth, crest, spine, scaly skin, tail, plates, spikes*).
- Develop a **Word Wall/Word Bank** about the topic, where field/topic-based vocabulary is displayed.
- Get the students to interview an expert in the field. They could write a letter inviting the expert into the classroom and prepare appropriate questions to ask.
- Once children have begun to build up some knowledge of the topic, they can match a picture (for example, a Stegosaurus) and a sentence that gives information about the dinosaur (for example, *Stegosaurus had a row of plates on its back*). You could also turn this into a barrier game using several pictures of types of dinosaurs and information about each of them. Student A has the sentences; Student B has the pictures. Student A reads out a sentence—*It has a row of plates on its back*—and Student B shows the appropriate picture. This has the advantage of providing simple models for the kinds of sentences students will later write.
- Use **Barrier Games** such as Find the Difference to describe the appearance of dinosaurs—for example, the differences between Stegosaurus and Triceratops. (See Figure 5–3.)
- Use the topic to develop research skills by visiting the library or using the Internet. If it is Internet-based information, it is important that you show students how to validate the information they find, for example, checking whether references are included and who the site belongs to.
- Watch a video and provide an **Information Grid** for pairs of children to complete as they watch.
- Before children watch a video, prepare two sets of questions, with one half of the class answering one set, in pairs, and the other half answering the other set, in pairs. Later, pairs from each half form groups of four and share their information.

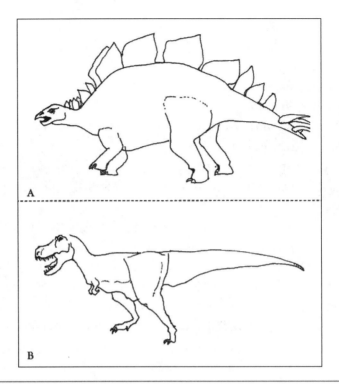

Figure 5–3 Find the Differences Between Dinosaurs

- Visit a museum and give different groups of children different questions to research. Children share information, as in jigsaw groups.
- As an ongoing activity during this stage, build up an information grid with the class that summarizes the information the students have gathered, to serve as an anchor chart. This could be developed on a large sheet of paper and displayed on the wall, with students adding information as they find it, using sticky notes, or writing directly on the grid. They could also enter information on a shared online site set up for the class. Information grids serve as working documents, so both you and the students can add to the grid as they discover more information. Alternatively, children can develop their own information grids, individually. In Stages 3 and 4 of the Teaching and Learning Cycle, these information summaries will be very important.

Stage 2: Modeling and deconstructing the genre

This stage aims to build up students' understandings of the *purpose, overall structure*, and *language features* of the particular genre the class is focusing on, in this case an Information Report. Choose a text that is similar to the one that students will eventually write themselves. Model texts may be commercially produced, teacher-written, or texts written previously by other students. Try to have this model text large enough for everyone to see it, to ensure that everyone is focusing on the correct part when you are discussing it. A Power-Point or interactive whiteboard allows you to visually emphasize different aspects of the text as you are focusing on them. You could also use a large sheet of paper. For our example, you would choose a short report about dinosaurs or about a particular dinosaur.

During this stage, introduce some meta-language—language to talk about language—as it is needed. Words like *connectives, genre, verbs*, and *tense* will make it easier for you to talk about the key features and for the students to self-evaluate their own texts later. Contrary to much debate about the place of the teaching of grammar, research and teaching practice in Australia has shown that students do not have difficulty understanding these concepts, and that providing a label helps to make explicit key aspects of writing (Schleppegrell 2013; Humphrey, Droga, and Feez 2012; Derewianka 2011; Williams 1999). The principle here, of course, is that these grammatical terms are taught *in the context of language use*. Here are some suggested steps to follow. Don't try to complete them all in a single lesson!

- Read and show the model report to the students, and discuss with them its purpose—to present factual information on a topic. (If students are already familiar with narratives, you could discuss with them the difference between the purposes of a narrative and of a report.)
- Then draw attention to the overall structure or "shape" of the text, and the function of each stage. (For example, Reports begin with a general statement, the purpose of which is to locate what is being talked about, and the rest of the report consists of facts about various aspects of the subject, often grouped under subheadings.)
- With more advanced students you might prefer to let the students themselves decide on the purpose, organization, and language

features. Get students in groups to examine several models of the same genre, and explain what they all have in common.

♦ Next, focus on any grammatical structures and vocabulary that are important in Reports. For example, you may want to focus on the verbs *be* and *have*, since these are very common in Information Reports. (Note, however, that here they will be used in the past tense since we are referring to things no longer in existence.)

♦ Also introduce grammar structures that are particularly relevant to the topic. For example, although scientists know a great deal about dinosaurs, there is much that is still speculative. We don't know for sure why dinosaurs became extinct, although there are many competing theories. Nor do we know why they grew so large. It is important for learners to be able to express these uncertainties, and this would be a meaningful context in which to introduce or remind students about how to use modality. Modality is the way in which speakers express degrees of likelihood or probability (e.g., *maybe, perhaps, might, could be*) or degrees of usuality (e.g., *sometimes, often, frequently*). Ways of expressing probability could form a word bank (e.g., *might have been, may have been, possibly, probably, perhaps, it is possible that*) on which students can draw when they come to do their own writing:

> Perhaps dinosaurs disappeared because the climate changed.
> Dinosaurs might have disappeared because the climate changed.
> They may have died from disease.
> They may have been warm-blooded.
> They could have become extinct because a meteorite hit the earth.

♦ Students in pairs do a **Text Reconstruction** of part of a report, reordering jumbled sentences into a coherent text. Alternately, you could mix up the sentences from two reports so that students must first sort out which sentence belongs to which report, and then sequence them.

♦ Use a **Dictogloss** (described in Chapter 7) to provide another model of the text type. The content of this should be taken from the current topic (e.g., you could choose a text that describes one of the dinosaurs the children are researching). In turn, this will also be a source of further information.

- ◆ Use the model text as a **Cloze Activity,** making the gaps according to the grammatical features or vocabulary you are focusing on. Children will also enjoy using a **Monster Cloze** or a **Vanishing Cloze**.
- ◆ Use part of the model text as a **Running Dictation**.
- ◆ Once the students have a clear idea of the characteristics of a report (or whatever text type you are focusing on), remind them of these characteristics and write them up as a chart that can be displayed on the wall. (Figure 5–2 may be useful as teacher reference here, but note that this is not intended for direct student use.)

Stage 3: Joint construction

At this stage, students are ready to think about writing, although they will not be writing alone yet. It will help you to understand the teaching purpose of this stage if you return to Chapter 1 and the example of Nigel talking with his parents. There we saw how the story Nigel told was jointly constructed—although the *meanings* were initiated by Nigel, his parents helped with the *wording*. This is a natural process, and for most adults an intuitive one. The joint construction stage of writing mirrors the same process. The students give suggestions and contribute ideas while the teacher scribes, and together the teacher and students discuss how the writing can be improved and whether the information is accurate.

The joint construction should be an example of the same genre, such as a Report on one type of dinosaur. At this stage the children will need to start drawing on the knowledge they developed in Stage 1. You should also remind students of the model texts they have looked at previously in Stage 2. Throughout the process, the teacher and students constantly reread together what they have written, with the teacher asking questions like: *Is that the best way to say it? Can anyone think of a more accurate word than that? Does anything need fixing up?* In the example that follows, the students and teacher have already written the first paragraph of the Report. They are now starting on the second paragraph. There is a large information grid on the wall of the classroom that summarizes all the information the children have collected about six types of dinosaurs.

T   well we've written our introductory paragraph . . and we've written some general information about stegosaurus . . . what do you think we should write now?

S1   we need a new paragraph

T   we do . yes . should we write something first though?

S1   oh we need another heading?

S2   we can say what it looked . . . how it looked.

T   what it looked like . good . who can remember the proper word to use here? what was the word that the writer used in the text we read about stegasaurus?

S3   I know . . . appear . . . appear

S4   appearance. it's appearance what things look like .

T   yes that's the word that one of the other reports used wasn't it? so appearance, remember it?—it means what something *looks* like. (*Teacher writes* Appearance *as a subheading.*) And this isn't the main heading of the whole report is it . . . it's a . . . ?

Several   subheading

T   so what are some of the things we learned about stegosaurus? who can remember something about its appearance?

S5   it has those . . . plates?

S7   plates on its back

S6   we can write *it has plates on the back* (*Teacher scribes.*)

T   let's read that sentence together.

All   (*Reading*) *It has plates on the back.*

S2   big plates (*Teacher adds* big.)

S7   big bony plates (*Teacher adds* bony.)

T   how is that now? . . . . look at that word (*Points to* has)

S4   oh I know . . . it *had*

T	why do you say that?
S4	they are all dead now so we say *had*
T	they are all dead now yes . . . who can remember that word we learned . . . it means they all died and they aren't any in the world now . look at the word wall
Several	extinct!
T	yes they are all extinct now . so we have to use the past tense . *had* . now let's read it again
All	(*Reading*) *it had big bony plates on its back.*
T	OK . . . now I'm reading this and I'm thinking what are those plates for? look at our information grid
S7	to . . . when they were fighting, for protect it?
S	protection
S5	but we don't know
S8	we read scientists don't know . . . only . . . . . . just have . . . think something
T	they don't really know the reason? so what could we say here then?

As this excerpt shows, during a joint construction the teacher can focus on all aspects of writing. It provides opportunities for teacher and students together to discuss the overall structure of the text, suggest more appropriate vocabulary, consider alternative ways of wording an idea, and work on using correct grammar, spelling, and punctuation. Remember that the children will by this stage have built up a good knowledge base, so the teacher may also need to remind them to look at the pooled work done by the class. (Note this teacher's reminder to look at the information grid and the word wall to find the precise terminology they need.) The joint construction is a time when there can be an explicit focus on how language is used, but, unlike the traditional classroom, discussion of grammar, vocabulary, spelling, and punctuation occurs in functionally relevant ways—in the context of actual language use, and at the point of need.

A joint construction also models the *process* of writing. As the children make suggestions, the teacher works collaboratively with them to create the text. She demonstrates that a writer makes changes, amends, adds words, and rereads what has been written. The children learn that the first thing they think of to write may not be the best choice to say exactly what they mean, or what the reader needs to know.

Once this first draft is complete, the teacher or a student can rewrite it on a large sheet of paper or reproduce it electronically so that it provides an additional model text that children can access as they move toward doing their own writing.

While the joint construction stage is teacher guided, it is not teacher dominated. Rather, as we can see from the example, the teacher's role is a kind of editor: she takes up the ideas of the students, leading the discussion of any linguistic aspects of the text that students are still learning to control and clarifying unclear wording. The joint construction is a very important part of the Teaching and Learning Cycle because it illustrates to students both the *process* of composing text and a *product* that is similar to what they will later write themselves.

In this context meta-language (language about language) can be explicitly modeled in the context of actual language use. It can then become a tool for both teacher and children to reflect on how language is used. Developing a shared meta-language encourages students to think more holistically about their writing and allows a teacher to give much more explicit feedback to children about their writing. This need not be complex or highly specialized: terms such as *genre, overall structure, time connectives, logical connectives, pronouns, tense,* and the names of the type of genre (here, *Report*) are all relevant in developing metalinguistic understandings. These can be introduced gradually and in context, and they will help students build up a language to talk about language, as well as draw their attention to significant aspects of their own writing.

Stage 4: Independent writing

This is the final stage of the cycle, when students write their own texts. They can do this writing individually or in pairs. In this case, they could choose a dinosaur to write about (but not the same one as used in Stages 2 and 3). By now note the considerable amount of scaffolding there has been for the writing. Students have developed considerable background knowledge about the subject, are aware of the linguistic characteristics of the genre, and have jointly constructed a similar text. Stages 1 and 2 provide scaffolding for the joint construction, and this in turn provides the scaffolding for the independent writing in Stage 4. This scaffolding will help ensure that the children have the knowledge and skills to be able to write their own texts with confidence.

As students write, remind them about the process of writing: doing a first draft, self-editing, discussing the draft with friends and later with the teacher, and finally producing a published text. The published texts can be displayed in the classroom or made into a class book. If you copy a few of the students' texts (with their permission), they can also serve as useful models and resources for other classes.

ADDITIONAL SCAFFOLDING FOR YOUNG LEARNERS AND EL BEGINNERS

The Teaching and Learning Cycle can also be used with very young students and those new to English, although the length of the text is likely to be shorter, and they are very likely to need *additional* support at the Independent Writing stage. One of the simplest genres to begin with is a personal recount. As you can see from Figure 5–2, a Recount reconstructs past experience, and is a retelling of an activity or a sequence of events in which the speaker or writer has been involved.

In one classroom, the teacher had planned a school excursion to a local dam. Excursions provide an ideal context for developing recounts. During the day, the teacher and some of the children took photographs and wrote brief notes of what they saw. When they returned to school, they shared their observations in the form of oral recounts. Later they relived the excursion through the photographs as the teacher helped the children talk about what they had done, using the sequence of photographs as prompts of the day's events: *we left school early in the morning; we got on the bus; we visited the national park; we had our lunch; we visited the dam*; and so on. After the oral discussion, the sequence of photographs remained on display as a prompt for the children's own writing.

Using time connectives such as *later, next, afterward,* and *finally* are important in structuring a Recount. Many young writers tend to rely on the connective *and then* for sequencing recounts and narratives, so in this class the teacher had been modeling a broader range of time connectives and had been focusing on these when she was reading to the children.

As Chapter 1 pointed out, as far as possible teachers should try to have the range of learners in their class complete the same or similar tasks—what will vary is the kind and degree of the scaffolding teachers provide. For children at the early stages of writing in English, provide a simple organizational framework and some suggested connecting words as they begin writing, and allow them, if they wish, to write in pairs. You could also provide a list of some of the vocabulary they will need to use.

In this class, the teacher provided the following outline as additional scaffolding for some children as they began to write their Recount:

On _____ our class went to _____.

First we visited _____. We saw _____ there.

Then we went to _____.

Next we visited _____ and saw _____.

Afterward we went to _____ and saw _____.

Finally we got back on the bus and _____.

We got back to school at _____. It was _____.

Here are some other ways to support learners who are new to English.

* If learners are already literate in their mother tongue, encourage them to continue to write in it. Literacy in the mother tongue is a major resource for becoming literate in English, and ideally the aim of full bilingualism will continue to be supported by the school even after the child is able to function in English. Where school resources are inadequate to do this, then use of the mother tongue in the early stages of learning English reduces the frustration children may feel

when they are unable to participate in classroom tasks that they would be well able to carry out in their mother tongue. If possible, provide a translation on a facing page (perhaps with the help of a parent or peer). Having a bilingual account will not only help learners understand the English version, but allow them to display their literacy skills, which may be considerable. In addition, bilingual texts allow monolingual English-speaking children to recognize that communication occurs through many languages.

◆ For a recount or a narrative, have learners draw a sequence of events or story map and dictate what they want to say. Write this text for them, which they can trace over or copy.

◆ Use **Picture Sequencing** with a group of students as a basis for a simple narrative.

◆ Use a **Dialogue Letter/Dialogue Journal** between yourself and the EL learner, or between the EL learner and an English-speaking buddy. These are ongoing written conversations where each partner writes a single short sentence responding to the other.

◆ Use **Jumbled Sentences**. Get learners to tell you a sentence about themselves, something they have done, or something they like. Or use a sentence taken from a text the class has read. Scribe it for them and then cut the sentence up, first into meaningful phrases: [Once upon a time] [there was] [a little spider]. Once the learner can read and order this, cut the sentence into single words. Learners rearrange the jumbled sentence, read it aloud, and rewrite it. If they are literate in their mother tongue, get them to write an equivalent sentence in their mother tongue, too.

◆ A variation on jumbled sentences is to write the same sentence on two strips of card. Cut one into the individual words. Students place the matching word on top of the uncut strip. This is useful for drawing attention to the shape of words and to the way they are spelled.

◆ Use a **Writing Framework**. Provide learners with an explicit framework for the kind of writing the rest of the class is doing when they begin to write independently. Figure 5–4 is an example of how even a fairly complex text type—a discussion—can be scaffolded in this way.

Figure 5–4 Discussion Framework (for students needing more scaffolding)

Title: _____

What the discussion is about, and my opinion

The topic of this discussion is . . .

My opinion is that . . .

Arguments for
There are a number of reasons why I believe this.

1. First

2. In addition

3. Finally

Counterarguments (arguments against)

1. On the other hand, some people argue

2. In addition

3. They also say

Conclusion

However, my view is that . . .

because . . .

A SCAFFOLDED APPROACH TO WRITING

It is easy to see how the notion of scaffolding applies to this kind of teaching. At no stage are learners expected to carry out alone a task with which they are not familiar, yet at the same time they are constantly being "stretched" in their language development and expected to take responsibility for those tasks they are capable of doing alone. At each stage there is systematic guidance and support until learners are able to carry out the writing task for themselves. Consider how different this approach is to the traditional one-off writing task, when students were expected to write a single and final copy at one sitting, or to some process-oriented approaches in which students were expected to make their own choices about a writing topic and how to approach it.

As we have seen, the cycle may take some time to complete. However, in the case of reports, for example, not only will students learn how to write a report, but they will also learn a lot about the topic (and thus develop particular knowledge in a curriculum area). As well, they will practice the study skills of note-taking and of locating, summarizing, and reinterpreting information. The cycle includes plenty of opportunities for reading, listening, and speaking, and you may decide to integrate it with focused teaching of these skills. In addition, students will learn how to write, edit, and evaluate any similar text that they might need to write at another time.

Of course, students will not know all there is to know about this genre after only one use of the cycle. It should be repeated throughout the year, and through the school, using appropriately chosen material for the age of the students. However, as they become more familiar with the particular text type, it probably won't be necessary to continue to go through Stages 2 and 3 in quite such detail.

> *At no stage are learners expected to carry out alone a task with which they are not familiar.*

It has sometimes been suggested that the cycle simply presents different genres as a series of "recipes" that students are then expected to follow slavishly. Creativity and the writer's voice, it is argued, will be stifled. However, making rules and expectations explicit to students does not limit their freedom and autonomy. On the contrary, it gives them the tools with which to be creative and autonomous. Once students are aware of the conventions of any of the genres, they will be able to manipulate them for their own purposes.

Good short story writers, for example, often don't follow the overall structure discussed earlier. They may begin with the resolution and narrate the story as a series of flashbacks, or they may manipulate the sequence in a whole range of other ways. But it would be foolish to suggest that good writers are unaware of traditional narrative writing; indeed, it is precisely this awareness that allows them to exploit and manipulate their writing in new ways, and to make conscious choices about how they write. We need to reflect this in the classroom. If students are to have real choices about what and how they write, they need to be shown what the range of options is. Otherwise, they may simply remain with what they know, writing about a limited range of things in the same way. And it is important to remember that the conventions that govern different types of writing have not been imposed by linguists, but simply describe what these genres look like in the real world.

ASSESSING STUDENTS' WRITING: WHAT THEIR TEXTS CAN TELL US

There is a range of purposes for classroom-based assessment: to report to other teachers and parents, to give feedback to the students, and to inform subsequent learning and teaching. Among the most important of these is the ongoing assessment teachers carry out to learn what their students are able to do. Only if we know students' current abilities can subsequent teaching be truly responsive, and only then can we plan how to take students further. Put another way, and using the Vygotskian idea of the zone of proximal development discussed in Chapter 1, we must know what the learner is able to do alone before we know what to scaffold next. This kind of assessment is not an extra item for which you must find additional time; it can occur during any normal classroom teaching. Here is a suggestion about how to analyze students' writing to find out both what they are able to achieve and the areas in which they need further help. To do this you will need to look at a piece of writing that represents what the writer can do alone. It need not be their first draft, but it should not yet have been discussed in a conference.

Here are two examples of narrative writing, both from EL learners. The first comes from a student who is still in the early stages of English, and the second comes from a younger child who is already fluent in spoken English. Take a moment to think about what each writer knows, and what kind of help they need.

Text 1: turtle and wolf

One day the turtle out the river to find the food. He go went the sun.

The sun very hot the turtle he want go back.

The turtle crying because he can't go back. the wolf thought the turtle he think turtle was singing. The wolf said "you don't singing to me I put you on the sun," "Don't worry I can get into my shell. "I threw you to the river.

"Don't do that."

The wolf threw turtle to the river. The turtle said "thank old mr wolf.

Text 2: Night

One night I was walking throgth the woods I heard something strange I didn't know what it was I looked I still didn't know what it was I looking it was an owl he led me to house he knocked on the door a which answer come little boy I might turn you into a frog all my prisoners are hiding somewhere so you can't escape if you try to they will catch you so I will turn you into a which their are stairs but their are prisoners hiding you can'not go up their because they have the stuf to turn you into a frog so I wouldn't try it she let me go I ran home as fast as I could I was home at last what happen I will tell you in the morning then I went to bed.

What were your first reactions to the two texts? If you were to look only at sentence grammar, you would probably be more critical of Text 1 than of Text 2. Text 1 has many more grammatical errors, particularly in the use of verbs, and it is quite clearly written by a second language learner. Text 2, despite the fact that it is written with minimal punctuation, has a much closer control of standard grammar. However, you probably also feel that Text 1 is a more coherent piece: we can follow the story line, and this is much harder to follow in Text 2.

Before you read further, look again at the discussion of the features of a Narrative discussed at the beginning of this chapter, and in Figure 5–2. Then consider the texts again, this time thinking about the question framework in Figure 5–5 as you read.

The questions in Figure 5–5 are designed to help you think in a systematic way about what you are reading, and about what the student knows and can do, as well as to highlight future learning needs. The framework takes a holistic and top-down view of writing, focusing first on the overall meaning, then on the overall organization, the ways that sentences are connected, sentence construction, and finally spelling and punctuation. It thus reflects the layout of the descriptions of the genres in Figure 5–2. Leaving spelling and punctuation until last is not to suggest they are not important, simply that correcting the spelling of a poor piece of writing results in a correctly spelled poor piece of writing—the piece of writing itself is not substantially improved! When helping students with their writing, spelling and punctuation must be considered in the final version, but only after other more fundamental aspects of writing have been considered first.

Your responses to these sets of questions may have given you a quite different perspective on the two texts. For Text 1, you will probably have responded positively to Questions 1, 2, and 3, and to some degree to 4. Your response to 5 and 7 will also probably have been quite positive. It is only when we look at 6 that difficulties are evident. So think about what that student *can* do and what he knows about writing (and how much of his ability to write would go unnoticed if sentence grammar were the sole focus of the assessment). By contrast, Text 2 is actually much less comprehensible and coherent, and compared to your assessment of Text 1 you probably found it in several ways a far less successful text.

An example of how the framework might be filled in for the writer of the first text is included in Figure 5–6. A framework like this will help you keep an ongoing profile of individual students' writing development. Try to jot down comments as you are conferencing with students or reading their texts. Even if these notes are brief, they will help you build up a clear idea of what kinds of texts your students are able to control, and any linguistic difficulties they

1. General Comments	2. Text Type	3. Overall Organization	4. Cohesion	5. Vocabulary	6. Sentence Grammar	7. Spelling
• Is the overall meaning clear? • Are the main ideas developed? • Does the writing reflect the writer's other classroom language experiences (e.g., what they have read or talked about)? • What is your overall impression compared to other things the learner has written?	• What kind of text is this? • Is this appropriate for the writer's purpose? • Has the writer written this text type before?	• Is the overall structural organization appropriate to the text type? • Are any stages missing?	• Are the ideas linked with the appropriate connectives? *(Note that these will vary with the text type; see Chapter 5)* • Is there an appropriate variety of these connectives? • Are pronouns used correctly (e.g., *he* and *she*)? • Do pronouns have a clear referent (e.g., is it clear what words such as *he, she, this, there,* etc., are referring to)?	• Is appropriate vocabulary used? • Is there semantic variety (e.g., does the writer use a range of words for *big*, such as *huge, massive, large, gigantic,* etc.)? *(Note that semantic variety will be appropriate for narratives and recounts, but probably not for more factual texts, such as reports and instructions.)*	• Is this accurate (e.g., subject-verb agreements, correct use of tenses, correct use of word order, etc.)?	• Is this accurate? • If the writer does not yet produce correct spelling, what does the writer know about spelling (e.g., evidence of sound–symbol correspondence)?

Figure 5–5 Question Framework for Assessing Writing

1. General Comments	2. Text Type	3. Overall Organization	4. Cohesion	5. Vocabulary	6. Sentence Grammar	7. Spelling
Meaning is clear and all elements of the story are present.	Narrative.	Good—has orientation, events, problem, resolution.	Used reference correctly throughout.	Good. Used vocabulary from the story.	Needs help with the past tense. Introduce more "saying verbs," such as answered, replied, begged	Spelling is good. Needs help with setting out of dialogue.

Figure 5–6 Assessment of Text 1

may be having. One teacher with whom I worked developed a system of color-coding, using one color for indicating positive achievements and another indicating the area where future teaching was needed.

An alternative way of using the framework is to use it to build up a *class profile*. To assess how well a group of students is able to use a particular genre, write the names of the students down the left-hand side and comment briefly on each one. You will then be able to see what abilities and difficulties they have in common.

Although this kind of assessment is time-consuming, you will find that you get faster the more you use it. It is also time well spent, because in reflecting on students' writing in this way, you are able to better target your future teaching to specific student needs. In doing this you are also differentiating the curriculum. This does not mean developing an individual program for every student, which for most busy teachers is a practical impossibility, but it does mean that the classroom program will be as responsive as possible to the individual needs indicated by the profile. Finally, the profile will indicate what students *can* achieve (as we saw in Text 1) as well as where they have difficulties, and will be a useful basis for giving feedback to the students themselves, to parents, and to other teachers.

> *When asked to edit their writing, students may focus almost exclusively on spelling and punctuation because they are unaware of what else to look at.*

If you simplify and adapt the question framework, you can also share it with your students to demonstrate how they might use it as to reflect, proofread, and evaluate their own writing. Often, when asked to edit their writing, students may focus almost exclusively on spelling and punctuation because they are unaware of what else to look at. One version of a self-assessment sheet is shown in Figure 5–7. It includes a space for children's own comments on their writing and for teacher comments. This kind of self-assessment, which structures for learners how to reflect on their writing, reinforces the importance of reflecting on what has been written and provides a valuable scaffolding tool for students to improve their own writing. It also helps students to give more thoughtful and specific advice to others when they are peer conferencing.

Self-assessment frameworks like this can also be used with younger children, including those in the early stage of literacy, as long as they are very simply worded and their purpose is clear to the children.

Clear Writing	Organizing the Ideas	Using Signaling Words	Careful Sentences	Correct Spelling
• Has a friend read your writing? Did your friend understand all of your ideas?	• Have you organized your ideas well? • Have you written an introduction? • Have you written several arguments? Have you included details to support each argument? • Have you written a conclusion and recommendation?	• What signaling words did you use to introduce each new argument? • What word did you use to introduce your conclusion?	• Have you read this aloud, sentence by sentence? Did you hear any mistakes? • Have you checked each sentence very carefully to make sure you haven't made any mistakes? • Did you check the endings of words?	• Did you check the spelling of words you are not sure of? • How did you check your spelling?
Your Comments or Your Friend's Comments	**Your Comments or Your Friend's Comments**	**Your Comments or Your Friend's Comments**	**Your Comments or Your Friend's Comments**	**Your Comments or Your Friend's Comments**
Your Teacher's Comments	**Your Teacher's Comments**	**Your Teacher's Comments**	**Your Teacher's Comments**	**Your Teacher's Comments**

Figure 5–7 Self-Assessment and Reflection Sheet for Writing: Argument

Here is one final comment about the approach to writing taken in this chapter. The more time you have spent on the stages of the Teaching and Learning Cycle, and the more planned and responsive the scaffolding, the more likely it is that students will write effectively, feel they have control over what they are writing, and gain confidence in using written language. Both you and your students will feel proud of their achievements. This is certainly preferable to spending endless time correcting mistakes in students' writing because they have not had sufficient support earlier in the process, and preferable, too, to setting up students for failure because they have been asked to write without sufficient scaffolding and knowledge of what is expected.

> *You and your students will feel proud of their achievements.*

In Summary

This chapter has illustrated the potential cultural and linguistic challenges faced by EL learners in writing across the curriculum. It introduces the notion of genres, their significance in school learning, and a pedagogy for their development.

+ Every genre occurs within a particular culture and has a distinct social purpose, overall structure, particular connectives and conjunctions to organize ideas, and particular language and vocabulary associated with it.
+ Explicit teaching involves strong teacher guidance in these areas, in the context of actual language use.
+ The Teaching and Learning Cycle aims to foster active student involvement and includes a focus on building the field, modeling the genre, joint construction, and independent writing, along with targeted teacher scaffolding that sets students up for success.
+ The Teaching and Learning Cycle provides a means of integrating subject teaching and language teaching.
+ Assessment of writing using a genre-based approach enables teachers to be explicit about EL learners' strengths and difficulties, and it can provide constructive feedback for learners, teachers, and parents.

To Think About

1. How could you use the Teaching and Learning Cycle illustrated in this chapter with your own students?
2. How is the Teaching and Learning Cycle similar to, or different from, the approach to teaching writing that you currently use?
3. What are the key genres that need to be taught at your grade level(s)?
4. What points in this chapter affirm your current practice? What is the most important learning for you in this chapter?
5. Tell a success story from your classroom. What was the context in which the writing occurred? What did the students achieve? What scaffolding did you provide?

Suggestions for Further Reading

Derewianka, B. 1990. *Exploring How Texts Work*. Portsmouth, NH: Heinemann and Primary English Teaching Association of Australia (PETAA).

———. 2011. *A New Grammar Companion for Teachers*. Sydney: Primary English Teaching Association of Australia (PETAA).

Gibbons, P. 2009. Chapter 6, "Scaffolding EL Learners to Be Successful Writers." In *English Learners, Academic Literacy, and Thinking*. Portsmouth, NH: Heinemann.

Humphrey, S., L. Droga, and S. Feez. 2012. *Grammar and Meaning*, Appendices 1, 2, and 3. Sydney: Primary English Teaching Association of Australia (PETAA).

Six

Reading in a Second Language and Culture

Barriers and Bridges

Literacy in a second language develops as in the first—globally, not linearly, and in a variety of rich contexts.

—Pat Rigg and Virginia Allen, *When They Don't All Speak English: Integrating the ESL Student in the Regular Classroom*

In this chapter we will examine the kinds of information that effective readers bring to text and suggest some of the reasons for why the reading process may break down for students learning to read in a second or new language. These breakdowns in the reading process are the potential "barriers" to reading with comprehension. The chapter continues with a range of strategies to use with students in three contexts: (1) before they begin to read a text, (2) during the reading itself, and (3) after the text has been read. These strategies are the "bridges" to text referred to in the title of this chapter: they provide scaffolding for students to bring meaning to a particular text, but also model reading strategies to support them in reading other texts. The chapter also contains discussion about the role and significance of phonemic awareness, and its link with the process of reading.

THE PROCESS OF READING

How well are you able to read this?

> Thr hs bn a It of dbat ovr th pst tn yrs abt th tchng of rding. Sme see rding as th mastry of phncs, othrs as a procss of prdctn whrby the rder uss bckgrnd knwldge and knwledge of th lngge systm to prdict mning.
>
> Thees diffreing veiws haev infelunced the wya raeding has bene tuahgt. Appraochse haev vareid betwene thoes who argeu that the taeching of phoincs is the msot imprtoant elmeent of a raeding prorgam, and thoes who argeu fro a whoel-language appraohc in whchi childnre laern to raed by perdicting maenngi.
>
> But it shou_be obvi_ to anyo_ readi_ thi_ th_ goo_ read_ use a rang_ of strateg_ to gai- mean- fro- writ- tex-.

As the final paragraph states, though with somewhat unorthodox orthography, good readers use a range of strategies to gain meaning from written text. In the first paragraph, almost all of the vowels have been omitted; in the second paragraph, all of the letters of each word are included, but they are scrambled; and in the third paragraph, only the beginning of each word is given. Despite this you were still able to bring meaning to the text quite easily. This is because as an effective reader, you used other kinds of information to read past the gaps and inconsistencies in the phonic information.

It is obvious that a lot more than phonemic awareness and phonic knowledge was involved in your reading of this text. Certainly this was helpful, but phonemic awareness and knowledge of phonics *alone* would not have enabled you to interpret the texts with meaning, nor would it have been sufficient for you to predict words as you were reading. You also drew on your background knowledge of the subject, or knowledge of the *field*, to predict what the text was saying. In addition, you drew on your intuitive knowledge of how English works: recognizing syntax and key vocabulary also played an important part in enabling you to predict the words you were reading.

A lot more than phonemic awareness and phonic knowledge is involved in reading.

Goodman (1967) was one of the first researchers to draw attention to three kinds of knowledge on which readers draw to gain meaning from text. He referred to these as *semantic knowledge* (or knowledge of the world, and specifically the field of the text), syntactic knowledge (knowledge of the structure of the language), and *graphophonic knowledge* (knowledge of the relationships between sounds and letters, and recognition of the phonemic patterning of the words in English). The next three examples illustrate how each of these kinds of knowledge enables you, as you are reading, to predict what follows:

> *The sun rises in the East and sets in the* _____.
> Your knowledge of the world, or field, of the text enables you to predict that the missing word is *West*.

> *This animal is a klinger.* This is *another klinger. There are two*
> _____.
> Your knowledge of how English works allows you to predict *klingers*, using other plural words as an analogy. The word is a made-up one, so your knowledge of the world doesn't help here!

> *The Australian indigenous flag is red, black, and* _____.
> Was this word hard to predict? You could have chosen any color, but unless you can bring specific cultural knowledge to this statement, the choice of colors would be random. So in this case you need an additional clue, this time one related to the sound of the word. You would have had no problem predicting the word *yellow* if I had written the example in this way:

> *The Australian indigenous flag is red, black, and y* _____.

> Australians, however, would almost certainly not need this clue, because they could draw on their knowledge of the field, specifically, Australian cultural knowledge.

These examples suggest a very significant point about reading effectively: when we *already know* something about the field of the text, and the syntax of English, then the process of reading is speeded up because we don't need to decode each word, one by one. But without field knowledge, including the specific vocabulary associated with it, and knowledge of the language, a reader has no option but to rely on basic "decoding" of a word. If you are new to English, and subject-based concepts and cultural knowledge are all new to you too, then you are likely to use the only source of information available to you, that is, sounding out words letter by letter. And even if EL students are able to decode the text by sounding it out, there is no guarantee that they will ultimately comprehend the *meaning* of it if the language or field of the text is unknown or unfamiliar. Nor will they be able to predict what follows as they are reading.

Here is another example to illustrate how the ability to sound out, or decode, a text may have little to do with whether or not you comprehend its meaning.

> If you are a disregarded entity with a single owner who is a foreign person and you are not claiming treaty benefits as a hybrid entity, this form should be completed and signed by your foreign single owner. . . . However, if you are a disregarded entity that is claiming treaty benefits as a hybrid entity, this form should be completed and signed by you. . . . A reverse hybrid entity should give form [–] to a withholding agent.

This text was part of an explanatory leaflet accompanying an income tax form. Although when I first read it I was able to recognize the overall "shape" of the text—the word *however* is an important clue here—I have no idea what the overall text means, yet I think of myself as a literate person! What I lack is any understanding of the field; my background knowledge of this field simply isn't adequate. And although I can recognize what each of the words might mean individually (because I have met them in other contexts), their use in this context is highly specialized, so the text as a whole isn't meaningful to me (though no doubt a person skilled in and familiar with the field of U.S. tax regulations would read this with ease).

If you reflect on your own reading, you'll be aware that you're able to read familiar material (e.g., an article on a topic about teaching) much faster than unfamiliar material (e.g., the text above, or an academic paper on a topic you know nothing about). When you are unable to bring personal knowledge and understanding of a topic to a text, you are effectively robbed of the ability to make use of a key resource for reading: *what you already know*. I will refer to this prior knowledge as "in-the-head" knowledge.

The notion of in-the-head knowledge has considerable implications for second language learners, who may not share the same cultural or field knowledge as the writer of the text, just as I did not share the field knowledge of the writer of the text noted previously. But for EL learners, there may also be a potential barrier posed by the language itself: the language system is also part of this in-the-head knowledge. If you are able to read another language yourself, but are still not very fluent in the language, you will find, once again, that your reading relies much more on graphophonic cues than does your reading in English. Consequently, you read much more slowly because the resources that are available to a fluent speaker of the language are not available to you.

> *What you already know about the topic is a key resource for reading.*

What I am referring to as in-the-head knowledge has its roots in schema theory. Schema theory, applied to reading, proposes that effective readers draw on particular kinds of culturally acquired knowledge and language to guide and influence the comprehension process. In one early but well-known study, two groups of adults, white North Americans and Native Americans, were asked to read and recall two texts that described a typical wedding of each group. There were clear cross-cultural differences in the way in which the same information was interpreted and recalled by the two groups (Steffenson, Joag-Dev, and Anderson 1979). This may help to explain why many teachers of EL learners feel that their students are unable to pick out the main points of a text or differentiate these central points from less significant details.

Schematic or in-the-head knowledge may be of two types: knowledge of the kind of genre or text, and knowledge of the field. From the headings alone in the three examples that follow, you will be able to predict a good deal about the kind of text and where it will occur, and about the actual content and information.

Bank Robbers Hold Hostages

Web Site Designer Required

The Sly Cat and the Clever Mouse

Your in-the-head knowledge has developed as a result of your familiarity with reading similar genres and reading about similar topics in the past; ultimately it comes from being participants in the culture in which these texts exist. At one level, reading confirms what we know (or challenges what we thought we knew). As we read we map our already existing experiences and knowledge onto the text. In this way, new knowledge that is presented in the text builds on and interacts with our existing in-the-head knowledge.

Of course, we also read to learn new things, and we certainly don't need to know every detail or perspective in advance, or every word, to make sense of the text. But our in-the-head knowledge has to be sufficient to provide us with some links, or "cognitive hooks," on which to "hang" the new information in the text. As students move into higher grades and subject learning becomes more specialized and complex, mother tongue speakers of English too may lack the necessary cognitive hooks to fully comprehend more academic texts.

What this discussion of the reading process should make clear is that *meaning does not reside solely in the words and structures of the text, but is constructed in the interactions between the text and the in-the-head, or schematic knowledge, of the reader.*

READER ROLES

As a result of a range of views about what reading is, there are many theories of literacy pedagogy. At different times (and for reasons that are frequently political rather than educational), approaches such as phonics, whole-word, whole language, and critical reading are put forward as *the* method that will lead to successful literacy performance. Alan Luke and Peter Freebody (1990) argue, however, that the issue is not to do with which method is the most appropriate; rather, each of these general approaches emphasizes particular aspects of literacy. It is not that one program affords literacy and another doesn't, but rather that different programs emphasize different "literacies." Luke and Freebody suggest that there are four components of literacy success, and that successful readers need the resources to take on all four related roles as they read. These are the roles of *code breaker, text participant, text user,* and *text analyst.*

Reader as code breaker

As a *code breaker*, a reader needs to be able to engage in the "technology" of written script. This kind of knowledge allows readers to decode text as they read. In English it includes being able to distinguish the sounds of English and how these relate to the way a written word "looks," left-to-right directionality, and alphabet knowledge. A balanced literacy program will not ignore these elements. But, as illustrated earlier, code breaking, though necessary, is not sufficient for the successful reading of authentic texts in real social contexts, and the importance of knowing the code does not justify its teaching in contexts devoid of any real meaning. In addition, overreliance on decoding skills means that children are limited in their use of other kinds of resources and in the other reader roles suggested by Luke and Freebody. Children who read slowly—painfully sounding out each letter, word by word—are often unable to carry meaning at the sentence level or across stretches of discourse, so they often lose the overall meaning of the text they are reading. Ironically, poor readers have often been fed a diet of remedial phonics instruction, yet for many young second language learners, as we have seen, this may not be the area in which they need support in accessing meaning. Remember, too, that sounds and letters are very abstract concepts, particularly when the sounds don't match those that children are accustomed to hearing in their mother tongue.

Poor readers have often been fed a diet of remedial phonics instruction.

Reader as text participant

As a *text participant*, the reader connects the text with his or her particular in-the-head knowledge—including knowledge of the world, cultural knowledge, and knowledge of the generic structure—in the sorts of ways discussed earlier in this chapter. Luke and Freebody cite an example of the ways in which cultural knowledge is related to reading comprehension, drawing on the work of Reynolds, Taylor, Steffensen, Shirey, and Anderson (1981). In this example, a mix of eighth-grade African American and Anglo-American students read a passage about "sounding," a form of verbal ritual insult predominantly found among black teenagers. While the African American students correctly interpreted the text as being about verbal play, the Anglo-American students in general interpreted it as being about a physical fight. Despite the fact that their decoding skills were as good and possibly better than the African American students, the Anglo-American students were unable to "read" the text in a way that matched the writer's intentions.

It is ironic, as Luke and Freebody have pointed out, that in many standardized reading tests the African American students, in general, may have scored lower than their middle-class Anglo-American peers. Yet in this example, which acknowledges the role of cultural knowledge, we see that the African American students in fact were the more effective readers of this text. Being a text participant, then, means having the in-the-head resources to match text with appropriate content and cultural knowledge.

Reader as text user

As a *text user*, a reader is able to participate in the social activities in which written text plays a major part and to recognize what counts as successful reading in a range of social contexts. For example, not all cultures value reading for relaxation or interest, and others may place great importance on the value of reading religious texts. The interactions that children have around literacy events construct their understandings about how they are expected to read particular texts. For example, parents may ask particular kinds of questions as they read a book aloud with young children, or teachers may model through their talk how to approach a character study in a piece of literature. At the higher levels of school, and in college or at university, we are faced with more complex ways to use texts when asked to write academic papers, and are required to read widely and integrate an extensive range of information into a single coherent text.

Reader as text analyst

As a *text analyst*, a reader reads a text as a crafted object, one that is written by an author who has a particular ideology or set of assumptions. An effective reader reads critically, recognizing in the text what is assumed, not said, implied, or unquestioned. Critical readers recognize that all texts, however authoritative they appear, represent a particular view of the world—that of the writer—and that readers are positioned a certain way when they read it. Clear examples of this reader-positioning technique are media advertisements that deliberately seek to manipulate the reader. There are numerous historical examples as well, from which we learn more about the writer and his or her perspectives on particular events than we do about history itself. Describing the colonizations of Australia or North America as "discovering" or "invading" the country depends on whether you are a colonialist or an indigenous man or woman. Critical reading entails recognizing the many other ways in which texts of all sorts are written based on a particular belief system or ideology, and understanding how these texts may manipulate the reader (see, for example, Wallace 1992, 2003, 2013).

Each of these four roles emphasizes a particular aspect of reading. Because they are all integral to effective reading, a well-balanced literacy program will plan to make provision for the coherent development of all of them. But they should not be seen as representing a developmental "sequence," for each role can be developed at *every* level of reading. Indeed, as we have seen, there are good reasons for not simply focusing on code breaking with early readers, and, as we'll explore later, even very young readers can be shown how to read critically.

IMPLICATIONS FOR EL LEARNERS

Many EL students are effective readers who enjoy reading, and many are able to read in more than one language. The evidence indicates that children who are bilingual use all their linguistic resources when producing and interacting with text (Wallace 2013; Hornberger and Link 2012; Garcia 2009), and that being able to read in one's first language is one of the most important factors in learning to read in subsequent languages (Cummins 2003).

But some children, particularly those whose first experience of learning to read is only in their second language, will need particular kinds of support in learning literacy. We need to remember that many, if not most, children's books in English are written with the assumption that their readers will be familiar with the cultural aspects of the story and will already be fluent in the spoken language.

The earlier discussion has made it clear that the knowledge readers bring to the text is critical to their ability to get meaning from it. But when children are *learning* to read, it is important that they initially develop these new and challenging reading skills in the context of familiar or comprehensible content. Most teachers would accept that a very basic principle of good teaching is to go from what students already know to what they don't yet know, to move from the given (already known) to the new (what is yet to be learned), and this is very much the case with the teaching of early reading.

However, this should not imply that teachers should avoid any books that contain unfamiliar content or cultural understandings. On the contrary, part of learning a language involves learning about the culture in which it is used, and learning new ways to use language in more specialized contexts. If we restrict what children read to the blandness of the basal reader, we do them a disservice by presenting a reductionist and limiting curriculum. So, rather than avoiding books that carry any unfamiliar cultural or field content, or new language (an almost impossible task anyway), the challenge for the teacher is to *build up* the knowledge and understandings that are relevant to the text the children will read. In this way, by the time the reader interacts with the text, the text will not be so unfamiliar. One major implication of this discussion is that what a teacher does *before* a book is read is an extremely important part of the overall plan for using it with the class, and it represents significant scaffolding for reading with comprehension.

> *What a teacher does before a book is read represents significant scaffolding for reading with comprehension.*

The earlier discussion also pointed to the role that familiarity with the language itself has in learning to read. Being unfamiliar with the language makes it almost impossible to predict the kind of information likely to follow. In one classroom, a student was asked to complete this sentence: *Although the light was red, the car. . . .* We would expect the sentence to end something like *the car continued* or *the car kept going.* Instead, the child completed the sentence to read *the car stopped.* He had not understood the word *although* and had responded to the collocation between red lights and cars stopping. If he had encountered *although* in reading, he would have been unable to predict the kind of meaning that followed it—that is, that the car did something *unexpected* in that context. The cues for predicting meaning that come from knowing the language would in this context have been unavailable to him. So, giving children an opportunity to gain some familiarity with the language of the book as well as the content before they come to read it is also important for comprehension.

Planning for reading: Activities for before, during, and after reading

Many reading activities that take place in classrooms are those that occur after a text has been read. They often focus on *assessing* students' comprehension by finding out how much has been understood. The activities below, however, are primarily focused on *teaching* about reading rather than *testing* what has been read.

Classroom reading activities should generally aim to fulfill two major functions:

- They should help readers understand the particular text they are reading.
- They should help readers develop good reading strategies for reading other texts.

In other words, it's important that the instructional activities you use for helping learners to comprehend a particular text *also* model the way effective readers read. For example, simply preteaching all the unknown words before children read a text does not help them to know what to do the next time they come to an unknown word. On the other hand, giving children strategies about what to do when they meet an unknown word not only helps them in that instance but it also makes explicit the strategies that can be transferred to other reading contexts. This reflects the discussion in Chapter 1 about scaffolding, and the notion that scaffolding should not only support students to complete a particular task but also develop students' autonomy so that they can later complete similar tasks alone.

A useful way to think about using a text with your class is to divide the planning into three sections (Wallace 1992):

1. What you will do before the reading
2. What you and the children will do together while the reading is going on
3. What you will do after the book or text has been read.

This overall plan is a useful framework that works whether you intend to read the book aloud yourself or whether you are planning for children to read by themselves or in small groups. The activities that follow are examples of what you might choose to do at each of these times.

First, before making decisions about specific reading activities, make sure you are very familiar with the text yourself! Consider what may be unfamiliar to the EL learners in your class so that you can preempt some of the potential barriers to meaning. As we have seen, these barriers may include both cultural and conceptual knowledge. Look not only at subject or field knowledge, but, in texts such as narratives, consider aspects of everyday life that may not be familiar to recently arrived children. Christmas, a visit to a beach, a visit to the zoo, a barbecue or picnic, an overnight stay with friends, birthday parties, play dates, school graduation, camps and excursions, surfing, watching a football match or baseball game, going to a disco, keeping pets, and many other aspects of life reflected in children's books are not taken for granted by all cultural groups. And there are considerable differences among families within any particular ethnic or cultural group, too. (Not all of these things will be part of your everyday life either, since they contain North American, British, and Australian examples!)

Also note aspects of the language that may cause difficulty for students. These may include unfamiliarity with the genre; unknown connectives and conjunctions; use of pronouns, auxiliary verbs, or tenses; density of the ideas in the text; or unfamiliar vocabulary, phrases, and idioms, including academic and subject-related language.

Before-reading activities

One way of understanding the purpose of these activities is to see them as representing "bridges" between the learner and the text they are going to read. Barriers to reading are those linguistic, cultural, and conceptual difficulties that you have identified in your own close reading of the text. The bridges are the interventions that occur through the scaffolding you provide, enabling students to get over these potential hurdles.

Before-reading activities aim to do the following. They:

- ◆ develop knowledge in relation to the *overall* meaning of the text (not every unknown word)
- ◆ prepare students for potential language, cultural, and conceptual difficulties
- ◆ remind students of what they already know (activate prior knowledge)
- ◆ support students to make predictions about the text.

As schema theory suggests, if students come to the text with a sense of what they will be reading about, reading becomes a much easier task because they have more resources to draw on. They will be less dependent on the words on the page and will be able to minimize the disadvantage of having less than native-like proficiency in the language. Because learners will have some sense of the overall meaning of the text, they are likely to be able to comprehend more linguistically challenging language than they might otherwise be able to comprehend. It has been found, for example, that EL learners who heard a story initially in their mother tongue better understood unfamiliar language structures of the story when it was later read in English. The text can therefore also serve the purpose of extending learners' linguistic abilities by providing models of new but comprehensible language.

Here are some examples of before-reading activities. They all provide a context in which the teacher can guide learners into understanding the major concepts and ideas in the text. All these activities involve some teacher-led discussion with students. These interactions with students are an opportunity for you to model particular vocabulary or language patterns that occur in the text; you can do this informally simply by using them as you build on students' ideas.

Predicting from a Visual

Show a key illustration from the book and give children time in pairs or groups to say what they think the topic is about or what the story will be. For example, based on a text about earthquakes the class would later be reading, one teacher gave the class a picture of the devastation after an earthquake and asked them, in small groups, to guess what had happened. As the children talked about the picture with the teacher, she developed a mind map on the board to collect their ideas. As suggested above, she also built on their suggestions by introducing some new vocabulary in the context of the conversation. Here is part of the conversation.

S   And in an earthquake the earth shake (sic). (*T writes "the earth shakes" on the mind map.*)

T   Right. Does anyone know another word, a special word, for the earth shaking?

S   *Wobble?*

T   Well I guess we could say it was *wobbling*, but there is a special word that we use. When the earth shakes we call it a *tremor*. (*T writes* tremor *on the mind map, above "the earth shakes."*)

The conversation continued in this way until, based on the ideas suggested by the children, much of the more technical vocabulary and other less familiar language had been modeled by the teacher. In other words, key vocabulary and language structures were used in a meaningful context and grew out of what children already knew. This is a very different way of preparing for a text than simply preteaching a list of vocabulary items. Several children quickly related these to words they knew in their first language. In the following activities, the teacher can play a similar role in the discussion.

Predicting the Main Ideas

Choose a short text, no more than six paragraphs. From each paragraph, carefully select four or five key words or some short phrases. These should be chosen on the grounds that they allow students to make some key predictions about the content of each paragraph. In groups, the learners predict the information and ideas they think will be in the text, based on the key words they have been given. After a class discussion about their predictions, they read the text itself. The example discussed here is from a text used with Year 7 students about the increasing usage of mobile phones and other electronic screen devices.

To begin with, paragraphs 1 and 2 were read with the teacher. These paragraphs carried general discussion about the speed of technological innovations and the need for people to take time out away from screens. Some discussion followed with the students about their own screen usage. They also looked at a photograph accompanying the text, which showed seven people in a café, all looking at or talking on their mobile phones. What was striking about the picture was that none of the people were looking at each other, not even those who were sharing a table.

The words chosen by the teacher from each of the remaining paragraphs follow. These were then given to small groups of students, who used them as clues about the information they predicted would be in the original text. Note these are the actual words from the text. (See how much you can predict yourself about the likely information in each paragraph!)

Para 3: *However . . . impact of innovation, masters or servants*?

Para 4: *joy of connecting, effect of ability to think deeply*

Para 5: *children and young teenagers, recent survey*

Para 6: *real world friends*

After students developed their ideas they were shared with the class as a whole, with interaction from the teacher who asked key questions (*What do you think the survey showed?*) and/or built on students' ideas to model some of the actual language of the text. In the transcript that follows the bold type indicates the text language from paragraph 5.

T   What do you think the survey showed?

S1   Maybe it means, like a lot

T   Right, it's probably going to tell us about how much time some children spend on the Internet—maybe television as well. How much time do you think they spent? Think about TV watching as well.

S1 I reckon many hours . . . many hours every week.

S2 And me, I spend heaps on my mobile, like even I'm in bed at night . . . at night

(General murmurs of agreement from students)

T And do you spend the same time watching TV too?

S2 Yeah TV too

T Do you think they spend the same amount of time on the Internet as they do watching television . . . who thinks that's likely?

S3 I see TV a lot . . . like last night I watch (name of show) and go to bed late . . . too late . . my mum she get mad say you sleep now *(Laughing)*

T So maybe the survey shows . . . maybe they spend the same time on both, maybe the survey tells us they **spend an equal amount of time surfing the Internet and watching TV**. How many hours every day do you spend surfing the net and watching TV, both together?

S3 Me I take more time on computer . . . not much TV . . is boring.

Once all the paragraphs have been discussed in this way, students are likely to read the original text with more engagement and interest (to find out whether their own predictions were right!), and with little difficulty in accessing overall meaning. One student commented, "I feel like I read this before." This activity can be used with a number of different genres, and with lower-level learners as well.

Predicting from the Title, First Sentence, or Key Words

Using any of these, get children to predict what kind of text they expect—for example, an information text or narrative—and what information they might find. Build on their suggestions and, as before and when appropriate, recast (reformulate) what students say using some of the vocabulary and language from the text.

Sequencing Illustrations or Diagrams

Give groups of children a set of pictures relating to the story, or a process, and ask the students to put them into a possible sequence. Ensure children use a left-to-right orientation as they put down their pictures.

Reader Questions

Give children the title of the book or a key illustration and encourage them to pose questions they would like answered. Before they read a recount about an earthquake, children wrote questions such as *When did it happen? Where did it occur? How many people were killed? How big was it?* The teacher posted these questions on the wall, and the children looked for answers as they read the text later.

Storytelling in the Mother Tongue

If you are able, tell the story in the children's first language (or invite a parent or other caregiver to do so) *before* reading it in English. If you have children who speak only English in the class, the experience will be valuable for them, too. It will demonstrate your respect and acceptance of other languages, position the second language learners in the class as proficient language users, and show children that all languages are a means of communication. Alternatively, tell the story as you show the illustrations, before reading it.

The more time you spend on before-reading activities, the easier the reading will be for the learners, and the more likely it will be that they read for meaning. Don't be tempted to reduce before-reading work to the explanation of a few key words. Of course, if the text you are using is part of a larger unit of work, much of this knowledge building will already be occurring in an ongoing way. One of the great advantages of an integrated approach is that reading occurs in a context where students are already developing an overall schema for the topic. In addition, comprehension is much more likely to be improved when vocabulary and language are associated with broad concepts and recur in an ongoing context, and involving student talk, than when instruction is in terms of single words or language items.

During-reading activities

Once students have some idea of the genre and content of what they will be reading, it is time for the reading itself.

During-reading activities aim to do the following. They:

- model good reading strategies and make explicit what mature readers do unconsciously
- engage readers actively with the text
- help learners understand how to read more effectively themselves.

The following activities are not intended to represent any particular teaching sequence, since not all would be used at all levels or with all kinds of text.

Modeled Reading

The first time a text is read, it's helpful to lower-level or younger learners for the teacher to read the text aloud using appropriate pausing and expression. This provides a reading model for the students. Try to bring the text to life; students need to see that print has meaning and is not simply a functionally empty exercise. With lower-level learners, remember that the more something is read or heard, the more comprehension there will be. So don't read a text just once! A favorite book used in shared book time can be read again and again. As you read, encourage the children to see whether their predictions were correct, but make clear that it doesn't matter if they weren't. Often our predictions

During-reading activities should model good reading strategies.

about things are wrong, but it is still important to have ideas and questions about the topic.

Pause and Predict (with narrative texts)

As you are reading, stop at significant points and ask questions such as *What do you think is going to happen? What's she going to do? If you were (character's name), what would you do?* The goal here is to engage learners in the process of meaning making, not to have them verbalize the "right" answers.

Shadow Reading

Read the text aloud while children listen and follow the text from their own copy. Ask children to read aloud along with you. Shadowing is a valuable activity because it demonstrates how meaning is made through text, and how intonation, stress, and the patterns of spoken language are related to the punctuation and to the words on the page.

Noticing Visual Layout and Text Features

Draw children's attention to the title as well as to visual features in the text, such as photographs, illustrations, graphs, charts, maps, and diagrams. Discuss with children what the functions of these visuals are. Also draw attention to text features such as headings, subheadings, captions, and the use of different fonts. These features should be seen as guides to the reader that help them organize the meaning of the text. They also play a prominent part in many electronic texts and are increasingly becoming a more significant part of literacy development.

Paying attention to subheadings is a good way to help children learn to chunk information because subheadings in a well-written text tell the reader what the following section will be about. With texts that don't make use of subheadings, have children try to think of a title for some key paragraphs as they read the text.

Skimming and Scanning the Text

These are important reading strategies with which students need to become familiar. When readers skim a text, they read it quickly to get an idea of the general content. When they scan they also read fast, but the purpose is to look for particular information. Searching down a telephone list, a train timetable, or a TV guide with the aim of finding a particular item are everyday examples of this. Make explicit the contexts in which we skim and scan, and point out that we read in different ways depending on our purposes for reading. Often skimming and scanning are associated with information texts. Some learners may have been taught to read in only one way—focusing on each word and every detail on the first reading. These students in particular will need practice in learning to skim and scan.

Explain that the purpose of skimming and scanning is to get a general idea of what the text is about and the main ideas, or to look for specific information. Students can also scan the text to check any predictions they made during the before-reading activities. Again, it doesn't matter whether these predictions were wrong; the actual process of having made predictions will encourage them to read the text more interactively. In fact, when students go into a text with a misconception, they are more likely to take note of the information presented there, because information that runs counter to one's expectations is usually more memorable than information that simply confirms what one already thinks. While the students are skimming the text on this first reading, they can also see whether they can find the answers to any questions they asked.

Rereading for Detail

After students have skimmed the text, they will probably need to read it again more carefully and thoughtfully. The purpose of this is to make sure they have understood the information. Get them to underline or make a note of words or phrases they don't understand. They can discuss these in pairs. Remind them of strategies they can use to work out the meaning of unknown words, such as the following:

> ➤ Read to the end of the sentence to see whether this helps in understanding the word.
> ➤ Look at the text that comes before and after the word; the word may be easier to understand later, with other clues to meaning.
> ➤ If there other sources of information, such as visuals and subheadings, use these to help work out the meaning.
> ➤ Think about the function of the word: is it a noun, verb, adjective?
> ➤ Look for the same word somewhere else; its meaning might be clearer there.
> ➤ Look for familiar word parts, such as prefixes and suffixes.
> ➤ Use an English–English or bilingual dictionary. Note that students should turn to a dictionary as a last resort and use it in combination with the other strategies. While dictionaries are a useful resource and students should be encouraged to use them when necessary, relying too heavily on a dictionary slows reading and works against the development of the strategies listed above. It should also be remembered that definitions often don't adequately explain a meaning in the particular context in which it is being used, and that students may often select a wrong or inappropriate meaning. This is also likely to be the case with translator software.

You can place a list of these strategies on a chart and add to them as appropriate. Remind students about these strategies whenever they read a new text. After they have finished reading, encourage discussion about how they dealt with the unknown words they came across.

Thinking Tracks: Making Thinking Explicit

As we have seen in the earlier discussion about the processes of reading, reading is a thinking and active process, not a passive one, and research suggests that allowing students many opportunities for responding to reading, as they read, supports reading proficiency (Allington 2009). (This is similar to what Luke and Freebody 1990 refer to as the role of text participant, discussed earlier in this chapter.)

Harvey, Goudvis, and Wallis (2010) also argue for the importance of teachers explicitly encouraging children's thinking during reading, and sharing this with others. The teacher can model this while reading aloud with children, using language like *This makes me think of . . . I wonder . . . This reminds me of/when. . . .* Children can then share their own thinking with a partner. As students become more skilled, these reading responses can become a regular activity while they are reading. Once children are familiar with talking about their thinking, Harvey et al. recommend the use of sticky notes on which children can "leave tracks" of their thinking through writing their responses to the text or perhaps asking questions. Proficient readers also frequently visualize what they are reading and in this way connect themselves to the text, so for these readers sticky note responses to text could be drawn rather than written.

Shared Book

With most learners, shared book (sometimes called *shared reading*) can be a highly effective reading activity. It involves using a big book (an enlarged text) or a text on an interactive whiteboard so that children have a shared focus of attention. With younger children, after you have introduced the book through a range of before-reading activities, read it aloud several times, encouraging children to join in as they remember or recognize words or phrases. In later readings, using a pointer to point to words as you read helps children link the sounds of words with their shape on the page, and it demonstrates left-to-right directionality and word spacing.

Shared book is also useful for more advanced readers, too, and provides a context to model how an experienced reader takes on the four reader roles. Developing good reading strategies also needs to continue in the later years, and often useful questions for learners can center around how they read the text, rather than what they are reading about. Questions like the following help to develop students' metacognitive awareness of the reading process:

> ➤ Why is the title important?
> ➤ If you imagine this (*referring to text*), what do you see?
> ➤ If you didn't know this word, how could you work it out?
> ➤ What do you think this word, *However*, is telling us about the ideas that follow? Is there another connecting word we could use that means the same thing?
> ➤ Why are words like *however* important?

For other suggestions for developing students' awareness of reading strategies and their own understandings about reading, see the section on margin questions in Chapter 5 of Gibbons 2009.

Word Masking

Once a big book or enlarged text has been read several times, mask some of the words with sticky notes. Ask children to predict what the word is. Allow time to discuss alternative choices. For example, if the word is *replied* and someone guesses *said*, respond positively to this and use it as a basis for discussion. Among the words you mask, include not only "content" words, but also "functional" words, such as pronouns and conjunctions. As we mentioned earlier, these functional or grammatical words are important in enabling readers to use syntactic cues.

In later rereadings you can use this activity to develop vocabulary knowledge by focusing on alternatives for some of the words. Ask questions like *What's another word we could use here? What other words instead of* said *could the writer use?* This is a good way to develop vocabulary knowledge in context and to build up word lists that can be displayed for children to use as a resource for their own writing.

Summarizing the Text

Harvey et al. (2010) argue for the importance of summarizing. If students are unable to summarize what they have read, chances are strong that they have not understood the text fully and that they are still unfamiliar with the content. Note that it isn't necessarily appropriate to summarize all kinds of texts. However, if this is something you want to focus on, here are some ways to help students practice summarizing skills.

> ➤ Suggest to children that they read the first sentence of each paragraph. This will often give them a clue about what information they will find in the paragraph.
> ➤ Suggest the use of sticky notes to identify key information, paragraph by paragraph.
> ➤ Get students to write a summary. Limit the maximum number of sentences or words they can use, pointing out that this means they must focus only on the most important points.
> ➤ Ask students to suggest a title for each paragraph.
> ➤ Either alone or with teacher support, have students write two or three sentences under each paragraph title and use these to write a short summary of the whole passage.
> ➤ If you are using a narrative, get students to retell it in shorter and shorter ways until it is as brief as possible. Write this up on the board and then discuss with students the kind of information that is now missing.
> ➤ Have students explain the key points to someone else in less than one minute.
> ➤ Get groups of students to decide on one sentence from the text that best sums it up or is most central to the text. There will probably be some disagreement about this, but the discussion should help students sort out key points and help you see how they are interpreting the text.

Jigsaw Reading

Another way to approach reading is to use a jigsaw technique. Prepare three or four different readings around the same topic. If you have varying reading levels in the class, include a simpler reading and a more challenging reading. Each group will become an "expert' on one of the readings, so children should be grouped according to the difficulty of the reading. Then they regroup so that new groups are formed where members have each read a different reading. They must share their information in a mixed group. This kind of activity gives reading a real purpose, since the aim is to share what one has read with others. It is also a useful way of having readers at different levels work collaboratively (even the poorer readers will be able to contribute in the group since their reading will have information that other members in the group don't have). Finally, it provides an authentic context for developing summarizing skills, since each group of experts must decide on the key points they are later going to share with others. Depending on the level of the students, it may be useful to focus on note-making skills and to provide an information grid to guide students in noting key information in their own reading, prior to regrouping in the mixed groups.

After-reading activities

These activities are based on the assumption that students are already familiar with the text and no longer have basic comprehension difficulties in reading it. The activities use the text as a springboard for new learning and may fulfill any of these three major purposes:

1. To use the now-familiar text as a basis for specific language study, such as to focus on a particular item of grammar, vocabulary, idiom, or phonemic or phonic knowledge that occurs in the text.
2. To allow students an opportunity to respond creatively to what they have read, such as through art or drama activities.
3. To focus students more deeply on the information in the text, such as by using information transfer activities that represent the information in a different form (e.g., a time line or a diagram).

Well-designed after-reading activities should require students to keep returning to the text and rereading it to check on specific information or language use.

Story Innovation

Story innovation can be a teacher-led or small-group activity. Using a familiar story as a basis, key words are changed to make a new story, while retaining the underlying structure. For example, students could change the characters in the folktale *The Elephant and the Mouse* to a whale and a little fish. While the central meaning of the tale should remain the same (the weak helps the strong and they become friends), key words and events are changed to fit in with the new characters. As the changes are made, the story is written up on a large sheet of paper or an interactive whiteboard. Children could also write a new ending.

Readers Theatre

In its simplest form, you provide a group of children with copies of a short story. Each child reads the dialogue of one of the characters, while other children share the narration. This can be practiced until it is word perfect and then performed to the class. Readers theatre is a much better context for children reading aloud than the traditional "reading around the class," since it allows them a chance to *practice* the reading (which is what adults would do if they knew they were going to read in front of others), and it provides a meaningful purpose for the reading.

> *After-reading activities require students to keep returning to the text and rereading it.*

Depending on their reading and language levels, some children can write scripts based on the story. Puppets can also be used in readers theatre. They are often successful with children who may lack confidence to talk in class but will take on a role when it is mediated through the puppet.

Story Map

A story map is a visual representation of the main features of a story. It can be drawn after a story is read, or it can involve an ongoing process of adding details as the story is progressing.

Time Lines

Texts that incorporate the passage of time lend themselves to a time line. These include narratives and some information texts (e.g., those that relate to events in history, or to the description of life cycles or processes). Children can also illustrate key events on the time line.

Hot Seat

This activity is usually based on a narrative text. Children are seated in a circle, with one chair being designated the "hot seat." The student in the hot seat represents a character from a book that has been shared by the class. Other students ask him or her questions to find out more about the character's life. Questions might include the following: *Where do you live? Can you tell us about some of your friends? What do you most enjoy doing? How did you feel when . . . ? What do you think of (another character in the book)?* Children take turns being in the hot seat. While they are free—and should be encouraged—to invent information, they mustn't say anything that is inconsistent with the story or with what has been learned from the other hot-seaters.

You can also play around with the time frame of the story by moving into the past or the future. Get children to stand and slowly walk counterclockwise in a circle, and as they are walking tell them they are time travelers going backward in time. Give the children a specific point in time, such as "Now it's seventy years ago and the old woman in the story is just a little girl." Continue the hot-seat activity as before, constructing an earlier life for one of the characters. Later, children can move clockwise around the circle, forward in time, until young characters in the story are now old people, or perhaps they have now died and are being remembered by others.

In this way the original story takes on a further life, and children will have a wealth of ideas for their own story writing. Rereading the original story, now that so much is "known" about the entire lives of some of the characters, also becomes a very thought-provoking and enriching reading experience.

A hot-seat activity could also be used in a history context, with children researching a particular era and then taking on the role of someone from that time.

Freeze Frames

Freeze frames are a kind of drama activity that shows a series of tableaux representing key stages in a story. Each tableau is a "still," with the students taking the role of specific characters. Simple props can be used. The audience members close their eyes while the group prepares the first tableau, and at a signal from the group they open their eyes and look at it for about ten seconds. Then they close their eyes again while the group prepares the second tableau, and so on until the story is told. The audience thus views the actions as a series of frozen frames. Groups will need some time to prepare this. They first need to decide what the key stages are (see the previous chapter for the overall structure of a narrative), then decide how they will represent them, and finally practice moving from one to the other as quickly as possible (otherwise the audience will not keep their eyes closed!). Since freeze frames do not require students to say anything at the presentation stage, even children with little English can participate in the freeze frame. At the same time, the preparation of the frames requires students to discuss important elements of the story and make decisions about how to portray the characters and events.

Cloze

Cloze activities, the device of deleting words from a text, focus on aspects of language, and they are also useful for bringing to learners' consciousness the strategies a fluent reader uses subconsciously. Traditional cloze activities can be based on either the text that has been read or on a similar text. When you make the deletions, you should keep at least the first and last sentences intact so that students have a context in which to read the text. Encourage students to first read the cloze straight through before they attempt to fill in the gaps. To provide extra support for lower-level readers, you can give learners a list of the words that have been left out.

Originally, cloze exercises were aimed at testing rather than teaching. However, in recent years their potential for developing learners' reading strategies has been recognized. A well-constructed cloze can give you information about what kinds of strategies children are using to predict meaning, and it can help children think about their own reading strategies. Traditional cloze involves deleting every sixth or seventh word, and it encourages readers to reference backward and forward in the text to work out what the missing words are likely to be. It therefore mirrors the kind of reading strategies used by proficient readers. However, cloze activities can also be used more selectively, with only certain kinds of words deleted. For example, you can choose to delete key content vocabulary that is integral to the topic, or grammatical items such as adjectives, connectives, pronouns, past tenses, and so forth. Cloze activities are often more successful when students work in pairs, since there will be discussion about why certain choices are made.

The aim in a cloze activity used for these purposes is not simply for children to get the "right" answer but to become aware of what they do when they read. After finishing a cloze, always allow time for discussion, when children can *justify* the words they have chosen and *explain* to others their rationale for their choice. To make this discussion easier, use a large version of the cloze so all children can see it together as they share their ideas for the missing words with the class. Remember that there is often a range of possible and appropriate words to fill "content" gaps, so you can accept any word that fits grammatically and has an appropriate meaning. This can be a time for vocabulary development. However, there is a much smaller range of options for grammatical items and often only one correct answer.

Monster Cloze

This is a whole-class activity, with the teacher as scribe. The "text" consists of only a title and gaps, so students need to fill in *all* the words. The original should be based either on the text the students have read or on a summary of it. Write the title of the passage on the board in full and discuss with the student what the passage might be about, including any predictions they can make about possible words. Students then guess the missing words (in any order), and the teacher writes in any correct words in the appropriate gap. (As a clue, you can point out that the words of the title are probably going to appear in the text!) After the sentences are partially completed, students should be able to predict more and more of the words of the passage by using their knowledge of the topic and of the syntax of the sentence.

You could also use this activity as a revision activity, based on a summary of learning from content areas, or at the end of a unit of work.

Vanishing Cloze

This is a further variation on cloze. Select a short excerpt from the text that the students have read (three or four sentences only, or a shorter section for beginners) or a summary of it. Write the excerpt on the board, and ask students to read it aloud together. Erase one word from anywhere in the text. Students read it again, putting back the missing word. Erase another word and repeat the process. Continue until all the words are removed, so that students are now "reading" from memory. It's important that after each word is removed, students repeat the reading; this requires them to replace more and more words each time. These repeated readings are especially helpful if the text contains a tricky grammatical structure or subject-specific vocabulary that the students are currently learning, since it provides a context for repetition that is both fun and challenging.

Text Reconstruction

Cut an excerpt from the text into paragraphs or sentences. Students must put the sentences or paragraphs in the right order and explain why they have chosen that order. This is a good context for focusing on text cohesion and drawing attention to reference words and conjunctions. To make this activity more challenging you could mix up two cut-up texts.

True/False Questions

Children decide on whether a number of statements about the text are true or false. Make sure that these involve inferential as well as literal comprehension. Literal statements can be checked directly against the information in the text, whereas the truth of inferential statements needs to be inferred from the text. Here are examples of both types.

> Sentence in the text: *The earthquake struck at three o'clock in the afternoon.*
>
> Literal statement: *The earthquake struck at three o'clock.* True or False?
>
> Inferential statement: *The earthquake struck during the daytime.* True or False?

In general, inferential statements (and questions) give you a better idea of how much readers have understood, since literal questions can often be answered correctly without comprehension of meaning.

"Key-ring" Words

Key-ring words are a strategy to help learners remember the meaning of more complex words, often words that name concepts, such as *nutrition*, *pollution*, *transpiration*, *negotiation*, *collaboration*, *friendship*, *metaphor*. These words can be taken from the text the students have read and/or words they have been introduced to in the course of a study of a topic.

> ➤ Cut cards into (approximately) five-by-three-inch strips.
> ➤ Have students write the word you have chosen at the top of the card along the longer side.
> ➤ They draw a r*epresentation* of the word that will help them remember and understand it. This drawing will be their personal mnemonic—they don't need artistic skills! For example, while demonstrating this with physical education and sports teachers, who were also responsible for teaching health and personal development, they suggested the word *agility*. My colleague drew what we thought the word meant and represented it with a stick drawing of someone jumping. The teachers told us this was not an adequate representation of the meaning of the word in the way it is used in their subject! To sports specialists it also includes the notion of time and direction. So we added a clock and a right-angled arrow beside the stick figure. (I will never forget what *agility* means!) Taking a word "off the page" and representing it visually, rather than through language, appears to cause it to be processed differently, and this process seems to help students remember the meaning. The drawing will also give you a good indication of how well the learners have understood the concept. Although this is primarily an individual

activity, it is a good idea, and an interesting process, to
have children share and explain their representations,
and to have others comment on it. You will be surprised at
how many different representations of a key concept word
are possible!

➤ On the back of the card, and if children are literate in their
first language, they can either explain or translate the word.

➤ Finally, punch a hole on the short side of the card and add it
to a key ring for each learner. These words build up to create
individual dictionaries. Cards could also be color-coded for
each subject or topic.

Questioning the Text

As we discussed earlier, being able to read critically is an important
part of being truly literate. To alert children to the hidden messages
of text, as well as the underlying assumptions about reality made by
the writer, teachers need to ask different kinds of questions and use
different kinds of activities from those normally associated with text
comprehension. Here are some examples.

➤ Focus on the pictures and on what the characters are doing.
For a book where family life is depicted, you might ask things
like *What is/are the mother/father/children doing? Do all
mothers/fathers/children do these things? Does everyone's
kitchen/family room look like this? What does your house
have that isn't in these pictures?* Seek to show children that
books do not necessarily depict the "whole truth," and that
other kinds of reality and role options also exist. Try to be
inclusive of all children's experiences.

➤ Discuss with children what the characters are like. Ask: *What
words are used to describe the names of characters? What
words can you find in the text that tell you about them?* This
will also require children to go back to the text to reread parts
of it with a more critical perspective.

➤ Make lists with the children of words or ideas that are associated with key people in the text. This is an interesting activity to use with information texts, too. In one upper elementary classroom, the children were comparing how a particular sports writer wrote about top male and female athletes, and what kinds of information and descriptive words were included (or omitted). They found that considerably more was written about the physical appearance of the women, including words relating to their attractiveness, than was written about the men. Conversely, much more relevant information (about their athletic prowess and previous career) was included for the men, but much less space was devoted to information about their family life. Yet until the children set out to look for these associations, or collocations, and list the kinds of information the text included, they had not noticed these differences. When helping children develop critical perspectives on what they read, remember that it is also important to look at what is *not* said.

➤ Have children rewrite a folktale, changing the key physical or personality characteristics of the characters.

➤ Talk with the children about stereotyping. In one classroom, the children were reading a story set in Fiji, which contained very stereotypical views of life on a tropical island. As one of the children in the class had recently arrived from Fiji, the teacher assigned him the role of informant, whom other children could question about everyday life in Fiji. Later, on the basis of what they had learned from their classmate, they decided that the book did not represent Fiji appropriately, and so a group of children rewrote it. They had learned a useful lesson: what you read is not necessarily "true."

Sometimes taking a critical perspective may lead into discussions that are highly connected to children's lives. Be prepared for this, and treat the personal stories that may result with empathy and sensitivity. Positive strategies and ways of action should result from critical discussions, such as the rewriting of the book about Fiji. Other actions could include making new and more inclusive illustrations for a text or, as Chapter 8 illustrates, writing a letter.

DEVELOPING PHONEMIC AWARENESS: HOW LISTENING AND READING INTERACT

In this section the focus is on the reader as "code breaker." An important foundation for decoding words and developing alphabetic knowledge is the ability to differentiate between the distinctive sounds of the language. On this basis children can develop knowledge of the phonic system and learn how the sounds are represented in print.

What is a phoneme?

The phonemes of any individual language are those sounds that make a difference in *meaning* between words. For example, in English, these words are distinguished from each other by a single sound (indicated in bold type). Try saying them aloud, and note that there are three distinct sounds in each word: b**a**n, b**e**n, b**i**n, b**u**n, b**ee**n. They differ in meaning only because of one sound.

In English the sounds of a word are not systematically related to its spelling, which is why there appear to be so many spelling "exceptions." The same sound, or phoneme, can often be written using a range of spelling patterns: *me, key, piece, peace, bee, Leigh*. Or the same spelling pattern may represent different sounds, as in *through, cough, though, tough, fought*. But when words are written in phonemic script, one symbol always represents one sound, regardless of how the word is spelled. So the two letters *kn* (as in *knot*) represent the single phoneme /n/.

In English there are around forty-four such distinctive sounds (a few more or less depending on the variety English you speak—British English, American English, Australian English, Indian English, etc.). These are made up of (again, with minor variations depending on the variety of English) twenty-two consonants, twenty vowels (including diphthongs), and two "semivowels." The two semivowels are the sounds we hear at the beginning of **y**ellow and **w**indow. As earlier examples illustrated, each of these forty-four sounds is able to make a difference in meaning to a word. Other languages may have far fewer, or many more, phonemes than English. One group of languages spoken in Namibia, Botswana, and Angola has around 141 phonemes! The numbers of vowels and the numbers of consonants also varies considerably between languages.

The phonemes of different languages are rarely exactly the same, although many phonemes in the student's first language may be close. This means that for EL learners, their own languages will not match all the sounds in English, and vice versa. Most language learners, especially in the early stages of learning the language, make use of the closest sound in their own language when the English phoneme is unfamiliar (and they probably "hear" it as the sound in their own language, too). For example, they may use the phoneme /s/ or /f/ for the *th* sound at the beginning of words like *think* and *thing*. Or they may not be able to either "hear" or produce the distinction between some of the vowel sounds of the five words in the first example. This is usually what is happening when we talk of someone having a "foreign accent."

In short, phonemic awareness is first and foremost about *listening to* and being able to *distinguish* the distinctive sounds of a language. It is the ability to understand and manipulate the sounds of a language *orally*. Activities such as rhyming, matching initial consonants, and recognizing the number of phonemes in a word all develop young children's phonemic awareness. Not surprisingly, phonemic awareness (being able to differentiate between distinctive sounds) is a strong predictor of later word-decoding abilities (being able to understand the relationship between the sounds of a word and the symbols used to represent sounds in writing) (Janssen, Bosman, and Leseman 2013; Adams 1990; Stanovitch 1986). Phonemic awareness is therefore an essential foundation for developing phonic knowledge—that is, learning to connect the sounds of English to letters when reading or writing.

Implications for classroom activities

Developing children's phonemic knowledge and alphabet knowledge on the basis of a familiar piece of language (such as a familiar story) follows four closely related principles about language teaching and learning. As this book has argued, sentence-based language items (such as sentence structure and grammar, vocabulary, and the sounds within a word) are generally more easily understood, and hence internalized, when they are taken from something that is whole, meaningful, known, and concrete rather than taught in isolation. In other words, as language teachers, our teaching progresses, as a general rule, in the following ways:

- *From whole to part.* This allows children to see where the language item has come from, where it fits, and its significance in the text as a whole.
- *From meaning to form.* Language forms, such as the phonemes of English, are a lot easier to make sense of if introduced in the context of a meaningful text.
- *From known to unknown.* New learning (in all teaching) proceeds more efficiently on the basis of what is already known.
- *From concrete to abstract.* Starting with a known, familiar story and then working toward more abstract ideas (such as phonemic awareness and alphabet knowledge) is a way of building on a concrete example to develop abstract knowledge about language.

As these principles suggest, one of the best ways to focus on developing phonemic awareness is to use known words that have come from a familiar text. Activities for developing phonemic awareness and alphabetic knowledge can be used as after-reading activities.

Examples of activities for developing phonemic awareness

Thumbs Up Thumbs Down

Using poetry, chants, songs, and rhymes that children are familiar with, select pairs of words, some that rhyme and others that do not. When children hear a rhyme they put their thumbs up, when they hear a non-rhyme, they put their thumbs down.

The same thumbs-up thumbs-down technique can also be used in other sound isolation activities. Students can listen for the same sounds across words—for example, all the words in a song or a poem that begin with a certain sound, or for the final or medial sound in pairs of words (adapted from Chen and Mora-Flores 2006).

What Word Is This?

Give children oral practice in blending sounds by saying (known) words slowly, breaking the words down into their phonemes and asking the children for the word.

> ➤ With beginner learners, start with chunking the words into syllables, pausing briefly after each syllable: el-e-phant
> ➤ Later, break words into the onset (first sound) and rime (remainder of the word): e-lephant, ch-ildren.
> ➤ Once children can do this easily, isolate all the sounds, beginning with a word with few sounds: c-a-t, before moving on to more complex words: e-l-e-ph-a-n-t.

What Sounds Can You Hear?

This is a more difficult activity and requires a reversal of roles from the previous activity. Give the children a word and ask children to tell you the first sound, the last sound, and then all of the sounds in the word.

BUILDING ON PHONEMIC AWARENESS: DEVELOPING PHONIC KNOWLEDGE

Phonic knowledge builds on phonemic awareness, because unless children can first recognize the sounds in a word they cannot be expected to write it. Phonic knowledge refers to the ability to match phonemes to their corresponding letters and combinations of letters. Initially phonics work needs to make use of words that are already familiar to students and that have been met in context. Children in the early stages of learning to read should never be expected to simply sound out words they have never met and can't say: we have seen that decoding does not in itself lead to reading with understanding. As Chen and Mora-Flores (2006) point out: "it's most important to understand that the knowledge of phonics is a tool . . . that children can call upon to attack challenging and unfamiliar words" (162).

Children in the early stages of learning to read should never be expected to sound out words they have never met.

Children also use both phonemic awareness and their knowledge of phonics when they are learning to write—in other words, when they begin to encode words they want to write themselves. This is a productive time for focusing on these skills because it is at this time that young readers and writers need to explore more systematically how the sounds of the language are related to spelling. Writing is therefore an important and relevant context for developing skills that are needed in reading, just as learning to read supports the development of early writing.

Working out how to write a word is a reasoning process that is based on the learner's ability to develop generalizations. Once a child has discovered that written words are constant and can be named, then, as discussed earlier, the sounds of the words can be related to the letters that represent the words. When children do not know the spelling of a word, scaffold *how* to work out a possible spelling:

- Encourage children to "have a go" at writing it using their existing knowledge about how sounds are written. (Often it is clear that children are developing considerable knowledge of this, even if they don't yet spell correctly—for example, CHN, CHRAN, ELFNT for *children, train,* and *elephant.*)
- Say the word slowly to them, phoneme by phoneme, or encourage them to articulate the word slowly themselves, and as they say the word to think about each of the *sounds* they can hear, focusing first on the initial sound and then on the final sound. (First and final sounds are usually more salient for young learners than medial sounds.)
- Ask them to think about what letter or letters could be used to write the sound, and draw analogies with other known words to help them recognize a common pattern.

Providing spelling lists of *thematically* related words to be learned by rote (perhaps related to a topic being studied) may assist in the learning of new vocabulary, but it is not likely to be helpful in teaching *about* spelling, since thematically related words are unlikely to have a spelling pattern in common.

Examples of activities to develop phonic knowledge

Alphabet Book

Children create their own alphabet book. As they become familiar with each letter they write it at the top of the page and, as they find them, they cut out magazine pictures or draw a picture that begins with that letter. Encourage the children to take the book home and share it with family, and to take pride in it.

Alternatively, they can create a similar book, but choose pictures depending on the first sound of the word (e.g., sh).

Progressive Words

This is based on the idea of a progressive brainstorm (see Chapter 3 for an explanation of a progressive brainstorm). Each group has a sheet of paper with one particular sound/spelling pattern that represents the same sound, with an example of a word that contains that pattern. For example, one group could have *ee*, as in *seat*; another *ea* as in *clean*. Other groups could have *ie*: *piece*, or *ey*: *key*. Each group also has a different-colored marker. Each group adds words that have the same sound and spelling pattern as the example. After five minutes the groups move clockwise to the next table, leaving their paper on the desk but taking their own colored marker. Each group then adds more words to those already there on the next sheet of paper. Allow five minutes for each group to write as many words as they can, before they move on. Remember to tell each group to keep the color marker they are using. At the end, review with the children what they have done, either by putting the papers up on a wall or reviewing them one by one. Encourage children to check that all the words are spelled with the right pattern and contain the same sound. Later they can be put up on a wall and children can continue adding to them as they find or think of other words.

Memory Reading Game

Using known words, create two sets of cards, one set with a picture on one side and the other set with words on one side. Turn the cards over. Each child has a turn at turning over two cards with the aim of finding a matching picture and word. If they are successful they keep the pair of cards; if unsuccessful they turn the cards back over and replace them in the same spot. The turn then passes to the next child. Children can work in a small group or in pairs. The winner is the player with the most pairs when all the cards have been taken.

An alternative to this is to choose high-frequency words that often can't be easily illustrated, for example, *the*, *he*, *she*, *and*, *this*, *but*. In this case both sets of cards will contain just the word. Frequent exposure to these sorts of "functional" words can speed up reading and help with comprehension and spelling.

CHOOSING BOOKS: A REASON FOR TURNING THE PAGE

There is considerable evidence to suggest that while overall language development supports reading, so too does reading support language development (Allington 2009; Wallace 1988, 1992). Language is learned through reading; it is not simply a prerequisite for it. Given appropriate texts, learners develop their language skills in the course of reading itself, because the patterns of language are "open to notice" in written language in a way that they are not in spoken language. So the more fluently and widely EL students read, the more they will gain exposure to the second language. At the same time, to become proficient readers students need to spend large amounts of time in reading. One implication of this is that students whose reading is less well developed or who need special support should spend more time actually reading. Unfortunately, class reading time may be the time when they are taken out of class for extra help, which may require them to spend extra time on isolated drill and practice activities instead of authentic reading (Harvey, Goudvis, and Wallis 2010). In similar vein, Chen and Mora-Flores (2006) caution teachers that as children are learning to decode, class time should still continue to be given to actual reading. Cummins (2003) also suggests that sometimes "phonics instruction drags out over too many years" and can be further developed through repeated and regular opportunities for reading (9).

Research also suggests that second language learners are able to determine the meanings of quite large numbers of unfamiliar English structures *if* they are presented in the context of meaningful sentences (see, for example, Elley 1984; Wallace 1988). This implies that particular language structures don't have to be in the active repertoire of learners (i.e., able to be used) to be understood in reading. As long as learners have a sense of the overall meaning of what they read, wide reading is an effective way of learning *new* language items, not simply of reinforcing or practicing old ones.

One clear implication of these views of the role of reading in language development is that the books children read must provide a rich linguistic environment. In the past, many books used in school were written simply to "teach reading." The major rationale for the choice of words was to present a particular sound or word as frequently as possible, not to present authentic language. This led to language such as: *See John. See Susan. Here is Rex. Run Rex run. Run Susan run. Run John run.* (Some older readers may remember books like this!)

We should ask ourselves what children are learning about reading if this represents their major reading diet, and whether this route to reading is the most productive for second language learners. Books like this are in important ways much more difficult to read than a complete story, especially for young readers, because it is impossible to predict what will come next. Thus learners are forced into total reliance on decoding words or whole-word recognition. Because they are led to concentrate on the visual and phonic characteristics of words, they are led away from an understanding of text as coherent language. As Wallace (1988) comments, "Books that set out to teach reading are frequently not so much books as strings of sentences that do not connect to build up any kind of text with a beginning, a middle and an end" (150). The pages quoted previously can in fact be read backward, putting the last sentence first, without any loss or much change of meaning! Learners are thus encouraged to think that reading is a random activity that can apparently start or stop at any point in the text, and that we read words or sentences but not continuous text. Such books also seem to assume, quite wrongly, that short words are "easier" to read. Yet we have all had the experience of very young children recognizing salient words in their environment, such as the McDonald's sign or their own name, or a word like *dinosaur* that represents an engaging topic. Texts like the one shown here are also functionally empty; there is little meaning to be had and no access to the rich models of language that are so important for EL learners. And, finally, as many children, their teachers, and their families know, books like this are mind-numbingly boring.

We don't, of course, want learners to learn lessons like this. Rather, as Wallace (1988) succinctly puts it, "We want to give learner-readers a reason for turning the page" (151). Good readers read for pleasure, to extend their worldview, to read more about what interests them, or to find out things they want to know or care about. And these are the sorts of purposes for reading we want children to have. Our learners should not be restricted to the familiar, the known, and the easy, or fed a watered-down version of written language. Rather, as the activities in this chapter aim to do, the challenge for teachers is to find ways of giving learners *access to* well-written children's literature and relevant information texts.

There are many criteria for choosing books, and it is beyond the scope of this chapter to discuss these in detail. But for very young learners who are learning to read in their second language, books that have the following characteristics will be supportive of early reading.

- ◆ They have repetitive language that becomes familiar to children so that they can begin to join in (e.g., *Run, run, as fast as you can, you can't catch me, I'm the gingerbread man*).
- ◆ They have a repetitive event that builds up into a cumulative story (e.g., *First the farmer, then his wife, then the child, then the dog,*

then the cat, then the mouse . . . all tried to pull up the giant turnip). Many stories include a repetitive structure of this sort, which decreases the comprehension load on EL learners. Once they understand the event, they are able to transfer their understanding to each repetition.

- They contain universal themes (e.g., good triumphs over evil), universal motifs (e.g., three sons or daughters, the two eldest of whom are bad, the youngest of whom is good), and the teaching of moral behavior (e.g., kindness gets rewarded). Traditional folktales are a good example of a context for universal themes, and for this reason they may offer a pathway to early reading for young learners who are very new to English.
- The illustrations clearly represent the meanings in the text and can be used as clues for understanding.
- The print is clear, with pages that are well designed and not too busy.
- They represent good, authentic models of language and don't sound contrived.
- Their content and language, while it might not be immediately accessible, can be "bridged" for EL readers.
- Their content and language can be used to extend children's knowledge about reading and about the world.
- They have content that is engaging to young readers.

For older learners who are reading longer factual texts, the following features are also important:

- The overall organization of the text should be clear. The better organized a text is, the easier it is to understand, and the more the reader is able to engage in higher-level processes such as summarizing and inferring.
- The text should have clear signaling devices. The structure and content of a well-organized text is highlighted by such devices as titles, headings, subheadings, visuals, clear topic sentences, and text connectives.

- The text should have appropriate conceptual density. New concepts should be spaced, and they should contain sufficient elaboration to make them understandable.
- There should be good instructional devices, such as a logically organized table of contents, glossary, index, graphic overviews, diagrams, and summaries.

In addition, the choice of books to use with your students will be affected by a number of other factors, such as their age, interests, and overall reading abilities. It will also be affected by your purpose in using the book. Will the book be used as instructional material aimed to extend a student's reading skills, and thus be a little ahead of the student's independent reading ability? Or is the book intended as part of a wide reading program, and thus something that children should be able to read fairly independently? In terms of the overall reading program, do children have access to a range of books, and a range of genre types? (Information texts need to be included at lower levels, too, because they are often more accessible to young learners than narratives.) As this chapter has suggested, how comprehensible a book is will also be determined by the kinds of activities you use and the kinds of interactions the children will be engaged in around the text. However, whatever the books you choose, seek to ensure that they will give children "a reason for turning the page."

In Summary

This chapter has argued that EL learners need access to a linguistically and culturally rich reading environment, and to a range of reading strategies to bring to the process of reading.

- A reader needs adequate "in-the-head" knowledge, both about the genre and the content of the text, to access the meaning of the text. Therefore, what the teacher does before students begin to read the text directly impacts on how effectively students are able to access the meaning of the text.

- Meaning does not reside simply in the words on the page, but involves a thinking and interactive process between the reader and the text.
- Effective readers take on four roles simultaneously as they read: as text decoder, text participant, text user, and text analyst.
- To support learners in these roles, teachers need to plan teaching and learning activities for using before, during, and after reading.
- Explicit teaching about literacy needs to be drawn from familiar and meaningful texts.
- Wide reading of engaging and authentic material needs to be an ongoing part of a literacy program at all levels and for all learners.

To Think About

1. Look at one of the texts that your students read. What specific cultural, conceptual, or language difficulties might your students face in reading the text? Suggest some before-, during-, and after-reading activities you might use.
2. Which reader roles are given most prominence in the literacy teaching practices at your school?
3. Is there anything you would like to change or add to in the literacy programs at your school?
4. What points in this chapter affirm your current beliefs and practices? What is the most important learning for you?
5. Make a key-ring card for the word *scaffolding*, and compare and explain it to a colleague.
6. Tell a success story about one of your learners and his or her literacy learning.

Suggestions for Further Reading

Chen, L., and E. Mora-Flores. 2006. *Balanced Literacy for English Language Learners, K–2*. Portsmouth, NH: Heinemann. (See Chapter 10 for excellent ideas on word work.)

Fountas, I. 2005. *Guided Reading: Essential Elements*. Portsmouth, NH: Heinemann.

Gibbons, P. 2009. Chapter 5, "Building Bridges to Text: Supporting Academic Reading." In *English Learners, Academic Literacy, and Thinking*. Portsmouth, NH: Heinemann.

Harvey, S., A. Goudvis, and J. Wallis. 2010. *Small-Group Lessons for the Primary Comprehension Toolkit*, Grades K–2 and Grades 3–6. Portsmouth, NH: Heinemann.

Wallace, C. 2013. Chapter 3, "Bilingual Learners in a Multilingual Primary School." In *Literacy and the Bilingual Learner: Texts and Practices in London Schools*. Basingstoke, UK: Palgrave Macmillan.

Seven

Listening

An Active and Thinking Process

Current views of listening emphasise the role of the listener, who is seen as an active participant in listening, employing strategies to facilitate, monitor and evaluate his or her listening.

—Jack Richards, *Teaching Listening and Speaking: From Theory to Practice*

The area of listening is often the "Cinderella" of language planning, sometimes neglected as a specific area of need, taken for granted or subsumed as part of speaking. Although effective interaction with others certainly depends on how well we understand what is said to us (including our ability to ask for clarification when we need it), this chapter will also show how the process of listening parallels that of reading. The chapter illustrates how listening occurs in four kinds of contexts, depending upon whether it is one way or two way, and whether it relates to everyday talk or to more academic, less concrete, and subject-based information.

But as Richards (2008) also points out, listening is not simply about comprehension. Like reading it is also a route to language development and "can provide input that triggers the further development of second language proficiency" (13). It is not something that can be taken for granted, any more than the teaching of oral language, reading, or writing. But helping learners to develop listening skills can be a challenging task for teachers: successful listening develops over time.

The chapter suggests a range of classroom activities for developing listening skills, with an emphasis on meaning-based activities. At the end of the chapter there are also suggestions for more focused work on the sounds of English (phonemes) and its stress and intonation patterns. Such activities overlap with those designed to develop phonemic awareness (discussed in the chapter on reading), and with pronunciation. These focused listening activities are important in some contexts and for some learners, but should not be overemphasized at the expense of meaning-based activities that have the potential to provide input for overall language development.

MAKING SENSE OF WHAT WE HEAR

The teaching of listening is often assumed to "happen" in the process of the teaching of speaking or reading; teaching programs and syllabuses often refer to "listening and speaking" as a single unit, so the specific teaching of listening may be overlooked. Yet in terms of learning, and second language learning in particular, listening is a key to language development: understanding what is said in a particular situation provides important models for subsequent language use. While most elementary classrooms are busy, engaging places for children, they are also frequently quite noisy. As you may have experienced yourself, background noise tends to interfere with comprehension far more if you are listening in a less-familiar language. And even if this noise is kept to a minimum, there is usually a level of background buzz that may make it very difficult for EL learners to comprehend what is said, even if it would be comprehensible to them in quieter contexts.

Like reading, listening is a route to language development.

The process of listening in many ways parallels the process of reading. Both involve comprehension rather than production, and both involve the active construction of meaning. Try this listening test with a colleague. One of you should read aloud a short paragraph from a book. The other should try to "shadow" the reader by repeating as closely as possible the words *as they are being read*. You will probably find that the person who is shadowing will be only a syllable or so behind the reader. Now do the same thing again—but this time with the reader reading the passage backward. How easy is it now to shadow? If you are the person shadowing, you will probably have found it to be a much more difficult task, and that you are much further behind the reader. Why should this be, given that the words are the same?

The answer, of course, is that the second reading doesn't make sense: there is no meaning for the listener. What the listener is hearing in the second reading is simply a string of unconnected words. To listen effectively we need to do more than simply recognize sounds and words. We need more than the acoustic information to gain meaning, just as in reading we need more than phonic information. Like reading, effective listening depends on the expectations and predictions about content, language, and genre that the listener brings to the text. So, just like reading, listening is an active process that depends not only on decoding the acoustic information but also on the listener's in-the-head knowledge about the world and about the structure of the language. That is why shadowing the first reading was much easier than shadowing the second reading: you were able to draw on more sources of information.

In the last chapter, we noted how earlier models of reading saw it as being no more than decoding words. Earlier models of listening paralleled this. The process of listening was seen as one where the listener segmented a stream of speech into its constituent sounds, linked these to form words, and then chained these words into clauses, sentences, and finally whole text. Nunan (1990) refers to this model of listening as "the listener as tape recorder," implying that the learner is a passive receiver of spoken language who takes no active part in making meaning. By contrast, more recent models of listening see the listener as what Nunan refers to as a "meaning builder." As in the process of reading, the listener is seen as taking an active role: listeners construct an interpretation of what they hear using not only the sounds of the language, but also, just as in reading, their available schema and knowledge of the language system.

We need more than the acoustic information to gain meaning.

When we think about the listening process, the notion of a "script" is useful. Just as in a play script, when the lines the actors speak are prewritten, in listening we draw on those "scripts" that are familiar to us through our previous experiences. Imagine, for example, that you meet a friend who has just returned from an overseas trip. When you ask her how the journey was, she comments:

> *It was good except for where I was sitting. They wouldn't let me move. The seat was. . . .*

What sorts of things do you think your friend is going to talk about? Who are "they" in this script? What are the sources of the knowledge you need to interpret this in order to predict what your friend is likely to say?

Anyone familiar with plane travel will have a good idea what is likely to be said. Perhaps the seat was too cramped, or perhaps she had requested an aisle or window seat but didn't get it. Maybe she was sitting next to someone unpleasant, or she was near a crying baby. *They* refers to the air stewards, or possibly the ground staff at check-in. The actors in this script are your friend and the steward (and possibly the ground staff) with whom she spoke about the problem, and possibly other passengers. The sources of knowledge that you used to interpret this snippet of conversation are your own experiences of air travel, or what you have learned from others' experiences. In other words, your "in-the-head" knowledge allows you to map key words onto the words you are hearing, and therefore predict meaning.

Again, note the similarity to the process of reading and the importance of in-the-head or background knowledge of the topic in understanding what we hear. Once more, it is clear that understanding what is said is not simply dependent on the sounds we hear. Consequently, listening tasks in the classroom, just like reading tasks, are far more demanding if children have no previous knowledge on which to draw. Lack of comprehension is likely to be due to this, just as much as to the fact that learners may find certain sounds difficult to discriminate. As we have seen, practice in sound discrimination is useful in the earlier stages of learning to read in a new language, and in learning to write, but as in reading it is not sufficient to ensure listening comprehension.

TYPES OF LISTENING

Nunan (1990) has suggested that listening occurs in four types of contexts, which he sets out as a matrix (see Figure 7–1). First, it may be one-way, where the listener is not called on to respond verbally (such as listening to the radio or to a lecture); or, it may be two-way, where two or more people take on the roles of listener and speaker in turn (such as in a conversation). At the same time, listening can also broadly involve two types of topic: everyday interpersonal topics, the sort of everyday chat we all engage in with friends; and more information-based topics, the kind of talk that occurs in the classroom or in contexts where the purpose is to gain information of some kind. Figure 7–1 shows how these four types of contexts produce a two-by-two matrix. Some examples of each of the four listening contexts are included.

Figure 7–1 Contexts for Listening

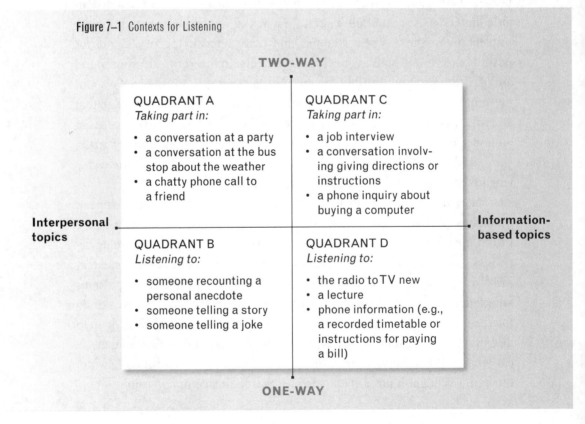

Of course, this is a very simplified picture of listening contexts; in reality the topics about which people speak cannot be classified so discretely, and it may sometimes be difficult to discriminate between what might be thought of as "chat" and "information getting." Nevertheless, this matrix does represent the broad range of contexts for listening, and it is useful as a programming device to check whether students are experiencing a *range of situations* in which to develop listening skills.

Generally, the easiest listening context for EL learners involves the sorts of situations found in Quadrant A, and to a lesser extent (because the topics may be less familiar) Quadrant C. Listening here is two-way, so listeners have a chance to ask for clarification or to signal that they don't understand. And as Chapter 1 suggested, most EL learners quickly learn to talk to others and comprehend what is said to them in face-to-face contexts, when the talk is about everyday and familiar topics and where the visual context itself can be an aid to comprehension, such as in some of the examples in Quadrant A.

However, not all situations that fall within Quadrant C are easy for learners. Understanding what is said on the phone can be quite demanding for any EL learners, including adults. As the discussion about the mode continuum in Chapters 1 and 4 suggested, more linguistic resources are needed the further we move away from "here and now" language. So, a phone call, even though it is two-way and may be about familiar topics, may be a difficult task: while speakers must make everything explicit through language alone, listeners must also reconstruct the intended meaning from language alone. In addition, they must do it in real time, without the time for reflection that is possible in reading.

One-way listening is generally more difficult than two-way because listeners don't have an opportunity to ask for clarification or to slow down the text they are listening to. Quadrant D tasks are also likely to involve less-familiar topics than those in Quadrants A and B, and probably represent the most demanding listening tasks of all for EL students, yet this is the kind of listening that is very common in classrooms since it occurs in all subject-based learning. The suggestions about making language comprehensible, including the use of message abundancy discussed in Chapter 2, are particularly important in these contexts.

IMPLICATIONS FOR TEACHING

As the previous section suggests, approaches to the teaching of listening should be primarily focused on meaning. To this end, here is a selection of listening activities that can be integrated within your regular program. They are divided into two groups, those that involve two-way listening and those that involve one-way listening. All the activities involve the learners taking some action, because it is by seeing what a learner *does* as a result of listening that we can most easily recognize whether effective listening has taken place.

> *Approaches to the teaching of listening should be primarily focused on meaning.*

Introducing how to listen

Many children in today's world are not used to quiet, and consequently they have never learned to listen perceptively to specific sounds. In preparation for listening in the educational context, the following two examples, though not specifically language based, help to sensitize young children to the need to listen actively and perceptively.

What Sounds Can You Hear?

Ask the children to be completely silent and to close their eyes. When the classroom is quiet, ask them to listen for any sounds they can still hear: these will be mostly from outside the classroom. Give them several minutes to concentrate on this task, and then ask them what they heard. Possible answers might involve a dog barking outside, a truck going past, someone coughing, a baby crying, people talking, a chair squeaking, and so on. As a follow-up to this task for older students, you could also ask which of these sounds they would not have heard a hundred years ago.

Sound Stories

Play three sounds to the class—such as the sound of children playing with a ball, the sound of glass breaking, and the sounds of someone shouting. In groups, the children produce a short (spoken) narrative that links the three sounds.

Two-way listening

One of the most important things that EL learners need to be able to do when interacting with others is to ask for clarification when they don't understand something. As we saw in Chapter 3, this interpersonal language is very important in collaborative work. As part of planning for listening, model and practice phrases like these:

Excuse me, I'd like to ask something.

I'm sorry, I don't understand. Can you repeat that?

I'm sorry, I didn't hear that. Can you say it again, please?

Did you say . . . ?

Sorry for interrupting, but would you mind repeating that?

Remind students to use phrases like these *whenever* they don't understand something. It is a good idea to have them written up on a poster and displayed so that their use becomes a classroom norm, both when students are talking to each other and to you. Be explicit about this, and point out that not understanding everything is OK, but that they should ask if they miss information or don't understand something. You do not want your students to become so accustomed to missing bits of what is said that they begin to accept this as an inevitable part of their school experience, and simply tune out if they do not fully understand what's been said.

You do not want your students to become so accustomed to missing bits of what is said that they begin to accept this as an inevitable part of their school experience.

Some students who are not familiar with these cultural norms may not be accustomed to these kinds of interruptions and see them as impolite, especially to a teacher. Reassure *all* students that you want to be sure they understand what you say, and that a polite interruption or a request for clarification will help them do this.

Any interactive problem-solving task is, of course, also a context for practicing interactive listening, for in these situations students will need to work out communication difficulties and clarify ideas. The spoken-language activities discussed in Chapters 2 and 3 are therefore also listening activities. Some additional activities are described below. Remember to encourage the students to ask for clarification or repetition whenever they need to.

Map Games

Give students identical maps, but with some road and building names removed. Map A should have the information that is not on Map B and vice versa. Collaboratively, but without showing each other their maps, the students must find out the missing names using questions like these:

> *What's the name of the road opposite the post office?*
>
> *What building is to the left of the post office?*

A variation on this activity is for students to have identical and completed maps. Both students agree on a starting point. Student A then directs Student B to a destination unknown to Student B. When the instructions are complete, the student who has been following the instructions should end up in the right place. Here's an example:

> *Go along the street.*
>
> *Turn left. You pass the post office on your left.*
>
> *When you get to the traffic lights, turn right.*
>
> *Just past the park there is a building.*
>
> *Where are you?*

Barrier games like this make ideal interactive listening activities since clarification questions are almost certain to occur as the listener seeks more information (*Did you say "left"? Can you repeat that? Is it near the station?*)

Split Dictation

■ ■

You will need two gapped versions of a text, with each text having different gaps. In pairs, students must complete the text by reading to each other the parts they have and filling in the blanks for the parts they don't have, so that collaboratively they complete the whole text. Students can take it in turns to read sentence by sentence (see Figure 7–2).

Figure 7–2 Split Dictation

PARTNER A

1. Insects have caused much suffering _____.

2. _____ have died of malaria.

3. This is a disease _____.

4. Insects _____.

5. _____ infects people with sleeping sickness.

PARTNER B

1. _____ for human beings.

2. Millions of people _____.

3. _____ that is spread by mosquitos.

4. _____ spread many other diseases.

5. The tsetse fly _____.

Dictogloss

This is a technique adapted from Ruth Wajnryb (1990). It is designed to develop listening skills, but is particularly valuable because it integrates this with speaking, reading, writing, and note-making skills. The aim for students is to reconstruct a written text that they will hear read aloud. The students' texts do not need to be identical to the original, but they should have the same information and be appropriately and accurately worded. The passage must be on a topic the students *already know something about.* (You could write the passage yourself, or you could use a passage from one of the students' textbooks in any curriculum area, or from a book related to a topic they are studying.)

1. The teacher reads a short passage twice (or more) at normal speed. The students just listen; they don't write anything at this point.
2. The teacher reads the passage a third time at normal speed, and this time, while the teacher is reading, the students individually write down as much as they can, as fast as they can. They should not try to write sentences, just key words and phrases. It is important that you make clear to the students that you do not expect them to write everything down. The aim is just to get as much information as they can. Handwriting and spelling are not important at this stage.
3. In pairs, the students compare and discuss the individual notes they have written. Together, they begin to reconstruct the original text they heard.
4. Two pairs of students then join to make a group of four. They repeat the same process, again adding to and adapting their notes. By using these four sets of notes, the group will almost always be able to produce a fairly accurate record of the original passage.
5. At this stage you can ask individual students to write out the passage based on their notes. Alternatively, the group can do it together. (Groups could use large sheets of paper and then put them on the wall for display.) Give them time to check their writing,

such as grammar and spelling. Then show the original passage (preferably on a screen or whiteboard so that everyone can see it together) and let the students compare what they have written with the original. Remind them that the aim is not to produce a text that is identical to the original, but one that has the same information and is appropriately worded. Discuss with students any differences between the texts, pointing out (and praising) variations that make sense and that show how the students were using their language knowledge, and helping them to see where the information or meaning may differ (or be incorrect).

At Steps 3, 4, and 5, encourage students to *reflect on* what they have written (e.g., to use what they know about English grammar to check for grammatical errors; to ask the question "Does it make sense?"; and to use the context to guess words they were unable to hear). This is a good context for talking *about* language in the context of actually using it. The completed text also provides a good model of written language.

Picture Prompts

This is a variation of dictogloss that is easier for young learners or those new to English. You will need to choose a text that has a number of simple sentences that tell a story, describe a process, or give information that can be illustrated. Again, the text must be on a topic that students know something about. In one class the teacher, as part of the study of the human eye, had chosen a text that described the parts of the eye and what each part does. The text began with the sentence "Light enters through the pupil."

1. Proceed initially as for the dictogloss, reading the text two or three times while students listen.
2. Then read sentence by sentence, pausing after each sentence while students individually draw a representation of the sentence. (This drawing is for the individual student only, to serve

as a mnemonic for the information they have listened to and to provide visual scaffolding for the subsequent writing.)

3. After the text has been read in this way, students write a sentence under each drawing. This will probably be quite close to the original.

4. They then move into pairs, then fours, as for the dictogloss, and collaboratively reconstruct the complete text.

One-way listening

Many reading tasks can be adapted to use as listening tasks. In addition, as we have seen earlier in the chapter, listening, like reading, is facilitated when students have the relevant schematic or in-the-head knowledge. You may find it helpful at this point to go back to the before-reading activities listed in Chapter 6 since many of these activities are as relevant for listening as they are for reading and can adapted to prepare for a specific listening task. They are especially relevant for developing the contextual knowledge needed for one-way listening, where learners will probably have fewer opportunities to ask questions.

One-way listening usually involves either listening for a specific piece of information (e.g., listening to a recorded message for the time of a train) or listening with the aim of getting general information (e.g., listening to the news). Make sure that the tasks you use provide a balance between these two purposes.

If You Are . . .

■ ■

This activity is adapted from Rost (1991). Students must follow instructions. These instructions vary depending on the characteristics of individual students, so this activity requires students to listen very carefully. As in the previous tasks, encourage students to ask you to repeat or clarify information. Here is an example.

Write your name on the paper. If you are a boy, write it on the left. If you are a girl, write it on the right.

Write your telephone number. If you are sitting beside a window, write it in red. If you are sitting anywhere else, write it in green.

How do you come *to school? If you take a bus to school, write the word* bus *inside a triangle. If you come by car, write the word* car *inside a square. If you walk, write the word* walk *inside a rectangle.*

You can make this a more complex listening task for more advanced students.

Hands Up

Give the students a set of questions based on a text they are going to listen to. As they hear a piece of information that provides them with any of the answers, they raise their hands. They should have a chance to look at the questions before they hear the text. Ensure, as much as possible, that the order of the questions reflects the order in which the information is given.

An alternative to this for younger children is to use an adaptation of the game of Musical Chairs. Instead of sitting down when a piece of music stops, children sit down when they hear the answer to a question.

Listening for Information

Provide the context for what the student will listen to: *You're going to hear some information about.* . . . This should be related to something students are currently studying. Students listen to any documentary program or video that presents a number of facts and figures. Prepare a blank information sheet for the students (see Figure 7–3). Students must transfer the information as they listen. For example, if students are listening to information about a country, as in the example, they listen specifically for particular pieces of information. If students already have a more extensive knowledge of the topic, encourage them to predict as many of the answers as they can *before* listening, so that they will be listening more actively and confirming or correcting their answers as they listen.

Figure 7–3 Listening for Information

- Name of the country
- Where it is
- Population
- What language(s) people speak
- Largest city
- ?
- ?

Spot the Difference

Prepare two versions of a story (A and B), two news bulletins, or two procedural texts that have minor changes of detail. Read Version A to the students and ask them to listen for overall meaning. Read it a second time so that students become familiar with it. Then give students a written version of the same text (Version A). With the text in front of the students, the teacher then reads the alternative version, Version B. Students must "spot the difference" between the written version they have and the alternative version they are listening to. They should circle the words or phrases on the print version when they hear differences.

Version A

Just as Jack had taken all the gold he could carry, the giant opened one eye and saw Jack. "Who are you?" he roared. He opened the other eye, and then he stood up. Jack could hardly see his head, it was so far away. He turned and ran and started to climb down the beanstalk as fast as he could. The giant strode after him, and Jack felt sure he was about to die!

Version B

Just as Jill had taken all the gold she could carry, the giant opened one of his eyes and saw Jill. "Who are you?" he shouted. He opened the other eye, and then he stood up. Jill could hardly see his head, it was so far away. She turned and ran and began to climb down the beanstalk as fast as she could. The giant ran after her, and Jill felt sure she was about to be killed!

Picture Dictation

You will need a short text that involves a sequence of events in time, such as a story, recount, or a description of a procedure. Students, individually or in pairs, have a number of jumbled pictures that match the text. Read the text to the children. As you read the text, students put the pictures in order.

Matching Game (Listening)

Students have several pictures, each labeled with a number (1, 2, 3). The teacher describes one of the pictures, giving each description a letter (a, b, c). Students then match the pictures with the description by saying which numbers and letters go together—for example, "3 goes with A." This is more challenging if the pictures are similar in most details.

Aural/Oral Cloze

Prepare a cloze activity with random or focused deletions (see discussion of cloze activities in Chapter 6). Write the title on the board and get children to predict what information the text is likely to contain. Read the complete text to the students while they listen, then read again as students fill in the blanks.

FOCUSING ON THE SOUNDS OF ENGLISH

As we saw in the previous chapter, a phoneme is a sound that makes a difference to the *meaning* of a word. For most young children, difficulty in discriminating between particular pairs of sounds and their pronunciation does not remain a problem for long, and extensive sound discrimination and pronunciation practice is rarely necessary. In fact, as Chapter 1 pointed out, many learners, in fact, very quickly begin to sound like fluent speakers of English, and because any discernible accent usually disappears quite quickly they may be perceived by some teachers as more competent in English than they are.

In later life, although older learners have other advantages in learning a new language, this ability to learn a new set of phonemes decreases considerably, and from adolescence onward, EL students, including adult learners, usually retain some evidence of their first language in their pronunciation. This is what we are responding to when we refer to someone "having an accent." Pronunciation may occasionally be an issue that older (postadolescent and adult) learners are themselves concerned about, and if this is the case then some pronunciation and sound discrimination may be useful. However, unless pronunciation interferes with comprehension, an ongoing overemphasis on the sounds of English is rarely necessary and may even be counterproductive. As English language teachers we should remember that there are many "Englishes" spoken across the world, and with increasing globalization and migration there will doubtless be increasingly more variation in how it is spoken. And it is in the nature of language to change, which is why most of us are unable to understand or speak the English of sixth-century Britain, or of the middle ages, and why we may also have difficulty with the language of Shakespeare!

One aspect of spoken English that some EL students may find hard to master is its stress system. This is an area that may need some focused work. In connected speech, many languages have equal stress on every syllable, whereas English stresses some syllables but not others. In <u>this</u> sentence, the <u>stressed</u> syllables are <u>marked</u>. Read the sentence aloud and note how the underlined words receive more stress. Notice, also, how the vowel in the word *are* "weakens"—that is, it changes from the way it would be pronounced if you said it in isolation. Most "function words," or grammatical words, change, or weaken, in this way, because they are not usually stressed in connected speech. Compare how you might say the following words in isolation and in a sentence, and notice how the vowels weaken. Be sure to speak as naturally as possible and at normal speed.

Was	She was playing.
Have	They have finished. (Probably further reduced to *they've*).
To	Give it back to him.
From	He's just got back from his holiday in Italy.

Of course, these words may be stressed if there is a reason for them to be, for example, if a speaker wishes to emphasize them, as in this example:

They have finished. No they haven't. Yes they <u>have</u>.

Also related to the stress system is the way that words are often "linked" in spoken English in continuous speech (as opposed to saying the same words individually). Notice how, in these examples, where one word ends in a consonant sound and the next begins with a vowel sound, the two sounds are linked:

Get it out please.	Ge-ti-tout please.
Put it in the bin.	Pu-ti-tin the bin.
He said I could take it.	He sai-dI-could-ta-kit.

If learners' speech sounds staccato-like (and this is likely to depend on their primary/first language), model how in continuous speech English speakers link the end of one word with the beginning of the next, as indicated above, and have students practice saying these phrases. (Note that the sounds of English spoken in different parts of the world vary, and the letter *t* may be pronounced close to /d/ in parts of North America and Australia, but the "linking" principle described here remains.)

Speakers of some languages, particularly some Southeast Asian languages, may have difficulties with the sounds /p/, /b/, /t/, /d/, /k/, /g/ in English when they occur at the *end* of a word. These may not be "heard" by children who speak a language where final consonants are not fully "released." Often these sounds represent critical grammatical markers in English, for example, markers for past tense (*jumped, opened, walked*) or plural endings; consequently, they may be missed when children write or speak. Sometimes what may appear to be a spelling or grammatical mistake has its roots in the learner not noticing a particular phoneme at the end of a word, or in his or her pronunciation.

Sometimes you may feel it necessary to focus specifically on the sounds of English, especially when focusing on phonemic awareness and pronunciation. The following activities may be useful for these purposes.

Jazz Chants and Raps

Jazz chants and raps can be great fun for children, including those they have written themselves, but they also provide an authentic context for a focus on the rhythms, stress, and intonation patterns of English, including the linking of words referred to earlier. Many other forms of "spoken language as performance" where there are opportunities for rehearsal—such as poetry, drama, or oral presentations— can provide excellent contexts for a focus on *how* something is said.

Minimal Pair Exercises

In these activities, the focus is on differentiating between pairs of words that differ only in one sound (phoneme), such as the ones below. Give students a list of pairs of words (such as *three, tree; bin, bean; bin, pin; cat, cap; thing, sing*). They listen to *one* of the two words being read and circle on their list the one they think they hear. (For younger children, you could use two drawings rather than words.) Such exercises may be useful for some older learners new to English who may find the sounds difficult to hear or to pronounce and who are also likely to be more conscious of sounding "different"; but in general, try to provide a greater contextualization for a task like this. After all, we rarely listen to words in isolation in real life, and, as we have seen, we use contextual clues to help us "hear" a sound correctly. You should also ask yourself these questions:

> ➤ Do these sounds make it difficult for the student to compre-
> hend what is said to him or her?
> ➤ Does the student's pronunciation of these sounds make com-
> prehension difficult for a listener?

If the answer is no, consider whether such exercises are really
relevant. In any case, remember that such focused practice is better
done regularly but in small doses, perhaps for a few minutes a day.

Say It Again

This activity is adapted from Rost (1991), who suggests it for focusing on phonological features, stress, and intonation. First, select a
scene from a video/DVD that the children will enjoy or find memorable, or that has high interest for them. This could be an excerpt
from a children's television drama or feature film. Students should
be familiar with the overall story line. Alternatively, you could use
an information video related to something the students are learning about.

Select some lines spoken by the characters/narrator in the video;
these are the lines that students are later going to practice. The lines
should be in chronological order but should not occur all together.
Write the lines on a chart or have them on a screen so there will be a
whole-class focus on them. Next:

1. Play the excerpt to the children.
2. After they have watched the video, read the sentences on the
   chart with the children. Ask whether they can remember who
   said them and where they occurred.
3. Play the scene a second time while the students listen for the
   sentences. Have them raise their hands each time they hear
   one. Stop the tape at this point and ask them to repeat the line
   exactly as it was said. Pay attention to all aspects of pronunciation, including stress, intonation, and vowel weakening. They
   may need several rehearsals with you!

4. Play the scene a third time. This time, stop the tape before the selected lines. The students say the line as you point to it. After several repetitions, continue the tape until just before the next sentence. If there is a story line, encourage the students to say the lines in character, not simply to repeat them as an exercise.

5. If students are enjoying the activity, play the tape once more and have individual students say the lines from memory.

Shadow Reading

Read a paragraph from a short story, preferably from a story that students are already familiar with. They should be able to see a copy. Students listen carefully to your reading, and how you say it. Then read it again, stopping after each sentence to give students a chance to repeat it. Students try to copy your pronunciation, stress, intonation, and pace as closely as possible. When the whole of the paragraph has been rehearsed in this way, read the paragraph again and this time have students "shadow" the tape by reading along with you as you read, remembering to pay attention to the stress and intonation patterns. They can then read it to a partner.

Another alternative, with a smaller class, is to have them move toward one of the walls of the classroom. Facing it, and standing about three feet away, they'll read the paragraph again (at their individual pace). Although the disadvantage of this method is that there is no audience, the advantage is that students are able to practice the reading by themselves, while you circulate and listen to them individually. Many older students appreciate this opportunity, and it can be very useful for rehearsing a subsequent oral presentation. If this is the case, also encourage the learner to reduce a full written version to brief notes or dot points as they gain confidence.

As Richards points out in the quotation that began this chapter, effective listening is a basis for the development of other language skills. Therefore it impacts on subsequent language learning. There are numerous opportunities for focusing on listening across the curriculum, and it is easily integrated with many regular teaching and learning activities. When you plan a unit of work or classroom program next, note these opportunities. Try to ensure that there is a balance of one-way and two-way listening, and that these occur both in contexts where students use everyday language and in those that require more academic and subject-based language.

Finally, remember that being a good listener *yourself* is all important. If we want children to become good listeners, we must ourselves become active listeners of what they say to us. Model effective listening by clarifying and checking that you have understood what children are saying, and build on their responses as an interested conversational partner. This behavior demonstrates the importance you place on active listening, and it is one of the most positive ways you can develop your students' listening abilities.

> *Being a good listener yourself is all important.*

In Summary

Listening is a thinking- and meaning-based process that also provides input for further language development.

 ◆ Listening ability develops in both one-way and two-way contexts. There should be a balance of both in an effective listening program.
 ◆ Listening to unfamiliar subject-related language is more difficult than listening to everyday familiar information, especially in one-way listening. Message abundancy, and other ways of providing comprehensible input, is therefore an important form of scaffolding in these more complex contexts.
 ◆ Just as it is possible to read in more than one way (such as skimming and scanning), it is also possible to listen in different ways (such as for overall gist or for specific information). Teaching and learning activities should reflect these purposes.
 ◆ Learning to ask for clarification is integral to interactive listening.
 ◆ Noticing the form of words, being able to discriminate sounds, and being able to recognize stress and intonation patterns are part of learning to listen accurately. However, as much as possible, learners

should focus on these aspects of listening in the context of meaning-oriented activities.

♦ Listening ability develops where there is a real purpose for listening, and where the focus is on listening for meaning. So, in the EAL context, the teaching of listening skills fits naturally into all curriculum areas. Designing listening tasks in the context of understanding and learning subject content provides many authentic situations across the curriculum for listening skills to be developed.

To Think About

1. Look again at the matrix on Figure 7–1. With a partner, think of some classroom activities that you use regularly and that involve listening, and locate them on the matrix. Is there a range of types of listening, in both one-way and two-way contexts, and involving both "everyday" and more academic contexts?
2. What situations occur in the classroom that may reflect a student's difficulty with listening in English?
3. Look at a current teaching plan, for example, a subject-based unit of work you plan to use. Where could you focus more specifically on developing listening skills?
4. What reading activities in Chapter 6 could also be adapted as listening activities?
5. Share some successful strategies. How do you help or encourage students to listen more effectively?

Suggestions for Further Reading

Goh, C. 2006. "Metacognitive Instruction in Listening for Young Learners." *ELT Journal* 60 (3): 222–32.

Nunan, D., and L. Miller, eds. 1995. *New Ways in Teaching Listening*. Alexandria, VA: Teachers of English to Speakers of Other Languages (TESOL).

Richards, J. 2008. *Teaching Listening and Speaking: From Theory to Practice.* Cambridge, UK: Cambridge University Press.

Ross, J. 2006. "ESL Listening Comprehension: Practical Guidelines for Teachers." *The Internet TESL Journal* 12 (2). Available at http://iteslj.org/, accessed 3/13/14.

Eight

Developing an Integrated Curriculum

■ ■

Learning Language, Learning Through Language, and Learning About Language

> *Five principles . . . guide the development and enactment of quality instruction for English language learners . . . academic rigor, high expectations, quality interactions, a language focus and quality curriculum.*
>
> —Aida Walqui and Leo van Lier, *Scaffolding the Academic Success of Adolescent English Language Learners: A Pedagogy of Promise*

This chapter brings together the ideas in this book and discusses some of the ways in which EAL teaching can be integrated into the regular classroom. It summarizes some of the main reasons for integrating language and subject learning, and outlines how this integration can be achieved in planning and practice. In this approach, the curriculum itself provides a context for language learning.

Part of the title of the chapter comes from a paper by Michael Halliday, entitled "Three Aspects of Children's Language Development: Learning Language, Learning Through Language, Learning About Language." This chapter shows how in a classroom that integrates subject content and language, these three aspects of language development are brought together.

WHY INTEGRATE?

When EAL first became generally recognized as a specialist area of teaching, probably around the middle of the last century in most English-speaking countries, the teaching of English language learners was often quite separate from what was going on in the mainstream curriculum. Students followed a special program, often focused on the grammatical structures and functions of English that were usually not related to the subject learning of the mainstream curriculum, and they were taught by a specialist teacher. Neither the learners themselves, nor what they were learning, were meaningfully integrated into the regular classroom.

Of course, some schools still choose to "pull out" some children who are new to both English and to the host country for a short daily program in the early stages of their learning. The focus of these programs is usually either the "survival" language so urgently needed by students who are very recent arrivals in a new country or a "sheltered" modified program related to the mainstream curriculum. This may be an appropriate choice for students who are new to the country and to English, or who may be very shy and lacking in confidence. In recent years, EL learners in schools have included increasing numbers of refugees, some of whom may have suffered great trauma, loss, and disrupted schooling. In a small group, away from the demands of the mainstream class, these learners may more rapidly gain confidence as they become familiar and comfortable with their new surroundings more easily. In addition they will have more opportunities to build a stable relationship with the teacher through one-to-one interactions.

However, the approach taken in this book has been based on the view that for most EL learners, the regular classroom offers the best opportunity to learn a new language, because it provides an authentic context for a focus on the language most relevant to subject learning. Language teaching is more effective when learners are presented with meaningful language in context, and the integration of EAL learning with curriculum content has for some time been broadly accepted as supportive of second language development (Echevarria and Vogt 2011; Mohan, Leung, and Davison 2001; Short 1993). Here are a number of reasons why this is the case.

◆ First, the integration of language and content is consistent with the notion that language is learned through meaningful use in a variety of contexts. The subject matter of the curriculum provides those contexts and thus a rationale for what language to teach. From a language-teaching perspective then, the curriculum can be seen as providing authentic contexts for the development of subject-specific genres and registers. In short, an integrated program takes a functional approach to language by placing its teaching focus on language as the medium of learning rather than on language as something separate from content.

◆ Second, as discussed in Chapter 1, there is evidence that it can take between five and seven years for EL learners to match their English-speaking peers in the effective use of the academic registers of school. Clearly, if this is the case, concurrent teaching and learning of both subject matter and language is a way of speeding up this process, and helping to ensure that children's classroom time is spent as productively as possible.

◆ Third, nonintegrated approaches—that is, instruction in language alone—is usually insufficient to enable children to succeed in mainstream studies (Collier and Thomas 1997; Collier 1995; Richards and Hurley 1990). As we noted earlier, if children are following a separate EAL program, the risk is that there will be little relationship between the language being presented in the language class and the language required for children to access and participate in curriculum learning. Since language is best learned in the service of other learning, the mainstream curriculum is an obvious source for language development; as one educator puts it, "Why go to the trouble of artificially recreating the mainstream classroom [in withdrawal classes] when the real thing is available next door?" (Clegg 1996, 10).

◆ In addition, situating language teaching within a curriculum area has the potential to support both language and curriculum learning in a reciprocal way. With a dual content-language focus, there is likely to be a continuous recycling of concepts, grammar, or vocabulary associated with particular curriculum knowledge. As we saw in Chapters 6 and 7, prior knowledge or familiarity with a topic greatly facilitates language comprehension and language learning. Equally, language-based tasks in a subject area can effectively recycle key concepts and knowledge in the process of focusing on relevant text types, registers, grammar, and vocabulary. In other words, content learning provides a "hook" on which to hang language development, and vice versa.

◆ Finally, it is important to recognize the benefits to all students of a culturally and linguistically diverse classroom, and a culturally inclusive and language-aware curriculum. As Clegg (1996) points out, "the language-rich diet of an EAL group can turn out to be nourishing for the whole mainstream class. It can help all the children use language for learning in ways which were not previously available to them" (12). We should recognize that separate provision for EAL learners impoverishes the school as a whole: it reinforces monoculturalism and monolingualism and puts the school at odds with the reality of the culturally diverse society in which it is situated. In the twenty-first century, characterized by globalization and large migrations of people, along with the many challenges and conflicts facing our planet, all children will increasingly need to navigate cultural and linguistic differences and learn to talk across cultures. The need for individuals to be cross-culturally literate extends far beyond the boundaries of school.

Though there are strong arguments for integration within the school, merely placing children in the mainstream classroom does not, of course, ensure it will actually occur or that learners will develop the academic language for learning. Content teaching that may be effective for some children is not necessarily good language teaching; at the same time, in the upper levels of the school, subject teaching may go beyond the knowledge base of language specialists. An integrated program, on the other hand, takes a functional approach to language, systematically relating it to the uses of language in the curriculum, so that curriculum topics will have both subject and specific language aims. When this occurs, the curriculum provides an authentic context for meaningful and purposeful language use. There is a range of ways in which integration has been interpreted and organized (for excellent summaries of these, see Davison and Williams 2001, 58–59). This chapter offers examples of how integration can occur. Broadly, it argues that all teaching, whatever the subject, needs to consider language outcomes alongside subject outcomes and activities. As Schleppegrell (2004) has argued: "Exploring the features of language used in schooling highlights the relationship between language and learning in ways that reveal the close connection between language and content in all school subjects" (4).

> *Merely placing children in the mainstream does not ensure that learners will develop the academic language for learning.*

INTEGRATING LANGUAGE AND SUBJECT LEARNING: WHAT DO WE NEED TO KNOW?

In this section we'll look at the language information that needs to inform all content teaching and learning. There are two sets of information that form the basis for planning an integrated program, represented by two questions:

1. What do children currently know about language, and what are their language-learning needs?
2. What are the language demands of the unit of work or topic?

The first question requires finding out about children's current language abilities. The second requires "unpacking" subject content for language—that is, finding the language that is embedded in the particular topic that children are studying. Each of these two areas is discussed below. An ideal model for EAL planning and teaching is one where a mainstream or subject teacher and an EAL specialist collaboratively plan and co-teach a program; however, the ideas that follow are equally relevant and achievable for a classroom teacher or subject teacher working alone.

What do children currently know about language, and what are their language-learning needs?

It is outside the scope of this book to address the extensive topic of assessment in depth. The approach taken here is that the most useful assessment of language for learning is that which provides information about children's mastery of the language of the classroom, in particular when it indicates the areas in which they require further scaffolding. This is better described as assessment *for* learning, rather than *of* learning, because its aim is to provide useful information about the current language development of children that in turn will feed into subsequent planning of teaching and learning. Such ongoing assessment is by its nature context-specific, so it will also indicate to the teacher the level and kind of scaffolding that is most relevant for particular tasks. Assessment-for-learning is essential information for planning any future work.

Ongoing assessment-for-learning can occur in a number of ways, some of them informal, some more analytical, and many of which you probably already use. With an assessment-for-learning orientation, most of the teaching and learning activities throughout this book can also provide informal assessment information so that assessment becomes an ongoing process. There is also good reason to argue that assessment activities should themselves be examples of worthwhile learning, and that the only valid way to assess something as complex as language development is to assess it in authentic contexts of use. All of the following can be valuable in helping build a profile of a learner's language use in authentic learning tasks:

> *Assessment activities should themselves be examples of worthwhile learning.*

- ◆ Your observation of how children work and interact with others, such as how far they make use of environmental print around the room, their level of interest in reading and writing, and how confident they are in speaking
- ◆ Your interactions with individual children, such as talking with them about how they have gone about solving a problem, listening to how

they have reasoned a math task, or discussing their understanding of what they are reading

♦ Portfolios of written work

♦ Oral presentations of what has been learned, to audiences other than the teacher, including PowerPoint presentations or short videos

♦ Ongoing reading assessments such as miscue analysis, reading conferences, children's own reading logs, teacher–student conferences, and retelling or rewriting what has been read

♦ Children's own self-assessments

♦ The outcomes of language-based tasks involving listening, reading, speaking, writing, or IT.

For EL learners in particular, it is also useful to carry out closer analyses of their spoken and written texts; this information can be very helpful not only as feedback to individual children but also for planning ongoing teaching. The section on assessment of writing in Chapter 5 (Figure 5–5) is an example of this. Because it describes how children's writing can be assessed against criteria that are specific to a particular text type, it has clear implications for follow-up work by the teacher. Many of the spoken activities described in this book can also serve as more systematic assessment tasks if they are based on explicit criterion referencing, as in Figure 5–5. Here is an example of how one of the collaborative activities could also be used as an assessment task.

Paired problem solving was described in Chapter 3. The task requires students to work in pairs to solve one of two problems (the example given in Chapter 3 was to design a paper boat that would keep a number of marbles afloat). Having come to a solution, two pairs cross-question each other about their solutions to their respective problems prior to solving the second problem themselves. If this activity were to be used as an assessment task, the aim would be to focus on the language involved in doing the task, rather than on the "best" solution to the problem. With this in mind, here are some of the criteria you may want to apply to evaluate what counts as a "successful" performance, from the perspective of language. The language is assessed as one pair of children is asking the other pair about how they solved their problem, and are then offering advice. (If possible, record children's talk; not only is it easier to assess, but it can also be replayed to children to help them reflect on their own performance.)

First, think about what this task requires children to be able to do. They need to do the following:

+ Describe their problem
+ Report their solution (use the past tense, use appropriate vocabulary, e.g., *tore, broke, fell apart, sunk, floated, flat-bottomed, pointed*)
+ Give reasons for the various solutions they have tried (e.g., *We did that because we thought . . .*)
+ Ask appropriate questions about the other pair's problem and solution (e.g., *What happened? What did you do then?*)
+ Give advice appropriately (e.g., *You could . . . Have you tried . . . -ing? Do you think you should have. . . ? Perhaps it would be better if. . . .*)
+ Acknowledge this advice (e.g., *That's a good idea. We could try that. No, I don't think that will work because. . . .*).

Used as an assessment procedure, these examples of task-related language can be translated into a set of criteria by which a learner's language can be assessed. Figure 8–1 is an example of how one child (Mario) was assessed on this task.

If a range of authentic classroom tasks are assessed against task-based criteria, even if only informally, these assessments will contribute to a profile of how learners use language for real purposes in the classroom. The assessment in Figure 8–1 indicates that Mario was able to report what he and his partner did, but did not use the range of modality by which English speakers are likely offer advice: *you could . . . it might be better if . . . maybe you should . . .* and so forth. In future tasks like this, this may be language that needs to be modeled more explicitly. And, of course, the language points identified here are also likely to relate to other contexts, too.

What are the language demands of the curriculum?

In this section the focus is not on long-term language planning but on single units of work, or topics. This is because at the topic or unit level (as opposed to long-term or year plans) it is possible to be quite specific about the language that will be encountered. Topics of work might include: Our Neighborhood; Minibeasts (insects and spiders); The Water Cycle; The First People of Australia/United States/Canada; Making a School Garden;

Criteria *Was the learner able to . . . ?*	NAME: Mario Comments
Describe the problem	Was able to do this quite clearly.
Report their solution: • Use the past tense • Use appropriate vocabulary • Give reasons for actions	Made some past-tense mistakes ("try," "putted") but meaning was clear. Vocabulary limited but showed good strategies for making meaning—"boat was not point at bottom" (flat-bottomed?). Not demonstrated.
Ask appropriate questions	Asked mainly WH questions. Question forms sometimes inaccurate—"how you did?" "why you do that?"
Offer advice appropriately	Used <u>maybe</u> throughout—"maybe you try like this." No other use of modality (e.g., you could have . . .). Overall communicated this well.
Acknowledge advice	Not demonstrated.
Other comments	Mario participated very actively in this activity—much more confident now—maybe because he felt he really had something to say. Focus: tense, question forms, modality

Figure 8–1 Example of Task Assessment: Shared Problem Solving

Although most teachers acknowledge the importance of language, it is often not explicitly planned for across the curriculum . . . it becomes the "hidden curriculum."

Symmetry and Patterning; Antarctica; Staying Healthy: Nutrition. A unit of work or a specific topic at elementary level typically lasts three to six weeks.

Most teachers think of planning for subject learning primarily in terms of subject content and subject learning, the tasks the learners will take part in, and the resources they will use. This section focuses on "unpacking" a specific unit, or topic, to determine what language children need to know in order to participate in learning in that topic.

Although most teachers acknowledge the importance of language in the classroom, it is often not explicitly planned for across the curriculum, so it becomes the "hidden curriculum" of schooling. The temptation, unless you are a language teacher, is to look "through" language to the content. Figure 8–2 provides a set of questions to help you start thinking about the language that is integral to a particular topic. The questions are intended to prompt

See Chapters 2, 3, and 4	See Chapter 7	See Chapter 6	See Chapter 5	See Chapter 8	See Chapters 3, 4, 5, 6, 8
• What spoken language activities will occur? • Are there sufficient opportunities for students to use language for learning, and to use literate spoken language?	• What listening tasks will there be? • What kinds of listening do they involve: One way or two way? Interpersonal or informational? • Are listening tasks built into the program?	• What texts will students be reading? • What are the possible cultural, conceptual, and linguistic difficulties that learners might encounter? • How will you develop learners' in-the-head knowledge prior to reading the text? • What other "bridges" to the text will be provided (e.g., during- or after-reading activities)?	• What writing tasks are there? • What is the key genre you will focus on or revisit? • What is the purpose of this genre, its overall organization, the types of connectives that are important to the genre, and the grammatical structures that are likely to occur?	• What key aspects of grammar will naturally occur (e.g., past tense, generalizations, interpersonal language for collaborative work, asking questions, language of comparison)?	• What specific vocabulary do children need to understand and use in this unit of work?

Figure 8–2 Finding the Language in the Content (based on a unit of work or topic)

you to think about your program through the "lens" of language, to help you hold language up to the light, to look *at* it rather than *through* it. The questions should help you to identify:

- the language demands (listening, speaking, reading, and writing) of the particular topic or area of study
- other opportunities for further language development, such as the inclusion of a listening activity.

Each set of questions is headed with a reference to the chapter in which the particular issues are discussed. You may wish to add other questions of your own.

Here is an example of how a classroom teacher and an EAL specialist working together identified some key language areas that would occur in a planned unit of work within the broad Social Studies area. The unit was based on a study of "Our Neighborhood" and was planned for a Year 5 class (usually the sixth year of elementary school in Australia). At the time there was a development plan for the local recreation park, part of which was to be rezoned as a car park (known in the U.S. as a *parking garage*). Because this was an area of concern for many young families in the neighborhood, and a real-life issue for the children themselves, the teachers decided that this should become a major part of the topic. Building on suggestions from the children, it was decided that they would research the issue by reading articles from the local paper, visiting the library where the development plans were on public display, and inviting key people to come to the school so that the children could listen to their views and ask questions. On the basis of this research, and their own ideas, they planned to write a class letter to the local paper identifying their concerns and suggesting recommendations. The teachers also suggested a class visit to the planned development site at the beginning of the unit. The engagement of the children in the unit created a rich context for language development in an authentic meaningful context that had relevance outside the school.

To unpack the unit of work for language, the teachers first listed the major learning activities that children would take part in, and then they "unpacked" these activities to show the language that children would need to be able to control in order to carry out those activities. Four of the activities, along with the unpacking of language, are shown in Figure 8–3. You

Major Planned Activities ⟶	Unpacking the Topic for Language
Children visit the site (local park). On return they will collaboratively recount the visit based on photographs taken.	Oral recount of the visit, using: • the past tense • time connectives: *first, next, afterward, later*
Invite key people to the school to speak about the issue from their perspective, and answer children's questions or concerns.	Formulating questions. Asking questions correctly and appropriately for this context (to a guest, someone not known by the children).
In groups, children share what has been learned and collaboratively make a list of key issues, for and against the development.	Using interpersonal language: giving opinions, expressing agreement and disagreement politely, building on others' ideas.
In groups, children will write letters to the local newspaper or articles for the school newspaper presenting opinions and making some recommendations.	Writing a persuasive argument, using: • appropriate overall structure (statement of position, arguments and supporting details, conclusion and recommendation) • appropriate connectives for presenting each argument: *first, second, in addition, therefore, in conclusion* • persuasive language showing writer's perspective (e.g., we feel *strongly* that; it is *clear* that the park is a *very important and popular* recreation area).

Figure 8–3 Unpacking the Content for Language

can see that the language section is quite detailed so that the teachers (and children) have a clear list of planned *language* outcomes for the unit of work. When looking at Figure 8–3 you may find it useful to refer also to the list of text types in Figure 5–2 and to the discussion of interpersonal language in Figure 3–5.

As the previous section suggested, teachers need to be aware of learners' language needs as part of this planning process. Among the needs identified by the teachers in this instance had been the need for more work on persuasive texts, as well as recurrent problems with aspects of sentence grammar such as the use of the past tense and questioning. As Figure 8–3 shows, the learning activities in this unit of work provide authentic and meaningful contexts for focusing on these particular language areas: there is a natural fit between learners' language-learning needs and the demands of the curriculum. Of course, there will always be areas of need that you have identified that cannot be addressed in a particular unit. Integration should not be forced! But it is important to refer to these whenever new units are being planned.

SELECTING LANGUAGE-BASED ACTIVITIES FOR THE UNIT

So far we have discussed two sets of information: (1) the ongoing language-learning needs of the learners, and (2) the language demands of the particular subject content in this unit of work. We turn now to the "how" of the teaching and learning activities—the processes of teaching and learning—and, using the unit discussed above as an example, illustrate some of the language-based tasks that scaffolded the focus language (not all are included). Note that these language-based tasks were chosen as a result of reflecting on children's needs *and* on unpacking the topic for language, so they had a clear pedagogical purpose.

The unit on the community concluded with the children writing jointly composed group letters to the editor of the local newspaper. A major language focus of the unit was therefore the writing of this letter, which was a persuasive text intended to present and argue for a particular point of view. The teacher followed the four stages of the teaching and learning cycle described in Chapter 5.

Building the field

The activities that led up to the major writing task included the site visit, a visit to the library where the plans for the proposed development were on display, the visit of a local council member to the school, and small-group discussions of the issues in class. So before they began writing, children had already gained a good knowledge of the issue. This is an essential criterion for any persuasive text if the writer is to have a "voice" that is credible and is to be taken seriously by a reader!

Modeling and deconstructing the genre

Although the text would be in the format of a letter, the body of the letter was a persuasive text that argued for a particular viewpoint, and this was the focus of this stage. It was not the first time that learners had used persuasive writing, but since it is a complex genre they still needed further scaffolding. Some of the activities are included below:

♦ The teacher reminded the children of the overall structure of the text and its key features (see Figure 5–2) using an interactive whiteboard; in this way, she was able to highlight aspects as they were discussed.

♦ Using the same texts, she focused on the structure of a paragraph. In most instances the topic sentence—often the statement of the argument itself—comes first in the paragraph, followed by supporting details, which may include personal experiences of the writer.

♦ In groups the children looked at three model examples (one of which was also a letter to an editor that the teacher had adapted), and the teacher drew their attention again to the overall "shape" of the text.

♦ Using different-colored highlighters, the children highlighted each section of the text (yellow for the introduction, blue for the conclusion and recommendation, yellow for each of the arguments, and red for the connecting words). They were also asked to highlight the first draft of their own writing in the same way, to help them check that their writing was appropriately structured.

♦ As a whole class they completed a Monster Cloze (see Chapter 6) using the first sentence of a persuasive text.

Joint construction

Together the teacher and children constructed a similar text to one they would later write. Since all the children wanted to keep the park untouched, the teacher suggested to them that this time they take the opposing view and think of reasons for the development to proceed.

Independent writing

This was completed in groups, with support from the teacher and peers. The children also had a self-assessment sheet (see Figure 5–7). Each group used this to reflect on their own writing. They also read what one other group had written and gave them feedback in the same way.

SUMMARIZING AND DOCUMENTING SUBJECT AND LANGUAGE OUTCOMES

The previous section discussed a possible process for making decisions about what language to include in an integrated unit, and it gave examples of the language and some of the activities used in one unit. In this section we look at how the outcomes of this planning process can be summarized and documented along with the subject outcomes.

Different countries and different states suggest, or require, a range of aspects of teaching and learning to be taken into account. At various times in the history of curriculum development, there has been a range of terms used to indicate educational intent. These have included aims, learning objectives, learning outcomes, levels, indicators, pointers, benchmarks, and standards (Brady and Kennedy 2014). In the United States, at the time of writing, the Common Core State Standards have generated debate among educators who are seeking ways to incorporate them into their planning, and in Australia a new National Curriculum is currently being introduced. More broadly, many curriculum documents, such as the new Australian National Curriculum, also now refer explicitly to aspects of subject-based literacy. And there is now an increasing recognition that children who don't come to school already speaking the major language of instruction do not thrive if they are treated as mother tongue speakers of that language. Consequently, there is an increasing acknowledgment that any teaching program needs to take account of this, and, as this book has argued, for all teachers to see themselves as teachers of language and literacy. In addition, individual schools or faculties often have their own preferred format for planning and programming.

Faced with a barrage of demands from both external and internal sources on what needs to be considered and documented in a teaching program (even before the teacher has set foot in the classroom), some teachers have suggested that this aspect of their work takes time away from planning what goes on in the actual day-to-day life of the classroom. Including a language perspective in all teaching, however, as this book has suggested, should not be an added burden. Nor should it be seen as something more to "cover" in an already crowded curriculum. Effective EAL teaching is not the icing on the cake, but the ingredients of it! It represents a particular way of thinking about teaching and learning and, in particular, the relationship between language and content learning.

Figures 8–4 and 8–7 are examples of a concise way of documenting an integrated program. Outcomes for both are brought together in a single table. Again, not all the language that *may* occur has been included. What is shown here is the language that is *essential* to an understanding of the content and the key concepts. The example provides a way to document planned integration. A similar page can be easily added at the beginning of every unit of work, regardless of what other planning format is used or required.

The topic of the first example in Figure 8–4 is common insects and spiders (called "Minibeasts" here). It included a study of the kinds of insects that live in the area, their descriptions and habits, their life cycles, how they differ from spiders, and their impact on humans. Sydney is home to a particularly dangerous spider (the funnel-web spider), so the unit included advice about how to avoid getting bitten!

> *Effective EAL teaching is not the icing on the cake, but the ingredients of it!*

Science Activities and Outcomes	Language Outcomes
Students will: • research some common insects in order to understand what all insects have in common, how insects change at different points in their lives (life cycles), and how they impact on other living things, including people • compare the differences between spiders and insects • study some of the spiders that are found in gardens and people's homes • know how to avoid getting bitten • produce an information report on an insect or spider that they choose.	Students will: • make generalizations (*All insects have . . .* , *Insects are . . .* , *Spiders have . . .*) • describe the appearance of some insects and spiders using appropriate specialist vocabulary (*head*, *thorax*, *abdomen*, *wings*, *antennae*) • explain how to avoid getting bitten (imperative: *don't put your fingers in holes in the garden*, *don't poke a spider with a stick*) • write an information report using an appropriate overall structure (e.g., headings and subheadings such as *appearance*, *habitat*, *food*, *life cycle*, and *other interesting facts*) • use time connectives for describing the sequence of a life cycle (e.g., *first*, *two weeks later*, *after this*, *finally*).

Figure 8–4 "Minibeasts" Integrated Unit

The topic of the second example in Figure 8–7 is health and nutrition. As in the unit on the local community, this topic also encouraged a critical and reflective perspective on the material the students were studying. The unit included a major focus on healthy eating and on how to choose a range of foods that represented the major food groups: grains, fruits and vegetables, proteins, dairy products, and "sweets and treats." Given the multicultural nature of the class, the teacher began by having the children identify the food they ate regularly at home, and on one day parents brought in a range of foods for children to share and enjoy. After this shared meal, the teacher introduced the notion of the "Food Pyramid" and the children decided where their favorite foods would belong (see Figure 8–5).

The teacher encouraged the students to value and celebrate the cultural differences represented by the range of cuisines, and this led to the children suggesting they should make a class recipe book. But at the same time the teacher drew children's attention to the fact that, while different groups may eat different foods, all humans have in common a need for healthy and sufficient food. She particularly wanted students to become aware of some of the global issues surrounding child poverty and nutrition in a number of developing countries. Later in the unit they looked again at a Food Pyramid diagram,

Figure 8–5 Dietary Range of Foods Eaten by Children in Australia

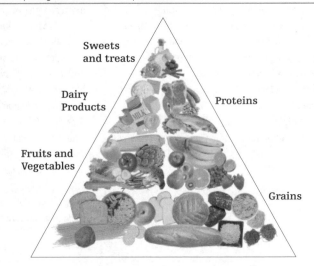

this time completed to show the actual diet of one child living in poverty in Timor-Leste (Figure 8–6). This version of the food pyramid was adapted from material produced as part of a campaign to raise money to support the work of Care Australia, an Australian humanitarian aid organization fighting global poverty and supporting the education of women and girls. The children discussed the major differences between the two diagrams and talked about how they felt when they looked at them.

This critical dimension to the topic meant that the unit of work related not simply to the children's own local experiences but to global issues and was a powerful way to bring an alternative perspective on issues that affected children of their own age. One of the "big ideas" of the unit of work was the notion of similarity and difference: all people have the same nutritional needs regardless of where they come from, but they meet them in different ways. Some food is healthy, some is much less healthy, especially processed and refined food. People in wealthier countries generally have sufficient food, those in very poor countries often do not; not all difference is because of choice. These ideas are reflected in the language outcomes (comparing and contrasting). This is significant language that represents the big ideas and concepts that are the enduring learning that will remain significant

Figure 8–6 Manuel's Dietary Range (adapted from material from Care Australia)

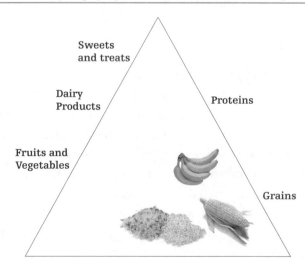

Health Activities and Outcomes	Language Outcomes
Students will: • learn how culture and climate shape what we eat • share some international food • learn about and show respect for cultural differences in food choices • understand that a need for good nutrition is important for everyone (Health Pyramid 1) • write a recipe for healthy food • understand that not everyone in the world has enough to eat (Health Pyramid 2) and express how they feel about this • prepare a PowerPoint presentation about nutrition for use with a Year 1 class (ICT).	• Key vocabulary: *grains, fruits, and vegetables, proteins, dairy products,* "sweets and treats," *processed, fresh* • Writing a recipe (Procedure) • Connectives for comparing (saying what's the same): *similarly, in the same way, the same as* • Connectives for contrasting (saying what's different: healthy and unhealthy food; different cultural choices; adequate and inadequate diets): *however, on the other hand, but, whereas* • Expression of personal reactions: *sad, upset, guilty, surprised, shocked,* etc. • Oral presentation skills.

Figure 8–7 Nutrition Integrated Unit

beyond the particular topic. Figure 8–7 shows the content and language integration of this unit.

LEARNING ABOUT LANGUAGE

Focusing on form

The final section of this chapter addresses a question that has concerned many teachers: how to focus on sentence grammar in a meaning-based approach to language teaching. In particular, certain aspects of English seem to be a recurring problem for some children, especially when they write, regardless of what their first language is. Teachers typically mention issues such as tense and the expression of time, articles, subject–verb agreement, and word order, and they note that these children make the same errors over many years no matter how much they are pointed out or corrected. In this context, even teachers who are committed to teaching language in ways that recognize its wholeness, and see it as a system for making meaning, may ask themselves, "Should we still teach 'grammar'?"

My own response to this is that it depends on what kind of grammar, and the context in which it occurs. Isolated language exercises *unrelated* to any other learning that's going on are not likely to be very helpful in addressing actual language use. Many years ago, in my own early days of language teaching, language was taught according to strict behaviorist principles that emphasized decontextualized repetition and drills, such as oral and written exercises that focused on tense forms, the use of prepositions, or the transformation of active into passive sentences or present into past. Most learners were able to complete these with a high level of accuracy. Yet these same learners very frequently failed to use them accurately (or avoided using them at all) in actual contexts of language use, when they were trying to say or write something meaningful. Depending on the approach taken, many of us may have had the same experience in our own learning of foreign languages. The reason may be that such learning remains "inert." It is only when we make *use* of a new piece of language that it becomes a resource for use in other contexts, and for the meanings that learners themselves need or want to convey. This is what is sometimes broadly referred to as "uptake" in second language-learning research. The learners' "agency" in this second context, their personal involvement in meaning making, is much less likely to be present in the first example.

But as this book has made clear, and as Michael Halliday's words at the beginning of the chapter suggest, there is certainly a place for children to learn *about* language, as well as learning how to *use* language and learning other subjects *through* language. To do this successfully learners should have at their disposal enough meta-language (language about language) that enables them to talk about it, and so that both they and the teacher are able to refer to specific aspects of language, especially written language (Chapter 5). This kind of talk is of considerable importance in developing metacognitive understandings about language and its use (Shleppegrell 2012, 2013; Derewianka 2011; Williams 1999). These understandings enable learners to take language "off the page" and hold it up for inspection. Most children who speak more than one language probably have an advantage here, since they are likely to have a greater awareness of the nature of language than monolingual children (Cummins 2000; Hornberger and Link 2012).

Many activities described in this book provide contexts for talking about language as well as focusing on grammatical accuracy. Among these are

Stages 2 and 3 of the Teaching and Learning Cycle, which focus on the modeling of a genre and discussion of its language features and a jointly constructed piece of writing where there is talk about language in the context of actual language use. Chapter 6 also suggested some principles that illustrate how there can be a focus on form, by moving from whole (the whole text) to part (which can include a particular aspect of grammar). Dictogloss, picture prompts, cloze activities, split dictations, and after-reading activities drawn from the text can all be tailored to focus on particular aspects of sentence grammar and accuracy.

For those who appreciate metaphor, here is one to represent how a study of language form can sit comfortably in a meaning-based approach to language teaching and learning. Imagine yourself standing on a hillside looking out across a panoramic view with a pair of binoculars in your hand. In front of you are fields, mountains, and forests. In the far distance, you can glimpse the sea and a boat. Your first gaze is at the whole vista ahead of you, the overall view from where you are standing. But, after a while, you use your binoculars to focus in on a particular part of the view, to home in on one detail of the landscape. You know how to locate this detail, where to train your binoculars, because you have already seen it as a part of the whole. When you have finished focusing on these details you will probably savor the whole panorama again, but this time with an enhanced sense of what is there. In this scenario, what you would not do is go up the hill with your eyes closed and look through the binoculars before you have looked at the view and located an area to focus on. If you did this, you wouldn't really know what you were looking at or where it belonged!

Looking at an isolated piece of language without its context is a bit like this. Not knowing why you are using the language, and having no sense of the social context in which it might be used, is like looking at a close-up of the view through binoculars before you know what you are looking at. In the same way, while your overall aim as a teacher will be to construct knowledge and develop understandings about the topic, and to use language meaningfully and purposefully, it does not prevent you, in the course of the topic, from at some point "training the binoculars" by helping your students focus "close up" on a detail of language. This may be a point of grammar, a spelling pattern, a group of meaning-related connectives and conjunctions, or the schematic structure of a particular genre. You may wish to spend some time on this "close-up view," but while you are doing so both you and the students know where these "parts" fit into the "whole," and how the focus on form is related to the meanings being made. Approaching the teaching of forms and parts in this way puts grammar, spelling, punctuation, and phonic and alpha-betic knowledge where they belong: as worthy objects of study in the service of meaning making and learning.

Figure 8–8 illustrates the relationship between learning language, learning through language, and learning about language. The "hourglass" illustrates how the focus of teaching and learning changes throughout the teaching of a

Figure 8–8 Focusing on Language as "Object"

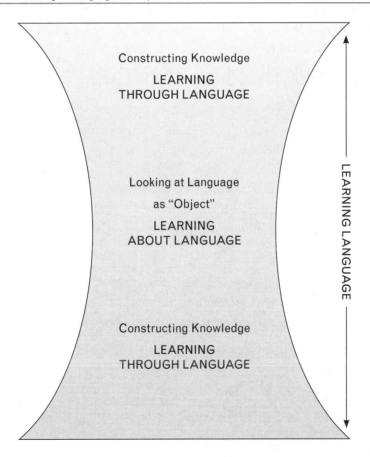

Constructing Knowledge

**LEARNING
THROUGH LANGUAGE**

Looking at Language

as "Object"

**LEARNING
ABOUT LANGUAGE**

Constructing Knowledge

**LEARNING
THROUGH LANGUAGE**

LEARNING LANGUAGE

topic, with the narrowing of the hourglass representing a focus on language it-self. Teaching and learning activities move at times from learning *through* language, to learning *about* language, to once more learning *through* language. In other words, teaching progresses from meaning to form, from whole to part, and back again. The focus on "language as object" is in the context of the overall meanings being made and the curriculum knowledge being constructed.

Creating mindful language users

Children's language development in school can also be strengthened by helping them become mindful of their own language use, so that they become able to reflect on and take responsibility for how they use language. This is the purpose of the self-assessment sheet on writing discussed in Chapter 5. This is, of course, what successful writers do: they are mindful of *how* they are writing. Helping children to be mindful in this way will also help them to avoid the kinds of recurrent inaccuracies in their language use that were discussed earlier. There are a number of ways that this mindfulness can be encouraged:

- Have children use a self-reflection sheet regularly while they are writing and to help them self-edit their writing afterward (see Figure 5–7).
- Encourage children to comment on their own editing (Figure 5–7).
- When conferencing with children or correcting their work, give specific feedback about one thing you would like them to do the next time they write:

   This is a great story. You've got a very interesting orientation and I like the resolution. But the next time you write a narrative try and focus especially on how you use the past tense.

- Get students to highlight, in their individual writing, any aspects you have been focusing on during the teaching and learning cycle, for example: *Highlight all the words you have used to connect your ideas, highlight the topic sentence in each paragraph, highlight your supporting arguments.* This will help you to see how well they recognize and are able to use the language, but also remind them of key language points relevant to the writing they are doing. You can personalize this for individual learners by making connections with their previous writing, for example, by asking them to highlight all the past tenses they have used in a narrative. Highlighting should occur before learners conference with you or hand in their writing. It is easy to do if students are using a computer, or they can use a regular highlighter.

> *Very effective speakers and writers reflect on how they use language.*

Of course, we do not want to make students unwilling to use language for fear of making an error, and certainly not every teaching and learning context is one that should, or needs, to be focused in this way! But very effective speakers and writers do reflect on how they use language, and for some contexts, such as in writing for an audience or in oral presentations, language needs to be mindfully constructed. Developing mindful language users is an important step in helping students develop autonomy and control over their language in ways that make them more powerful speakers and writers in school and beyond.

In Summary

In this chapter, we have looked at a number of reasons for supporting the integration of EL learners into the mainstream class and what this means in practice:

- Language is best learned through meaningful use in a variety of contexts, and the whole curriculum can be viewed as a resource for language development.
- An integrated curriculum takes into account both the language-learning needs of the learners and the key language that is required to learn subject content.

- All units of work, or topics, should be "unpacked" for language and clearly relate subject activities and outcomes to language outcomes.
- In an integrated unit, children will learn language, learn through language, and learn about language.
- The "language-rich diet" of EL teaching benefits all students and supports all children in using new language in ways that are central to academic learning.

A Final Word

The potential for learning is not finite or bounded. And the potential for learning in school should not be restricted by a learner's lack of knowledge of the language of instruction, because this would deny EL learners their right to be full members of the school community. They should not be expected to prove themselves linguistically before they can claim this right. The responsibility for their second language development belongs to the school and to their teachers.

Regardless of the educational constraints that impact both teachers and students, sometimes imposed by government policies or education systems, it is critical that *individual* teachers remember that they can and do make a difference to children's lives. The notion of scaffolding has been a recurrent theme throughout this book. It represents an approach to teaching and learning whereby individual teachers can maintain high expectations of their students and reject the inequality of an alternative or watered-down curriculum, or a curriculum that, for reasons of language, students are unable to access. Teachers who hold these beliefs are likely in their own practice to:

- Link to, and build on, what children bring to school: their language, culture, understandings, and experiences
- Provide the kind of support, or scaffolding, that is responsive both to the particular language development needs of second language learners and to the language demands of the mainstream curriculum
- Hand over to students the responsibility to use what they have learned independently, in new contexts and for their own purposes, and encourage them to do this

♦ And, echoing the story of the choir in Chapter 1, create classroom cultures that are futures-oriented, where children are treated as the people they can become.

We know that some students begin their school life with less of what Delpit (1988) has referred to as "the accoutrements of the culture of power" than other students. Some critical theorists refer to this as "cultural capital," and part of that cultural capital is the ability to control the spoken and written codes of the dominant society. As we have discussed, it would be wrong to assume that children who are not fluent in these codes will automatically acquire them through the process of being in school without specific kinds of support. In the words of Julianna, with which this book began, EL learners need to be able to use English not only for day-to-day purposes but "for school work and strangers"—for academic learning and ultimately for negotiating their place in the wider society. This book has suggested some ways in which schools and individual teachers can help make this happen.

> *Individual teachers can and do make a difference to children's lives.*

To Think About

1. If you already integrate subject content and language, what advice would you give to a classroom or subject teacher wanting to do the same? If you don't currently use an integrated approach in your school, how could you apply some of the suggestions in this chapter to your own situation?

2. What do you think the implications are of a whole-school integrated approach for those in senior leadership positions in a school?

3. Do you agree that it is important to develop learners' "mindfulness" about language? How can mindfulness be encouraged?

4. The final section of the chapter lists four overarching practices that are significant for EL learners. There are, of course, many others. What would you add to this that reflects your own personal belief about teaching EL learners?

5. In what ways has this book affirmed your current practices? What has been the most important learning for you?

Suggestions for Further Reading

Cummins, J. 2000. Chapter 10, "Transformative Pedagogy: Who Needs It?" In *Language, Power, and Pedagogy: Bilingual Children in the Crossfire*, ed. J. Cummins. Clevedon, UK: Multilingual Matters.

Davison, C., and A. Williams. 2001. "Integrating Language and Content: Unresolved Issues." In *English as a Second Language in the Mainstream: Teaching Learning and Identity*, ed. B. Mohan, C. Leung, and C. Davison. London: Longman.

Gibbons, P. 2009. Chapter 8, "Planning for a High-Challenge, High-Support Classroom: Setting Up EL Learners for Success." In *English Learners, Academic Literacy, and Thinking*. Portsmouth, NH: Heinemann.

Houk, F. 2005. *Supporting English Language Learners: A Guide for Teachers and Administrators*. Portsmouth, NH: Heinemann.

Walqui, A., and L. van Lier. 2010. Chapter 6. In *Scaffolding the Academic Success of Adolescent English Language Learners: A Pedagogy of Promise*. San Francisco: WestEd.

Glossary of Teaching Activities

Note: Where activities are described fully in the chapters, only a brief description is given here.

After-Reading Activities   These activities include the following: Story Innovation, Readers Theatre, Story Map, Time Lines, Hot Seat, Freeze Frames, Cloze, Monster Cloze, Vanishing Cloze, Text Reconstruction, True/False Questions, Story Innovation, "Key-Ring" Words, and Questioning the Text. See Chapter 6.

Alphabet Book   This is to develop early alphabetic knowledge. See Chapter 6.

Aural Cloze   This is a cloze exercise that focuses on listening skills. See Chapter 7.

Barrier Games   Barrier games are usually played in pairs, and involve solving a problem of some sort. Each player has different information that they both need if they are to solve the problem. See Chapters 3 and 5.

Before-Reading Activities   These activities include the following: predicting from a visual; predicting the main ideas; predicting from the title, first sentence or key words; sequencing illustrations or diagrams; reader questions; storytelling in the mother tongue. See Chapter 6.

Cloze   Cloze activities are pieces of text with some words deleted. See Chapters 5 and 6.

Describe and Draw   This is a barrier game in which each child in a pair takes it in turns to describe something he or she is drawing, or has drawn. His or her partner then has to draw the same thing. See Chapter 3.

Dialogue Letter/Dialogue Journal   As the name suggests, this is a conversation that is written down. It may be between the student and teacher, or between an EL learner and an English-speaking buddy. Figure G–1 is an example. Note how the teacher's models are taken up by Mario. See Chapter 5.

Dictogloss   This is a technique adapted from Ruth Wajnryb (1990) designed to develop listening skills, and integrating this with note-taking, speaking, reading, and writing. See Chapters 5 and 7.

Donut Circles   In two concentric circles with equal numbers, children face each other and have a short conversation. One circle then moves on and the process is repeated. See Chapter 3.

During-Reading Activities   These activities include the following: modeled reading; pause and predict; shadow reading (in addition, see Chapter 7); noticing visual layout and text features; skimming and scan-

Figure G–1 Dialogue Journal

What did you do yesterday, Mario?

I go buk beets.

What did you do at the beach?

at the beach I swimmin.

Do you like swimming?

YES I like

Do you like a swimming

Yes I enjoy it very much, Mario!

ning the text; rereading for detail; thinking tracks; shared book; word masking; summarizing the text; jigsaw reading. See Chapter 6.

Find My Partner   This is played with five or six children who each have a picture card that differs from others only in small details. They do not show their cards. Two cards are identical, and one is marked by a cross. Through questioning, this child must find the other identical picture. See Chapter 3.

Find the Difference   In this barrier game pairs of students have two similar but not identical pictures. Through questioning and describing they must collaboratively find the differences. See Chapter 3.

Hands Up!   Students have a set of questions based on a text. The text is read aloud, and as students hear the information that answers a question, they raise their hands. See Chapter 7.

Hot Seat   This is a role-play activity that can involve the whole class. One student takes on a character role, and the remainder of the class asks questions about his or her life. See Chapters 3 and 6.

I'm Thinking of . . .   In a small group each person chooses an object to describe from a set of pictures related to a topic being studied. Other students guess what is being described. See Chapter 3.

If You Are . . .   This listening activity requires students to follow different instructions depending on other information that relates to them. See Chapter 7.

Information Grid   This is an information transfer activity whereby information in a text is represented in another way. It requires students to pick out main points from an information text and is a good resource for research and later writing. See Figure G–2 and Chapter 5.

Inquiry and Elimination   This activity helps develop reasoning skills and practices question forms. See Chapter 3.

Dinosaur	When It Lived	What It Looked Like	What It Ate	Other Features and Interesting Facts
Ankylosaurus	70 million years ago	Big and heavy. Bony plates on its head, neck, and a club at the end of the tail.	Only plants	As big and heavy as a tank
Stegosaurus		Plates on its back–one or two rows but we're not sure. Bony spikes on its tail.		Plates were to control its temperature. Called the stupidest dinosaur because its brain was only the size of a walnut!
Tyrannosaurus	100 million years ago	Very short arms. They couldn't reach its mouth.	Meat	Very fierce
Diplodocus		Very long. Long neck.		The longest dinosaur, as long as 7 cars or 16 people. Lived in North America.

Figure G–2 Information Grid

Jazz Chants and Raps   These focus attention on the rhythms, stress and intonation patterns of English. See Chapter 7.

Jigsaw Groups   This is a form of grouping where each group of children become "experts" in one aspect of a topic, with different groups becoming experts in different aspects of the topic. Then they regroup and share this information in the new group (their "home" group), where each member has become an expert on a different aspect of the topic. See Chapter 3.

Joint Construction   This activity is an important part of the teaching and learning cycle that models both the product and process of writing. Teacher and students write the text collaboratively (in the focus genre).

The teacher scribes while the students contribute ideas, with the teacher leading the process and acting as "editor" when needed. See Chapter 5.

Jumbled Sentences   This activity helps early learners to understand how sentences are structured by focusing attention on meaningful chunks, and individual words, in a sentence. It can also serve as a scaffold for emergent writing. See Chapter 5.

Key-Ring Words   These are students' own visual representations of key concept words, drawn on small cards and fixed on a key ring. If the word is known in another language, they may also write this, or an explanation, on the back of the card. See Chapter 6.

Listening for Information   This listening activity develops students' skills in listening for key information. See Chapter 7.

Map Games   These are barrier games using two incomplete maps with different information that must be completed through questioning. Alternatively, students may use two completed maps and give each other directions, with one student not being aware of the destination. See Chapter 7.

Matching Game (Listening)   In this listening activity students must match a number of pictures to descriptions that are read aloud. See Chapter 7.

Memory Reading Game   This memory game is designed to support word recognition skills. See Chapter 6.

Mind Map   This is a way of collecting and organizing information, often carried out initially as a brainstorm, with students recalling what they already know about a subject and the words and concepts they associate with the key word. In this case these ideas will often reflect very different categories and levels of generalization. So, after the initial brainstorm these random associations can be reorganized and classified by the teacher and students together. Sticky notes can be used to record the suggestions so that ideas can be more easily moved around. As the topic progresses, new categories, subcategories, and information are added. See Chapter 5.

Minimal Pair Exercises   These are designed to help children hear the differences between the phonemes of English. See Chapter 7.

Monster Cloze   This variation of a traditional cloze is a whole-class activity where only the *title* of the passage is written on the board. It involves prediction and vocabulary knowledge. See Chapters 5 and 6.

Opinion Clines   This activity requires students to physically place themselves along a continuum depending on whether they agree or disagree with a contentious statement. In this process they interact with others to decide where they stand relative to others' opinions. See Chapter 3.

Paired Problem Solving   Two pairs solve different problems, and later each pair explains to the other how they solved it. The listeners give advice and later solve the other pair's problem. See Chapter 3.

Picture Dictation   In this listening activity students have a number of individual pictures corresponding to a narrative, sequence of events, or procedure. The text is read aloud, and as they listen, students sequence the pictures. See Chapter 7.

Picture Prompts   This is similar to Dictogloss, but with an extra drawing stage before the initial individual writing stage. See Chapter 7.

Picture Sequencing   Use a set of pictures that tell a simple story, or that illustrate a sequence such as the life cycle of an insect. In groups of five or six (corresponding to how many cards there are) children in turn each describe their card, without showing it. On the basis of the descriptions, the group decides on the correct sequence for the cards, which are then laid down. See Chapter 3.

Problem Solving Groups of children solve a problem through discussion and then report back to the class about their solutions. See Chapter 3.

Progressive Brainstorm This is a brainstorming activity involving groups writing down their ideas about a topic on a large sheet of paper. After a set time they move on, adding or responding to the ideas of the next group. The papers stay in the same position throughout the activity, but each group is identified with a different-colored pen. See Chapter 3.

Progressive Words This is a variation on the Progressive Brainstorm where children list words that have the same spelling pattern *and* pronunciation. Each paper has a model of a word that illustrates the spelling pattern. See Chapter 6.

Running Dictation This is a team game that can be a very noisy activity! Students should be in teams of about six. Before you begin, write a short text on a large sheet of paper, starting each sentence on a new line. Place the text on a wall somewhere outside the classroom (e.g., in a corridor outside the room). The first member of each team runs out of the class to the text and reads (and tries to remember) the first sentence. He or she runs back into the class and dictates it to his or her team, who write it down. When they have finished, the second member of the team runs out, reads and memorizes the second sentence, returns, and dictates it. This continues until a team has completed the text. If a member forgets the sentence on the way back (this happens often!), he or she can go back and read it again, but of course time is lost if they do this. Point out to students that they should try to think about the meaning of their sentence—simply trying to memorize a sentence as a string of words is much harder than remembering something meaningful. However, make sure that you use a text that is within your students' capabilities to understand, and one connected with a topic the children are studying. See Chapter 5.

Say It Again This is a listening activity in which students "shadow" a character in a video. It provides practice in pronunciation, stress, and intonation. See Chapter 7.

Shadow Reading   Children first follow and then "read along" with the teacher. They try to follow the pronunciation, stress patterns, and intonation patterns as closely as possible. This is a useful "rehearsal" if children are later going to read aloud, for example, in readers' theatre. See Chapters 6 and 7.

Sound Stories   This is a listening activity in which children find a connection between several sounds. See Chapter 7.

Split Dictation   This is a listening activity in which pairs of students each have part of a text. By dictating the parts they have to their partner, each student completes the text by filling in what is missing. See Chapter 7.

Spot the Difference   This activity is aimed at developing students' skills in listening for information. See Chapter 7.

Story Map   This is a visual representation, drawn by the children, of the characters and events of a story. It can prompt learners if they are retelling a story. Alternatively, before they write their own Narrative, they can draw a story map to organize the overall structure and main ideas See Chapters 5 and 6.

Talking Points   This activity is based on a statement, or list of statements, that relate to a topic, and that are factually correct or incorrect, or contentious. It stimulates interaction, thinking, and learning. See Chapter 3.

Teacher-Guided Reporting   As a child retells about something he or she has learned or discovered, the teacher provides scaffolding to support the child's retelling. This includes prompting, asking for clarification, recasting, or questioning. See Chapters 2 and 4.

Text Reconstruction   Students reconstruct a text that has been cut up into sentences or paragraphs. They should be able to explain the sequence they have chosen. This is a good activity for focusing on the cohesive links across sentences, such as pronoun reference and conjunctions. See Chapters 5 and 6.

Thinking Tracks   This is a during-reading activity where children note key points as they read. See Chapter 6.

Thumbs Up Thumbs Down   This activity develops phonemic awareness. See Chapter 6.

Vanishing Cloze   This is a cloze variation in which words are gradually removed one by one from a very short text. On each occasion, children read the text aloud, each time replacing the missing words. See Chapters 5 and 6.

Wallpaper Activity   This is a brainstorm activity. Give students sticky notes to write down one thing they know about a topic, or one idea they have about a controversial issue. Place the sticky notes on the walls of the classroom. Students walk round and read other students' ideas. Later they can comment on the ideas of others: *I agree with the one that said . . . I didn't know that . . . I don't think that's right.* See Chapter 5.

What Can You Hear?   This is a listening activity designed to introduce students to focused listening. See Chapter 7.

What Did You See?   This activity for beginner EL learners practices vocabulary, usually related to a topic. See Chapter 3.

What Sounds Can You Hear?   This activity develops phonemic awareness and phonic knowledge. See Chapter 6.

What Word Is This?   This activity develops phonemic awareness skills for emergent readers and writers, or those new to English. See Chapter 6.

Word Wall/Word Bank   This is a display of words that are relevant to a particular topic or text type. They are organized according to types of meanings (see Figure G–3). Other examples could be ways of describing size (*huge, enormous, gigantic, large*) or feelings (*happy, delighted, joyful*). In the example in G–3, words that are likely to appear in the same genre are listed together (connectives for Narrative and "saying" verbs for introducing dialogue in Narrative). See Chapter 5.

Writing Framework   This provides additional scaffolding for those learners who require it in the final Individual Writing stage of the Teaching and Learning Cycle. See Chapter 5.

Figure G–3 Word Wall

CONNECTIVES FOR DISCUSSION WRITING

First	On the other hand
Second	However
Also	Nevertheless
In addition	Therefore

CONNECTIVES FOR NARRATIVES

One day	The following morning
After	In the end
A week later	Finally
Later on	At last

"SAYING VERBS" FOR NARRATIVES

said	cried
explained	yelled
shouted	whispered
growled	replied

References

Adams, M. 1990. *Beginning to Read: Reading and Thinking About Print*. Cambridge, MA: MIT Press.

Alexander, R. 2008. *Towards Dialogic Teaching: Rethinking Classroom Talk*. 4th ed. North Yorkshire, UK: Dialogos.

Allington, R. 2009. "If they don't read much . . . 30 years later." In *Reading More, Reading Better*, ed. E. H. Hiebert, 30–54. New York: Guilford.

Ball, T., and G. Wells. 2009. "Running Cars Down Ramps: Learning About Learning Over Time." *Language and Education* 23 (4): 371–90.

Barnes, D. 1976. *From Communication to Curriculum*. Harmondsworth, UK: Penguin.

Baynham, M. 1993. "Literacy in TESOL and ABE: Exploring Common Themes." *Open Letter* 2 (2): 4–16.

Brady, L. 2006. *Collaborative Learning in Action*. Frenchs Forest, NSW, AU: Pearson Education Australia.

Brady, L., and K. Kennedy. 2014. *Curriculum Construction*. Frenchs Forest, NSW, AU: Pearson.

Bruner, J. 1978. "The Role of Dialogue in Language Acquisition." In *The Child's Conception of Language*, ed. A. Sinclair, R. Jarvella, and W. Levelt. New York: Springer-Verlag.

Carrasquillo, A., S. Kucer, and R. Adams. 2004. *Beyond the Beginnings: Literacy Interventions for Upper Elementary English Language Learners*. Clevedon, UK: Multilingual Matters.

Chang, G., and G. Wells. 1988. "The Literate Potential of Collaborative Talk." In *Oracy Matters*, ed. M. Maclure, T. Phillips, and A. Wilkinson. Milton Keynes, UK: Open University Press.

Chen, L., and E. Mora-Flores. 2006. *Balanced Literacy for English Language Learners, K–2*. Portsmouth, NH: Heinemann.

243

Christie, F. 1990. "The Changing Face of Literacy." In *Literacy for a Changing World*, ed. F. Christie. Hawthorn, Victoria, AU: ACER.

Clegg, J., ed. 1996. *Mainstreaming ESL: Case Studies in Integrating ESL Students into the Mainstream Curriculum.* Clevedon, UK: Multilingual Matters.

Cloud, N., N. Genessee, and E. Hamayan. 2000. *Dual Language Instruction: A Handbook for Enriched Education.* Boston: Heinle and Heinle.

Collier, V. 1995. "Acquiring a Second Language for School." *Directions in Language and Education. National Clearing House of Bilingual Education* 1 (4): entire issue.

Collier, V., and W. Thomas. 1997. *School Effectiveness for Language Minority Students.* Washington, DC: National Clearinghouse for Bilingual Education.

Cummins, J. 2000. *Language, Power and Pedagogy: Bilingual Children in the Crossfire.* Clevedon, UK: Multilingual Matters.

———. 2003. "Reading and the Bilingual Student: Fact and Fiction." In *English Learners: Reaching the Highest Level of English Literacy*, ed. G. Garcia. Newark, DE: International Reading Association.

Davison, C., and A. Williams. 2001. "Integrating Language and Content: Unresolved Issues." In *English as a Second Language in the Mainstream: Teaching, Learning and Identity*, ed. B. Mohan, C. Leung, and C. Davison. Harlow, UK: Longman.

Dawes, L. 2008. *The Essential Speaking and Listening: Talk for Learning at Key Stage 2.* London: Routledge.

Delpit, L. 1988. "The Silenced Dialogue: Power and Pedagogy in Educating Other People's Children." *Harvard Educational Review* 58 (3): 280–98.

Derewianka, B. 1990. *Exploring How Texts Work.* Sydney: Primary English Teaching Association of Australia. Reprinted 1991. Portsmouth, NH: Heinemann.

———. 2011. *A New Grammar Companion for Teachers.* Sydney: Primary English Teaching Association of Australia.

Des-Fountain, J., and A. Howe. 1992. "Pupils Working Together on Understanding." In *Thinking Voices: The Work of the National Literacy Project*, ed. K. Norman. London: Hodder and Stoughton.

Driver, R. 1983. *The Pupil as Scientist?* Milton Keynes, UK: Open University Press.

Echevarria, J., and M. Vogt. 2011. *Response to Intervention (RTI) and English Learners: Making It Happen.* Boston: Pearson Education.

Elley, W. 1984. "Exploring the Reading Difficulties of Second-Language Readers in Fiji." In *Reading in a Foreign Language,* ed. C. Alderson and A. Urquhart. London: Longman.

Fountas, I. 2005. *Guided Reading: Essential Elements.* Portsmouth, NH: Heinemann.

Garcia, O. 2009. *Bilingual Education in the 21st Century: A Global Perspective.* West Sussex, UK: Wiley-Blackwell.

Genesee, F., K. Lindholm-Leary, B. Saunders, and D. Christian. 2006. *Educating English Language Learners: A Synthesis of Research Evidence.* New York: Cambridge University Press.

Gibbons, P. 2001. "Learning a New Register in a Second Language." In *English Language Teaching in Its Social Context,* ed. C. Candlin and N. Mercer. New York: Routledge.

———. 2003. "Mediating Language Learning: Teacher Interactions with ESL Students in a Content-Based Classroom." *TESOL Quarterly* 32 (2): 247–73.

———. 2008. " 'It Was Taught Good and I Learned a Lot': Intellectual Practices and ESL Learners in the Middle Years." *Australian Journal of Language and Literacy* 31 (2): 155–73.

———. 2009. *English Learners, Academic Literacy, and Thinking: Learning in the Challenge Zone.* Portsmouth, NH: Heinemann

———. 2012. "Scaffolding Academic Language and Literacy with School-Aged English Language Learners." *The European Journal of Applied Linguistics and TEFL* (2): 51–64.

———. 2013. "Scaffolding." In *The Encyclopedia of Second Language Acquisition,* ed. P. Robinson, 563–64. New York: Taylor and French/Routledge.

Goh, C. 2006. "Metacognitive Instruction in Listening for Young Learners." *ELT Journal* 60 (3): 222–32.

Goodman, K. 1967. "Reading: A Psycholinguistic Guessing Game." In *Language and Literacy: The Collected Writing of Kenneth S. Goodman. Vol. 1: Process, Theory, Research,* ed. E. Gollasch. London: Routledge.

Graves, D. 2003. *Writing: Teachers and Children at Work*, 20th ed. Portsmouth, NH: Heinemann.

Halliday, M. 1975. *Learning How to Mean: Explorations in the Development of Language.* London: Arnold.

———. n.d. "Three Aspects of Children's Language Development: Learning Language, Learning Through Language, Learning About Language." In *Oral and Written Language Development: Impact on Schools* (*Proceedings from the 1979 and 1980 IMPACT Conferences*), ed. Y. Goodman, M. Hayssler, and D. Strickland, 7–19. Newark, DE, and Urbana, IL: International Reading Association and National Council of Teachers.

———. 1993. "Towards a Language-Based Theory of Learning." *Linguistics and Education* 5: 93–116.

Halliday, M., and R. Hasan. 1985. *Language, Context and Text.* Geelong, Victoria, AU: Deakin University Press.

Hammond, J. 2008. "Intellectual Challenge and ESL Students: Implications for Quality Teaching Initiatives." *Australian Journal of Language and Literacy* 31 (2): 128–54.

Haneda, M., and G. Wells. 2008. "Learning an Additional Language Through Dialogic Enquiry." *Language and Education* 22 (2): 114–35.

Harvey, S., A. Goudvis, and J. Wallis. 2010. *Comprehension Intervention: Small Group Lessons for the Primary Comprehension Toolkit, K–2.* Portsmouth, NH: Heinemann.

Hawkins, E. 2007. *Choir of Hard Knocks.* Sydney: Random House Australia.

Hornberger, N. H., and H. Link. 2012. "Translanguaging in Today's Classrooms: A Biliteracy Lens." *Theory into Practice* 51 (4): 239–47.

Houk, F. 2005. *Supporting English Language Learners: A Guide for Teachers and Administrators.* Portsmouth, NH: Heinemann.

Humphrey, S., L. Droga, and S. Feez. 2012. *Grammar and Meaning.* Sydney: Primary English Teaching Association Australia (PEETA).

Janssen, M., A. Bosman, and P. Leseman. 2013. "Phoneme Awareness, Vocabulary and Word Decoding in Monolingual and Bilingual Dutch Children." *Journal of Research in Reading* 36 (1): 1–13.

Krashen, S. 1982. *Principles and Practices in Second Language Acquisition.* Oxford, UK: Oxford University Press.

Luke, A., and P. Freebody. 1990. "'Literacies' Programs: Debate and Demands in Cultural Context." *Prospect* 5 (3): 7–16.

Lyle, S. 2008. "Dialogic Teaching: Discussing Theoretical Contexts and Reviewing Evidence from Classroom Practice." *Language and Education* 22 (3): 222–40.

Mariani, L. 1997. "Teacher Support and Teacher Challenge in Promoting Learner Autonomy." *Perspectives: A Journal of TESOL Italy* 23 (2).

Martin, J. 1984. "Language, Register, and Genre." *Children Writing: Study Guide*, ed. F. Christie. Geelong, Victoria, AU: Deakin University Press.

———. 1986. "Secret English: Discourse of Technology in a Junior Secondary School." *Proceedings from the Working Conference on Education*. Macquarie University, Sydney.

———. 1989. "Technicality and Abstraction: Language for the Creation of Specialized Knowledge." In *Writing in Schools*, ed. F. Christie. Geelong, Victoria, AU: Deakin University Press.

Martin, J., F. Christie, and J. Rothery. 1987. "Social Processes in Education: A Reply to Sawyer and Watson." In *Current Debates*, ed. I. Reid. Geelong, Victoria, AU: Deakin University Press.

Martin J., and D. Rose. 2008. *Genre Relations: Mapping Culture.* London: Equinò.

Maybin, J., N. Mercer, and B. Stierer. 1992. "Scaffolding Learning in the Classroom." In *Thinking Voices, The Work of the National Oracy Project*, ed. K. Norman. London: Hodder and Stoughton.

McKay, P., A. Davies, B. Devlin, J. Clayton, R. Oliver, and S. Zammit. 1997. *The Bilingual Interface Project Report.* Canberra, AU: Department of Employment, Education, Training and Youth Affairs.

Mehan, B. 1979. *Learning Lessons.* Cambridge, MA: Harvard University Press.

Mercer, N. 1994. "Neo-Vygotskian Theory and Classroom Education." In *Language, Literacy and Learning in Educational Practice*, ed. B. Stierer and J. Maybin. Clevedon, UK: Multilingual Matters.

———. 1995. *The Guided Construction of Knowledge: Talk Amongst Teachers and Learners*. Clevedon, UK: Multilingual Matters.

———. 2000. *Words and Minds: How We Use Language to Think Together*. London: Routledge.

Mercer, N., L. Dawes, and J. Kleine Staarman. 2009. "Dialogic Teaching in the Primary Classroom." *Language and Education* 23 (4): 353–70.

Mohan, B. 2001. "The Second Language as a Medium of Learning." In *English as a Second Language in the Mainstream: Teaching, Learning, and Identity*, ed. B. Mohan, C. Leung, and C. Davison. London: Longman.

Mohan, B., C. Leung, and C. Davison. 2001. *English as a Second Language in the Mainstream: Teaching, Learning, and Identity*. London: Longman.

Newmann, F., and Associates. 1996. *Authentic Achievement: Restructuring Schools for Intellectual Quality*. San Francisco: Jossey-Bass.

Nunan, D. 1990. "Learning to Listen in a Second Language." *Prospect* 5 (2): 7–23.

Nunan, D., and L. Miller, eds. 1995. *New Ways in Teaching Listening*. Alexandria, VA: Teachers of English to Speakers of Other Languages (TESOL).

Olivos, E., and L. Sarmiento. 2006. "Is There Room for Biliteracy? Credentialing California's Future Bilingual Teachers." *Issues in Teacher Education* 15 (1): 69–84.

Painter, C. 1988. "The Concept of Genre." Paper commissioned by Queensland Department of Education, Australia.

———. 2000. *Into the Mother Tongue: A Case Study in Early Language Development*. London: Bloomsbury.

Pianta, R., J. Belsky, R. Houts, and F. Morrison. 2007. "Opportunities to Learn in America's Elementary Classrooms." *Science* 315: 1795–96.

Reynolds, R., M. Taylor, M. Steffenson, L. Shirey, and R. Anderson. 1981. "Cultural Schemata and Reading Comprehension." In *Center for the Study of Reading Technical Report No. 201*. Urbana-Champaign, IL.

Richards, J. 2008. *Teaching Listening and Speaking: From Theory to Practice*. New York: Cambridge University Press.

Richards, J., and R. Hurley. 1990. "Language and Content: Approaches to Curriculum Alignment." In *The Language Teaching Matrix*, ed. J. Richards. Cambridge, UK: Cambridge University Press.

Rigg, P., and V. Allen, eds. 1989. *When They Don't All Speak English: Integrating the ESL Student in the Regular Classroom*. Urbana, IL: National Council of Teachers of English.

Ross, J. 2006. "ESL Listening Comprehension: Practical Guidelines for Teachers." *The Internet TESL Journal* 12 (2). Available at http://iteslj.org, accessed 3/13/14.

Rost, M. 1991. *Listening in Action*. New York: Prentice-Hall.

Rowe, M. 1986. "Wait Time: Slowing Down May Be a Way of Speeding Up." *Journal of Teacher Education* 37: 43–50.

Schleppegrell, M. J. 2004. *The Language of Schooling: A Functional Linguistics Perspective*. Mahwah, NJ: Lawrence Erlbaum Associates.

———. 2012. "Academic Language in Teaching and Learning." Introduction to the Special Issue. *The Elementary School Journal* 112 (3): 409–18.

———. 2013. "The Role of Metalanguage in Supporting Academic Language Development." *Language Learning* 63: 153–70.

Short, D. 1993. "Assessing Integrating Language and Content." *TESOL Quarterly* 27 (4): 627–56.

Sinclair, J., and R. Coulthard. 1975. *Towards an Analysis of Discourse: The English Used by Teachers and Pupils*. London: Oxford University Press.

Stahl, R. 1994. "Using Think-Time and Wait-Time Skillfully in the Classroom." *ERIC Digest*. ERIC Clearinghouse for Social Studies. Available at www.ericdigests .org/1995-1/think.html, accessed 3/27/2014.

Stanovitch, K. 1986. "Matthew Effect in Reading: Some Consequencess of Individuals' Differences in the Acquisition of Literacy." *Reading Research Quarterly* 21 (4): 360–407.

Steffensen, M., C. Joag-Dev, and R. Anderson. 1979. "A Cross-Cultural Perspective on Reading Comprehension." *Reading Research Quarterly* 15 (1): 10–29.

Swain, M. 2000. "The Output Hypothesis and Beyond: Mediating Acquisition Through Collaborative Dialogue." In *Sociocultural Theory and Second Language Learning*, ed. J. Lantolf. Oxford, UK: Oxford University Press.

———. 2005. "The Output Hypothesis: Theory and Research." In *Handbook of Research in Second Language Teaching and Learning*, ed. E. Heinkel, 471–83. Mahwah, NJ: Lawrence Erlbaum Associates.

Thomas, W., and V. Collier. 1999. *School Effectiveness for Language Minority Students*. Washington, DC: National Clearinghouse for Bilingual Education.

Vygotsky, L. 1978. *Mind in Society: The Development of Higher Psychological Processes*. London: Harvard University Press.

———. 1986. *Thought and Language*, ed. and trans. A Kozulin. Cambridge, MA: Harvard University Press.

Wajnryb, R. 1990. *Grammar Dictation*. Oxford, UK: Oxford University Press.

Wallace, C. 1988. *Learning to Read in a Multicultural Society: The Social Context of Second Language Literacy*. New York: Prentice-Hall.

———. 1992. *Reading*. Oxford, UK: Oxford University Press.

———. 2003. *Critical Reading in Language Education*. Basingstoke, UK: Palgrave Macmillan.

———. 2013. *Literacy and the Bilingual Learner. Texts and Practices in London Schools*. Basingstoke, UK: Palgrave Macmillan.

Walqui, A. 2007. "Scaffolding Instruction for English Language Learners: A Conceptual Framework." In *Bilingual Education: An Introductory Reader*, ed. O. Garcia and C. Baker. Clevedon, UK: Multilingual Matters.

Walqui, A., and L. van Lier. 2010. *Scaffolding the Academic Success of Adolescent English Language Learners: A Pedagogy of Promise*. San Francisco: WestEd.

Wegerif, R., and N. Mercer. 1996. "Computers and Reasoning Through Talk in the Classroom." *Language and Education* 10 (1): 47–64.

Wells, G. 2000. "Dialogic Inquiry in Education: Building on the Legacy of Vygotsky." In *Vygotskian Perspectives on Literacy Research: Constructing Meaning Through*

Collaborative Inquiry, ed. C. Lee and P. Smagorinsky. Cambridge, UK: Cambridge University Press.

Williams, G. 1999. "Grammar as a Semiotic Tool in Child Literacy Development." In *Language Teaching: New Insights for the Language Teacher*, Series 40, ed. C. Ward and W. Renandya. Singapore: Regional Language Centre, SEAMO.

Wong Fillmore, L. 1985. "When Does Teacher Talk Work as Input?" In *Input in Second Language Acquisition*, ed. S. Gass and C. Madden. Rowley, MA: Newbury House.

Wood, D., J. Bruner, and G. Ross. 1976. "The Role of Tutoring in Problem Solving." *Journal of Child Psychology and Psychiatry* 17 (2): 89–100.

INDEX

instructions
  activities to provide, 70–72
  providing clear and explicit, 42–46,
    54–56, 108–109
  time required to provide clear, 60–61
integration
  activities, 64–74
  of EL learners, 17–19, 59–60, 207–11,
    221–24
  units for language development, 218–24
interpersonal function of language, 63,
  74–77, 186–87
interviews, 5, 113, 186
"in-the-head" knowledge (schema
  theory), 92–94, 136–42, 185, 194, 215
IRE pattern (Initiation, Response, Evaluation), 31–32, 88–89

jazz chants and raps, 200
jigsaw activity, 58, 112, 159
joint constructions, 28, 53, 110, 117–20,
  219
journal writing, 84, 91–92
jumbled sentences, 123

"key-ring" words activity, 166–67
knowledge, reading, 136–38, 185

language. *See also* academic language
  conversational, 9
  focus, 218
  "here and now," 7–8
  stretched, 26–27
language development
  activities, 121–24
  assessment for learning, 211–13
  content development activities for,
    218–20
  dialogic approach, 32–34
  grammar and, 224–28
  as the hidden curriculum, 214–18
  integrated units focusing on, 221–24
  with integration of EL learners,
    207–11

interpersonal function in, 63, 74–77,
  186–187
IRE pattern (Initiation, Response,
  Evaluation), 31–32
listening, 183–87
modeling, 28, 34–35, 54–56, 65–66, 89
mother tongue to promote, 29–30
problem-solving dialogue, 26
purpose of, 108–109
self-assessment and reflection in, 228–29
spelling, 97, 119, 128–32, 169, 172–75
subject development and, 59–60
through reading, 175–79
language development activities, 29–30,
  218–19
Language of Schooling, The (Schleppegrell), 96
language-based activities. *See also*
  activities
  building the field, 218
  content development, 218–20
  dialogue letter/dialogue journal, 123
  discussion framework, 124
  history reading, 161–62
  independent writing, 110, 120–24,
    219–20
  joint constructions, 28, 53, 110, 117–20,
    219
  literate talk, 53, 81–83, 87
  message abundancy, 42–46
  modeling and deconstructing the genre,
    115–17, 218–19
  mother tongue, 25, 29–30, 121–25, 151,
    233
  personal recount genre, 106, 121–22
  running dictation, 117
  vocabulary, 73, 106, 121–22
  writing frameworks, 28, 123
  for young learners, 121–24
learner, self-contained, 11–12
learner development. *See also* scaffolding
  for academic language, 4–11, 32–33,
    45–46, 81–82
  cognitive gap, 13–14